Something Magic

Something Magic
The Baltimore Orioles, 1979–1983

CHARLES KUPFER

McFarland & Company, Inc., Publishers
Jefferson, North Carolina

All images courtesy National Baseball Hall of Fame Library, Cooperstown, New York.

LIBRARY OF CONGRESS CATALOGUING-IN-PUBLICATION DATA

Names: Kupfer, Charles, author.
Title: Something magic : the Baltimore Orioles, 1979–1983 / Charles
    Kupfer.
Description: Jefferson, North Carolina : McFarland & Company, Inc.,
    Publishers, 2018 | Includes bibliographical references and index.
Identifiers: LCCN 2018020893 | ISBN 9780786499359
    (softcover : acid free paper) ∞
Subjects: LCSH: Baltimore Orioles (Baseball team)—History. |
    Sports—Maryland—Baltimore—History.
Classification: LCC GV875.B2 K87 2018 | DDC 796.357/64097526—
    dc23
LC record available at https://lccn.loc.gov/2018020893

BRITISH LIBRARY CATALOGUING DATA ARE AVAILABLE

ISBN (print) 978-0-7864-9935-9
ISBN (ebook) 978-1-4766-2677-2

Front cover: Baltimore Orioles first baseman Eddie Murray at
the plate in the 1983 World Series (National Baseball Hall
of Fame Library, Cooperstown, New York)

Printed in the United States of America

McFarland & Company, Inc., Publishers
    Box 611, Jefferson, North Carolina 28640
    www.mcfarlandpub.com

To all the fans in Section 13
(before the red line)

Memorial Stadium chants in unison—"Edd-ie, Edd-ie, Edd-ie"—and when Eddie swings at a 1-1 pitch we know it's gone even before the ball rockets off his bat in a tremendous arc, moving slowly and even gently through the air, perfectly visible, stage-lit against the deep green of the grass, the right fielder not moving, just turning his head to watch it go, and it's like the perfect arc of youth, a constellation made up of baseball, booze, girls and loud music ... we know the parabola must start downward somewhere, and in the·split second it takes to react to the home run, you see that this is life, a luminous rise and a steady, frictional wearing down, a curve disintegrating in the sure pull of gravity, Eddie Murray dropping his bat and starting the slow trot around the bases, the crowd coming to its feet, the ball finally crashing into the bullpen. And you're rising up with a great emotional surge swelling inside you. You're standing on the aluminum bench with Ed and Charlie stamping your feet. You're waving your arms wildly in the air. You're looking up, past the glowing towers of lights, at the floodlit sky. You're yelling like there's no tomorrow.—excerpt, "Capitalist Poem #25," by Campbell McGrath, *Capitalism*, Campbell McGrath (Hanover, NH: Wesleyan New Poets/University Press of New England, 1990), p. 35–36. Copyright Campbell McGrath; quoted with permission.

TABLE OF CONTENTS

ACKNOWLEDGMENTS

My sporting interests arose during a childhood marked by dislocation and movement, since my parents lived through the 1960s. I was born as Charles Jan Dyke II in 1962 at Walter Reed in Washington, D.C., moving to Baltimore soon thereafter. My first baseball memory was of admiring the Orioles cap of a friend at my fourth birthday party, 1966. Next, my mother and I headed to Seattle, where my awareness of sports clicked "on." This made me a Seattle Pilots fan, a distinction I still cherish. Marty Pattin burning one in, Tommy Davis rapping a base hit or Tommy Harper rounding first—all remain vivid for me. We moved back east in 1970, to Bethesda, Maryland. I vainly searched the standings for Pilots information, not yet understanding franchise relocation. My initial Oriole game was a 1970 home contest against Milwaukee. I recognized the Brewers as the former Pilots, which marked the first time I wondered how pro sports really worked. I also watched the dismantling of the Senators, epitomized by the 1971 Denny McLain trade. Such episodes intensified my sense that the grown-ups running things were not always trustworthy, a fitting skepticism given the era. The Orioles offered the antidote of reliability.

I grew up following baseball in clinical detail, listening to Bill O'Donnell and Chuck Thompson on WBAL and WTOP, and Shelby Whitfield on WWDC; poring over the sports pages of the *Washington Post*. To call 1970s *Post* sportswriters superb is a vast understatement. Shirley Povich, Thomas Boswell, Bob Addie, John Feinstein, Jane Leavy, Robert Fachet, Ken Denlinger, Dave Kindred, Leonard Shapiro, Mark Asher, Michael Wilbon, William Gildea, and all the others under editor George Solomon during the 1970s provided an education in first-class sports prose. I looked forward to seeing what ran under each byline and began to recognize reporting skill and writing excellence. Upon moving to Baltimore for college, 1980–1984, I added the *Sun, Evening Sun,* and *News-*

American to my daily repertoire, admiring writers such as Bill Tanton, Bob Maisel, Alan Goldstein, Jim Henneman, John Steadman, Vito Stellino, and Phil Jackman. Other media figures such as Vince Bagli and "Stan the Fan" also gave me the chance to immerse in passionate and informed sports discourse. Journalism in general and sportswriting in particular remain my favorite literary genres, meriting scholarly analysis as surely as poetry or fiction.

Thanks go to many teachers and coaches at Sidwell Friends, and professors at my three universities: Johns Hopkins, Oxford, and the University of Texas. The JHU campus was awash in Orioles spirit, and Stephen Dixon was its best Writing Seminars professor. Playing MCR cricket at St. Catherine's College, Oxford, gave me new perspectives on ball-and-stick games. Philosophy tutor Brendan McLaughlin supported my distraction with his inimitable broad smile. In graduate school at UT, Terry Todd was the greatest mentor for taking sports seriously, along with his wife, Jan Todd. William Goetzmann, Shelley Fishkin, and Mark Smith were similarly supportive, as were my cohort peers Kathleen Rice, Tevi Troy, Gehrig Coleman, and Jonathan Silverman. It was valuable to delve into Longhorn/Astros/Rangers/Missions baseball for nine great seasons.

My best professional break came when Doug Noverr and Larry Ziewacz, of Michigan State, gave a rookie Ph.D. his chance and hired me. At Penn State Harrisburg, Hannah Murray, Simon Bronner, Michael Barton, John Haddad, Anne Verplanck, Anthony Buccitelli, Troy Thomas, Yvonne Simms, Spero Lappas, Glen Mazis, Ron Coffman, Sr., Jeremy Plant, Cat Rios, Cathy McCormick, and Greg Crawford all provided me solidarity. Cindy Leach shared her memories of Orioles Magic. Henry Kortezky, librarian and Phils fan, kindly gave me old periodicals from his stash. Ev Fuller, of the Wildcard Fantasy Baseball League in Harrisburg, regaled me with Oriole stories, and our league is a fine source of baseball camaraderie. Two PSH American Studies graduate students were wonderful research assistants: David Misal, and Christopher Haraszkiewicz. Both helped their analog professor in digital ways. Skidmore's Dan Nathan is a scholar whose love of Baltimore sports matches his editorial talents. At the National Baseball Hall of Fame Library and Museum, Ken Roussey, of the photographs division, was incredibly helpful and forthcoming with photographs and assistance. It is fitting that he is in Cooperstown.

In Camp Hill, John Harles of Messiah College is a great friend and fellow writer. Corinna and Peter Wilson introduced me to Corinna's father, George Vecsey. Getting to know a sportswriting giant was a thrill. Mike Berney, probably Camp Hill's most ardent baseball fan, was enthusiastic.

Dan Morra and Leslie Hays are go-to guys for Harrisburg Senators culture. Vivian Blanc and Lawrence Altaker were helpful beyond measure. Muriel Kaiser supported my baseball interests. Her two (sequential) husbands, Charles Jan Dyke and Carl Kupfer, had varied attitudes towards sports. But Carl Kupfer was always up for a catch, and let me throw balls against the garage door for hours at a time. My Dyke patrimony is basketball-oriented (the Dutch are tall) and Iowa-focused, but Jan did tell me that grandfather Lt. Col. Lester M. Dyke spent Opening Day mornings quaffing at the Army-Navy Club before dozing through the Senator game. I appreciate the Washington connection. Mary C. Dyke went to high school with Marty Pattin in Charlestown, Illinois, and talked to him on my behalf, providing me a rewarding Pilot connection. In 1991, Kimberly Wolf, of Pikesville, accepted my proposal of marriage, delivered in section 13 of Memorial Stadium. I remain grateful. While Kim might occasionally repine regarding her assent, I never will, not least because our four children, Willie, Teddy, Sandy, and Heidi, are my best sources of motivation and amusement. Coaching Willie in Challenger/Disabled Little League taught me even more about baseball's powers. Siblings Sarah Kupfer, Janny, Peter, and Tommy Dyke, and Abigail Klinect, offer me varying forms of motivation that anyone with brothers and sisters can understand. Tommy is a Cards fan & Peter a Cubs fan, but Janny picked the Orioles. Sarah served under fraternal impressment as a sounding board and researcher. Cousin Roger Seidenman, a fellow baseball academician, is a reliable source of good Baltimore-focused analysis. Morris Wolf was happy to have a Baltimore fan in the family and we discussed many of this book's themes over 18 years. Bobbie Wolf and Jerry Fine are lifelong O's fans and thus good company. My other in-laws, such as Leo Sorokin, David Morgan, Kelly O'Neal and Anthony Pollina, mostly have northeastern orientations, so are puzzled when told that baseball matters beyond the Boston-New York axis.

Friends who liked sports built the foundation from which this book emerged. Dan Ainsworth, Senator-Nat loyalist, was my first baseball fan-friend. David Martin, the first to drive, logged many miles between the beltways and induced me to broaden my horizons from Section 13 to Section 34. Edward Meigs was another reliable driver always ready for a game. His boyhood disenfranchisement as a Senator fan prompted fruitful ruminations. Campbell McGrath, one of whose poems serves as this book's epigraph, was the friend who knew that reading, writing, and baseball are complementary. We greeted rookie Mike Boddicker together in Comiskey Park. Mark Shaw, who claimed not to like baseball in high school, wound up walking to scores of games with me from JHU. Other section 13 crew members included Arthur Linde, who pretends never to have liked the Orioles but who certainly did; Henry Steuart, devout Yankee rooter who treated a flock of Bird fans with toleration; Gary Davison, JHU tuba player who visited Loudy Loudenslager with me; Michael Rossides, who lacks the baseball gene but puts up with his friends; Dedrick Schmidt, still the model of a catcher; Mehmet Gurgun, a Pittsburgher who did not remind me of Stargell's series-clinching HR more than necessary, Al Shuldiner, a Met fan until his DC sons started dragging him to Nationals games; David Barnes, a Nat fan with an Oriole past; Ross Bunnell, Bosox fan who bid farewell to Yaz at Memorial Stadium, Dennis Chien and Matt Perkins. Baseball friends met later included Bucs fan Mark Mravic, who helped me process 1979's Series through "confrontation therapy," Dave Andres, Dodger fan who saw the charms of Memorial Stadium, and Dave Harding, hockey fan, whose blasé approach to baseball made his willingness to sit through games and conversations remarkable. Matthias Maass' love of sports and scholarship reinforces our friendship.

All the fans, workers, and players at Memorial Stadium were sources of comradeship and inspiration. It boggles my mind that Mark and I could go to games on a $3 student ticket, or visit the park after the season was over as the Orioles sold off their remaining stock of souvenirs. We spent time sitting on folding metal chairs chatting with Ken Singleton, Cal Ripken, Jr., Jim Palmer, Joe Altobelli, Ernie Tyler, and the like. They cheerfully and patiently answered our questions; those were different days. We chatted over the bullpen fence with Denny Martinez, Sammy Stewart, Tim Stoddard, Elrod Hendricks, Tippy Martinez, and other Orioles. I spent too many hours at Memorial Stadium to figure; those are some of the happiest times in my life. If I ever had a spiritual locus, it was there. Of course, the sweetest parts of life don't last—a lesson no Pilot fan could forget. But *Something Magic* really did happen in a red-brick ballpark on 33rd Street in Baltimore. As the words over the front gate said, "*Time will not dim the glory of their deeds.*"

INTRODUCTION:
BALTIMORE AND BASEBALL,
1858–1972

The origins of baseball in Baltimore are, like the origins of the sport itself, difficult to pin down. While a newspaper story published in 1905 suggests that some form of the game was played in the city as early as 1825,[1] the best extant example of a birth certificate for the New York Game—that is, the oldest version that fans today might recognize—may be the one reported on by James H. Bready in 1998. Bready found a July 12, 1858, article in the *Baltimore American* announcing that a new team, the Excelsiors, was being formed, "[p]rincipally with the view of promoting physical exercise and healthful recreation."[2] Their first game was a road win against a team from Washington, D.C. This was the first time, but far from the last, that the national capital's baseball destiny intertwined itself with that of Maryland's main city.

During the late 19th century, American enterprise organized itself. Vocations and avocations that formerly depended on informal arrangements suitable for a society on the move took advantage of new stability offered by a settled continent to become professionalized. Licensing bodies and boards of directors rose during the Gilded Age and set about formalizing a host of American enterprises. Associations of all kinds sprang up as like-minded Americans gathered themselves around vocations and avocations. Often, the end was commercial. This was the real dawn of corporatization as the American social and economic norm.

Baseball went through the same process. The localized, city-by-city phenomenon of pickup teams playing haphazardly morphed into standardization and association as central governance emerged. The New York Knickerbockers played a key role, popularizing their version of the game with codified rules.[3] Later, sportswriter Henry Chadwick took up baseball's cause against the rival English game of cricket, arguing that American fans should not embrace a colonial sport and framing the choice as a matter of national pride or lack thereof.[4] (Chadwick, it should be added, nevertheless firmly believed baseball to have British roots.) He developed the box score and wrote voluminously, touting the game's appeal to players and spectators alike.[5] The Knickerbockers were New Yorkers of the professional class with the leisure time to practice and the wherewithal to play as amateurs. But by the post–Civil War years, the drive to win outstripped the need for genteel pretensions, and in 1869, the Cincinnati Red Stockings abandoned sham amateurism for honest commercialism with a lineup paid to play and win. Their excellence was the Red Stockings' main appeal. Totally outclassing their foes, they barnstormed to a 65–0–1 record, even playing before President Ulysses S Grant.[6] The clear superiority of the professionals was a lesson no observer could deny.

Baltimore did not have a National League team at first, but because of the city's size and strategic East Coast location, it was an attractive market for the National Association, American Association, Union Association—all of which fielded teams in the city during the 1870s and 1880s—and later the Eastern League. All fielded teams in Baltimore during the 1870s and 1880s. In 1872, the National Association's Lord Baltimores featured a host of favorite players and a popular pep song, "Lord Baltimore's Nine:" "Of all the manly games in vogue, / Enumerate them all, / There's none you'll find that can compare / With that known as Base Ball."[7] The American Association's franchise, born in 1884, was first to call itself the Orioles. Backed by a brewing family, the Von der Horsts, the team built a new stadium at Greenmount Avenue and 25th Street, cultivating a rivalry with the mighty St. Louis Browns, playing on Sundays, and selling plenty of beer at games.[8] A loyal Oriole fan during this time was August Mencken, Sr., a prosperous Baltimore cigar manufacturer who liked bringing ballplayers home to dinner, thrilling his young sons, August, Jr., and Henry Louis Mencken.[9] Also in 1884, a different Baltimore franchise took up in the fledgling Union Association, challenging both the National League and American Association. Playing on the league's name, locals informally tabbed the Baltimore team "The Onions."[10] Like their league, the Onions lasted but a season, finishing third. Lack of stability and capital bedeviled every baseball outfit but the lordly National League, and when the American Association collapsed in 1891, Baltimoreans dreamed of seeing their city join the senior circuit. Those dreams came true in 1892.

The National League Orioles made their mark in baseball history as

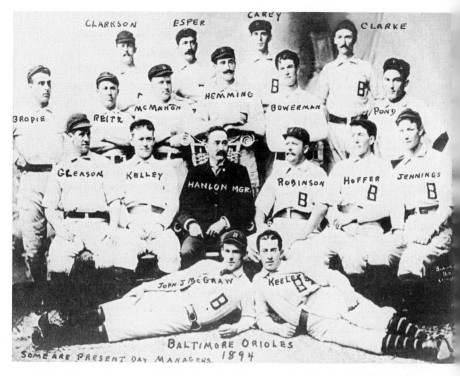

The 1894 Orioles won the National League pennant and were Baltimore's first baseball champions. They won pennants in 1895 and 1896 and took home the Temple Cup in 1896 and 1897 but were out of the league after 1899.

a dynasty, as well as one of the most colorful major league teams ever. Built into champions by manager Ned Hanlon, they featured stars such as John McGraw, Hugh Jennings, Wilbert Robinson, Joe McGinnity, Joe Kelley, Steve Brodie, and Wee Willie Keeler. The Orioles won three pennants in a row, from 1894 to 1896, and two Temple Cups, in 1896 and 1897. These triumphs occasioned parades and civic glee on a massive scale. Crowds of 30,000 showed up for big games. But it was the fabled Oriole style that made them important.

Baseball historian Robert W. Creamer termed them "the greatest team of all time until the 1927 Yankees came along," adding that they were "a nova, a sudden manifestation in the baseball skies that flared brilliantly."[11] Lee Allen, lauding their feistiness, joked that they ate "gunpowder and warm blood" for breakfast, "feasted on scrap iron for lunch," "nailed umpires to trees," and—more literally—were "a team whose stars peaked together and whose best years came at the same time."[12]

It was that spirit that also made the Orioles controversial. Besides making Oriole Park groundskeeper Tom Murphy a virtual member of the team, since his grooming, dirt-packing, and manicuring was designed to help the home team, they also resorted to extra-legal measures in their search for a winning edge. Ostentatiously sharpening their spikes on the dugout bench was intimidating, not just to opponents, but to umps—for the men in blue were not immune from intentional spikes.[13] Catcher Robinson was a master at flipping his mask into the base path to trip up runners; third base coach Clarke would frequently break for the plate, appearing to any pitcher's peripheral vision as a runner stealing home; runners from first might cut around second base if the umpire's eyes were elsewhere. To Baltimore fans, it was a matter of local pride and amusement; to McGraw and his mates, their style exemplified an indomitable will to win. Opponents and out-of-town fans, on the other hand, thought the Orioles were dirty. When Boston's Beaneaters finally outpaced them for the 1897 pennant on the last day of the season, many considered it a victory for sportsmanship and clean play. *The Sporting News* editorialized that Hanlon's team played "the dirtiest ball ever seen."[14]

Because of the team's star appeal, Orioles fans assumed that their favorites were safe when the National League moved to contract by four teams before the 1900 season. But a series of tricky financial maneuvers involving dual ownership with Brooklyn put Baltimore on the chopping block. Fans were irate, barely cheered up in 1901 when the city landed a franchise under John McGraw in Ban Johnson's new American League. That squad, which moved to New York in 1902 to become the Highlanders and Yankees, marked McGraw's last stop before the Giants.

Loath to see Baltimore without a team, Ned Hanlon purchased the minor Eastern League's Montreal franchise, moving it to Baltimore in 1903.[15] Hughie Jennings would return to manage in 1904 and 1905, but it was former outfielder Edward Dunn, joining in 1907, who forged these minor league Orioles into Baltimore favorites. Under Dunn's management, the Orioles became a minor league power, shifting to the International League, moving into Oriole Park in 1916, and winning seven straight pennants from 1919 to 1925. They resembled a major league team in terms of talent and box office success. Their only lean years came when the upstart Federal League placed the Terrapins in Baltimore in 1914, and fans hungry for major-league status flocked to the new club. This forced Dunn to sell off his talent, including homegrown pitcher Babe Ruth, to stay afloat. The Feds went under in 1915, and the Terrapins' major contribution to baseball history was to lose their protest lawsuit, giving the major leagues a coveted anti-trust exemption.

Fans eager for the return of major league baseball flocked to Terrapin Park in 1914. When the Federal League folded after 1915, the stadium was renamed Oriole Park. The International League Orioles moved in, remaining until a fire in 1944.

Parochial and segregated, Baltimore's white fans settled into a half-century of minor-league baseball with the Orioles. The city's many African American fans enjoyed some of the best teams ever to play in the Negro Leagues, including the Black Sox, from 1916–1934.[16] At various times, the Black Sox boasted stars Jud Wilson, John Beckwith, Satchel Paige, and Leon Day.[17] Later, stars like Joe Black, Junior Gilliam, and Roy Campanella, played for the Elite Giants. The Elites won the championship in 1949, and their final season, 1951, marked the end of an era.

Baseball was due for massive change just like the rest of the United States during the post–World War II years, Baltimore included. Oriole Park burned down in 1944, and the International League Orioles moved into huge, hastily retrofitted Memorial Stadium, just blocks away. It did not escape notice when the 1944 Junior World Series games in Memorial Stadium outdrew the World Series in Sportsman's Park. The Braves' move from Boston to Milwaukee in 1953, and the Athletics' shift from Philadelphia to Kansas City in 1954 showed that long-fixed major league arrangements were in flux. Meanwhile, Brooklyn's Walter O'Malley jousted with New York Parks Commissioner Robert Moses about building a new stadium, and dreamed longingly about Los Angeles. Bounty was abundant for those who would grab it. In Baltimore, fate put Browns owner Bill Veeck into the guise of likely savior. While teams such as the Braves, A's, Dodgers, and Giants made the franchise wave a westerly one, the iconoclastic Veeck was willing to go in another direction.

The Browns, long a second-class sibling to the Cardinals, survived largely by dint of owning Sportsman's Park. The situation of the successful and popular Redbirds paying rent to keep the Brownies afloat was unusual if not preposterous.[18] The brash Veeck bought the struggling Browns on July 3, 1951.[19] Straight off, he declared his intention to run the Cardinals

Follow the American League's "Parade of Stars"

ST. LOUIS BROWNS . . . 1950

Top row, left to right: Tom Ferrick, pitcher; Sidney Schacht, pitcher; Sherman Lollar, catcher; Al Widmar, pitcher; Tommy Fine, pitcher; Donald Lenhardt, outfielder; Kenneth Wood, outfielder; Joe Ostrowski, pitcher; Roy Sievers, outfielder; Les Moss, catcher.

Middle row, left to right: Art Peters Club House Attendant; Bill Durney, Traveling Secretary; Clarence Marshall, pitcher; Roy Coleman, outfielder; Tommy Upton, infielder; Wm. Sommers, infielder; Dick Starr, pitcher; Ned Garver, pitcher; Lou Kretlow, pitcher; Ed Redys, Batting Practice Pitcher; Dr. Bob Bauman, Trainer.

Lower row, left to right: Wm. DeMars, infielder; Hank Arft, infielder; Harry Dorish, pitcher; Owen Friend, infielder; Ralph Winegarner, Coach; Earle Brucker, Coach; Zack Taylor, Manager; Johnny Tobin, Coach; Bob Dillinger, infielder; Dick Kokos, outfielder; Leo Thomas, infielder; Cliff Fannin, pitcher and Frank Overmire, pitcher.

out of town. Doubters—and there were many, given Veeck's penchant for overstatement and fondness for the grand gesture—figured he had his eyes on Milwaukee and was merely trying to placate the DeWitt family, which sold him the Browns but announced their hopes for the team to remain in St. Louis.[20] Grantland Rice was moved to doggerel: "Stalwarts have hunted to charging lion, deep in the jungle veldt. / Brave men have stood to the tiger's rush seeking his costly pelt. / Hunters have tackled the elephant, never a job for clowns. / This world is packed with daring deeds—but Veeck has purchased the Browns."[21] John Lardner preferred sarcasm: "Many critics were surprised to know that the Browns could be bought because they didn't know the Browns were owned."[22]

But for all the guffaws, and for all his showmanship tricks, Veeck was an artful baseball man whose Indians won the World Series in 1948. While the only player on the Browns who qualified as a star was pitcher Ned Garver, Veeck's plan to outlast the Cardinals was not totally far-fetched. The Cardinals' owner, lawyer Fred Saigh, had legal problems. Saigh hated Veeck, who nettled him with provocations such as hiring Card favorites Rogers Hornsby as manager and Harry "The Cat" Brecheen as pitching coach. But the attorney's indictment for tax evasion in mid–1952 cut into the effectiveness of his campaign to remind fans that, whereas the Browns were a baseball circus featuring the likes of Eddie Gaedel, the Cardinals were, as their scorecards promised, "A Dignified St. Louis Institution."[23] Veeck watched hopefully as Saigh talked with Houston businessmen anxious to move the Cardinals to Texas. At the same time, Veeck dickered with Milwaukee, Baltimore, and Los Angeles.[24] Had Saigh sold to out-of-towners, Veeck might have wound up running St. Louis's remaining ballclub. Instead, Anheuser-Busch boss Gussie Busch emerged with a lucrative offer to take the Cardinals off Saigh's troubled hands and keep them in St. Louis. "I wasn't going to run Gussie Busch out of town," Veeck later recalled, "And I certainly wasn't going to run Anheuser-Busch out of town. Busch wasn't buying the club himself, the brewery was buying it.... I had been knocked out of the box."[25]

Milwaukee looked good to Veeck, but Perini's Braves made it their own, so he turned his attentions to Baltimore. There was plenty of support from Baltimore's political establishment, led by Mayor Tommy D'Alesandro, Jr. Owners knew this, and appreciated the Orioles' high attendance

Opposite: **The end of the 1950 season saw the St. Louis Browns finish in seventh place, 40 games behind the pennant-winning Yankees. It had been six years since St. Louis's only pennant and five since the team had finished at or above .500.**

in a newly refurbished ballpark. So major league owners were not necessarily averse to a return to Maryland. But they were averse to Veeck, and welcomed the chance to ease the maverick out of their corral.[26] Convening their annual meeting in Tampa, they forbade Veeck permission to move in 1953, forcing the cash-strapped Browns' owner to consider selling his team. According to Browns general manager Bill DeWitt, Veeck might have grabbed lucrative Los Angeles but declined.[27] The iconoclastic owner had been negotiating already with a group of Maryland civic boosters who wanted to purchase a share in the club. It was relatively simple to up the local ante. Local attorneys Clarence Miles and Zanvyl Krieger, with help from the Gunther Brewery, led a consortium of investors anxious to return to their city the major league imprimatur. The inexhaustible D'Alesandro kept peppering big league owners with his message of positivity. At the end of the 1953 season, Veeck struck a deal with Baltimore forces. The few embittered Browns fans in St. Louis mourned, but after a territorial concession by the Washington Senators, and with the massive enthusiasm unleashed by the big leagues' return to Milwaukee as precedent, major league owners approved the sale and move.[28] Baltimore was back.

Back in the Show: The Coming of the Oriole Way, 1954–1965

In Baltimore, memories die hard. The return of major league baseball was seen as restoration. Poet and fan Ogden Nash set the tone with "You Can't Kill an Oriole," in which a reanimated Willie Keeler runs through the city, with fire back in his eyes and his jaw full of tobacco, to rouse the old greats of the 1890s with the news that the Orioles have returned.[29]

"CITY GETS THE BROWNS, Baltimore's 51-Year Drouth Finally Ends," exulted the September 30, 1953, banner headline in the *Sun*.[30] The *Washington Post* also played the theme: "Orioles Have Brilliant History and 11 Players in Hall of Fame," adding a tone of justice to the tale, penned by Herb Heft: "And so, after 50 years, the American League yesterday atoned for the shabby treatment it gave Baltimore fans when it took away their major league baseball franchise."[31] Longtime Washington Senators owner Clark Griffith overrode nephew Calvin's opposition and supported the transfer, a rare instance of a sports tycoon take a gracious approach to a new competitor. Clarence Miles assured Baltimore fans that there was no question of importing the Browns' name or adopting any other but "Orioles": "That's a proud old Baltimore name and it would be unthinkable to run a ball club here and call it anything else."[32]

Bill Veeck bought the Browns in 1951. His hopes of overtaking the Cardinals took a blow when Gussie Busch bought the National League squad in 1953. Veeck eyed a move to Baltimore, but fellow owners would approve the shift only if Veeck sold his club.

They opened on the road, losing to the White Sox on April 13. But as in the 1890s, the reborn Orioles started off 1954's home season on April 15 with a parade up Howard and Charles streets, all the way from Camden Station to the renamed Memorial Stadium on 33rd Street. Spectators roared their approval from the sidewalks while manager Jimmy Dykes and the players waved from open convertibles, preceded by bands and floats.[33] Vice President Richard Nixon did first pitch duties, and the Orioles obliged a packed house with a 3–1 victory, paced by pitcher Bob Turley, supported by home runs from catcher Clint Courtney and third baseman Vern Stephens.[34] The glow of Baltimore's restoration shone all season, even though the team resembled the desultory Browns more than Keeler's fearsome pennant winners, finishing at 54–100. They did avoided the cellar by a game, slipping past the forlorn A's who were playing it out in Philadelphia.[35] They made positive history on September 10, when Joe Durham debuted as the Orioles' first black position player, taking the field while Baltimore was still a segregated city.[36]

The mid-to-late 1950s were glory years for pro sports in Baltimore. Most of the excitement took place on Memorial Stadium's gridiron, where the Baltimore Colts put together one of the National Football League's all-time great teams. Like the Orioles, the Colts had a phoenix-from-the-ashes component that made protective Baltimore fans cling to them all the more fiercely. The team started when Baltimore investors purchased the defunct Miami Seahawks of the All-American Football Conference, in 1946. A fan contest renamed the team in honor of Maryland's thoroughbred heritage, and the AAFC Colts took the field in 1947. The upstart AAFC struggled in its competition with the National Football League, gaining a partial merger.[37] The Colts expired, only to reappear when the

The relocated Browns became the Baltimore Orioles in 1954. They would lose the same number of games, 100, as they had the year before, but attendance jumped from just under 300,000 to more than 1 million.

Memorial Stadium, hastily refurbished after Oriole Park burned down in 1944, was home to the NFL Colts in addition to the Orioles, who would play there through the 1991 season.

Dallas NFL team went under in 1953.[38] Behind the adroit scouting of GM Don Kellett, who made the famous phone call that netted free agent quarterback Johnny Unitas in 1954, the Colts improved on the field and dominated the city's sportscape.[39] It was Kellett and head coach Weeb Ewbank who formed the brain trust, while a hallowed assortment of stars including Unitas, Lenny Moore, Artie Donovan, Raymond Berry, Alan Ameche, Gino Marchetti, and Gene "Big Daddy" Lipscomb took the Colts to the top of the pro football world. They won the so-called "Greatest Game Ever Played," besting the New York Giants during overtime in the 1958 championship game, and they repeated as title winners in 1959.

In the meantime, the Orioles were a lower-division regular. But just as the Colts laid the basis for success by empowering smart management, the Orioles made a fateful hire at the end of the 1954 season. Chicago White Sox manager Paul Richards' contract was up. The Pale Hose, after years of mediocre drift, were on a definite upswing, which famed *Chicago Tribune* columnist Arch Ward attributed to Richards' systematic approach to building a winner. Deaf to Ward's pleas to rehire the brainy Texan, the Comiskey family let Richards go. The Orioles, done with Dykes, snapped

Richards up, offering "The Wizard of Waxahachie" a dual appointment as manager and GM. "I'm running the show," explained the new Baltimore chief.[40]

`At age 45 upon taking the helm, Richards had, during his eight years as a big-league catcher, given lie to the old barb about "the tools of ignorance." He was known for his cerebral approach, relying less on savvy and hunch than on his own brand of systematic baseball analysis. While managing in the minors, Richards hit upon a formula he called "batting average with bases on balls," that he felt captured a hitter's general effectiveness better than conventional metrics. Later statistics-minded baseball students would call this "on-base percentage," but by any name, Richards was first to track it.[41] In 1955, Richards published a book, *Modern Baseball Strategy*, which laid out his ideas in theory and practice. The book contained no magic formulae, but rather packaged solid insight with specific suggestions for how to handle everything from a starting staff to a run-down. One example among hundreds was his take on the pick-off move. "Many coaches and managers teach pitchers to come to a complete stop when holding runners on first," he noted, adding that this could be a mistake for some hurlers because, "The good base runner can sometimes get a better jump after a stop." He added that, regardless of the rule book definition of "full stop," he taught the pitcher to "come down and allow his hands to make contact with his body," because, in the American League at least, "The umpires will consider this a stop."[42] "Pitching is the backbone of any baseball team, and a good staff can keep a mediocre team in the pennant race almost indefinitely," he pronounced, adding that no two pitchers were alike, which meant that a manager had to figure out how to handle each one properly.[43]

It was his emphasis on pitching and defense that prompted implementation of vertical formula from top to bottom throughout the Oriole system. Richards blended keen diamond knowledge with understanding about off-field factors. "Pitching and defense keeps you in games, and if you have a chance to win the fans will keep interested and have hope," he observed.[44]

It was not for nothing that Richards weighed the fans' loyalty. In those Baltimore days, the Colts reigned supreme. Orioles front-office employee Joe Hamper admitted that, "The Colts ... were almost like a religion to the sports fans of the city, and we were second-class citizens. The Colts sold out the stadium and everybody, myself included, was a fanatic Colts fan."[45] And in fact, there was potential for fan disaffection when it came to baseball. First off, the Orioles had a slower start at the gate and on the field than the Braves did in Milwaukee, disappointing American League owners hoping for a replica of Wisconsin's instantaneous success. Second, the racial tensions of Baltimore—never far from the surface—seemed worse on the diamond than the gridiron. D'Alesandro, a quintessential machine pol who liked each vote, nevertheless was very much a product of his place and time. Once, he was asked by reporters to compare Baltimore's paltry economic development with Pittsburgh's aggressive urban renewal. "You've gotta remember," the mayor lamentably quipped, "Pittsburgh's got all those Melons. All we got is watermelons."[46] It was lines like that, reflecting the still-staunch commitment to segregation in the city, which prompted the NAACP to warn the American League that 1954's move into Baltimore meant a move into Jim Crow land. Local *Afro-American* sports scribe Sam Lacy, who went on to become the dean of Baltimore sportswriters, pointedly contrasted the Orioles' slow approach to integrating their roster with the Colts' record as the most racially liberal organization in sports.[47]

Richards' identity as a Texan did him no favors in the eyes of African American fans, nor did rumors of a lukewarm attitude towards integration. Richards responded angrily to accusations of racism, and there is no evidence that he was particularly insensitive or intransigent. But suspicions lingered. In order to shore up the connection to black Baltimore, the Orioles and D'Alesandro pragmatically sponsored "Connie Johnson Day" in honor of the Orioles' first black pitching star. But asked about Richards' racial attitudes in later years, Johnson himself surmised, "I don't think he liked blacks too much."[48]

With that kind of baggage in tow, the Orioles might have found themselves controversial. But they were not, perhaps because the Colt fever raging throughout Baltimore in the mid–late 1950s allowed Richards and his team to operate under the protective shade of a winner which lifted fans' moods. So all-encompassing was the era of good feelings generated by the Colts, who drew fans from both sides of Maryland's color line and from every stratum in socially stratified Baltimore, that there was simply no room for sports gloom. Richards' arrival removed the last whiff of the Browns, allowing the team to re-make itself as Baltimore's own.

There were two main thrusts to Richards' plans to overhaul and improve the Orioles: vertical integration of instruction and talent acquisition. First, he systematized what coaches and managers taught players throughout Spring Training and the minors. He wrote and distributed a manual distilling the major points from his book, stressing his belief that learning how to react properly in any game situation would mean victories

down the road. "More games are lost rather than won," Richards would
insist, as he walked everyone through a series of situations and explained
how all Orioles should react.[49] Richards' protégée Dick Williams, who
went on to a Hall of Fame managing career, was an Orioles utility man in
those days. He described what it was like watching Richards teach during
spring training. "They began by taking the whole ball club to the on-deck
circle," Williams explained, relating the Waxahachie Wizard's message as,
"This is what we do here. This is what we do going up to the plate as far
as looking at the coaches and getting the sign is concerned." From there
it was on to the plate itself, where "They talked about every play, offen-
sively and defensively.... Same thing between home and first ... how to
run the bases. First base, breaks and leads. Offensive and defensive plays
at first, second, short, third. Same thing in the outfield. All phases of the
game."[50] According to Williams, the first around-the-diamond tutorial
took three full days. Years later, catcher Elrod Hendricks explained the
result of having a major league roster made up of players trained in what
came to be called The Oriole Way. "Never beat yourself.... We let the other
team make mistakes and beat themselves and when the opportunity came
we'd jump on it."[51]

What made Richards unusual and lent him a wizard's aura was not
the actual strategy and tactics he taught. These were hardly radical. But
Richards was unapologetic about his system and its mandate for correct
instruction. He preached a baseball version of mindfulness. The sport is
not often kind to intellectuals operating within its borders. It likes high-
brow writers praising it from outside, or retired participants putting out
funny memoirs with the help of friendly sportswriters. But if a player gets
too literary, labels like "egghead," "rebel," or "loner" soon circulate. So
learned Jim Brosnan, the bespectacled pitcher whose diaries *The Long
Season* and *Pennant Race* chronicled the 1959 and 1961 seasons, or Jim
Bouton, whose *Ball Four* broke the sports book mold with its irreverent
expose of the 1969 Seattle Pilots. But Richards' book was direct and uncontroversial, and as for his authorship, he was ever blunt about the wisdom
of institutionalizing basic baseball theories and methods. The Orioles
offered him a laboratory in which to put his ideas into practice.

These ideas were put forth plainly in *Modern Baseball Strategy*, published by Prentice-Hall in 1955. With a foreword purportedly by Leo
Durocher, the book bore the seal of respected baseball men. Richards'
opening chapter, "Why I Wrote This Book," makes the revealing point
that, after a lifetime of studying the game, he felt compelled to record his
knowledge in systematic form as much to codify his lessons for himself

as for the reader.[52] Richards covers every scenario from the hit-and-run to the squeeze play, from junk pitches to superstitions. On every page, he stressed the need for every player to be thoroughly drilled on the proper play for each scenario. He blended anecdotes from game situations with instruction on how—and, most crucially, *why*—certain situations called for certain reactions, every time.

The other phase of Richards' organizational overhaul was talent acquisition. The Browns' unproductive farm system needed improvement, so a commitment to scouting was imperative. Richards plunged right in, as in 1955, when he talked with the father of a young Arkansas-raised infield prospect still playing in high school and considering his options. The teenager's name was Brooks Robinson, and his father was worried about the Orioles' losing ways and brief track record. "They lost a hundred games in Baltimore last year," Richards admitted, "We're gonna lose a hundred this year. If your boy can play, he'll get a chance to play here."[53] But Richards exuded confidence bordering on certainty that the losing would stop once the youngsters learned and matured. The Robinson family liked what they heard.

As if to underscore the fact that the new Orioles were no longer the old Browns, Richards immediately pulled off the biggest trade in baseball history in 1954, a 17-player doozy with the Yankees that unloaded pitchers Don Larsen and Bob Turley while importing catcher Gus Triandos and a host of others.[54] Quantity and quality were part of the tear-down and rebuild. Robinson himself understood that Richards aimed at totally over-hauling the Orioles roster and way of doing things. In those days, flush with authority and the power to spend, Richards "signed a lot of young players and handed out huge sums of money," according to the young infielder's recollection. But no matter the situation, "He always looked like he was thinking," Robinson recalled. Except for his only preferred topic, baseball, Richards was a man of few words. Hungry for game knowledge, Robinson and his Oriole teammates hung on each lesson.[55] As the organization reinvented itself and institutionalized a new vision of what it meant to be an Oriole ballplayer, fans enjoyed some highlights on the field. None was more sweet than the 1958 All-Star Game, awarded to Baltimore, which served as a sort of national coming-out party reaffirming that the Orioles were back. That game saw pitcher Billy O'Dell retire all nine batters he faced to save a 4–3 American League triumph.[56]

In July 1960, the team started a new initiative aimed at shoring up community relations and attendance. Since the team's arrival, attendance had bounced around the 1 million mark; slightly above in bumper seasons,

Signed in 1955, third baseman Brooks Robinson played 23 seasons for the Orioles. He would go to win the 1964 MVP Award, 16 consecutive Gold Gloves and election to the Hall of Fame in 1983.

below otherwise. This was respectable, but hardly signaled the bonanza that Milwaukee experienced with the Braves at first. So the franchise founded the Oriole Advocates, a 75-member group of men and women from local businesses who were committed fans anxious to lend a hand to their favorite team. Their work focused on promotions and public relations, including such off-field endeavors as the Junior Orioles, a fan club for kids that kicked off in 1963 with 750 youngsters, rising to 20,000 members by 1977. Also, the Advocates contributed time and funds to in-park events such as cap night, paying for and distributing the giveaway souvenirs. They played a leading role in refurbishing Babe Ruth's childhood home as a museum.[57] Over the next decades, the Orioles Advocates formed a cadre of pro-baseball civic leaders who would become politically valuable in the late 1970s when the team went through ownership changes and sought a new ballpark.

From the start, Richards had a premonition that what he wanted to do would take years to institutionalize itself. Turning defeat into victory was neither easy nor quick. He once joked with reporters, "Someday, boys, maybe in four or five years from now, Baltimore will have a fine young team in the field. When the day finally comes and a pennant is hoisted on the stadium flagpole, all I ask is that you observe a moment of respectful silence in memory of old number 12."[58] He almost made it through 1961. The expansion Houston Colt .45's lured him back home to Texas. But by then, his Orioles plan was a success. Incremental improvement through 1959 saw the Birds rise to a near-.500 record before breaking through in 1960, when they went 89–65 and nipped at the pennant-bound Yankees' heels before finishing second, eight games back.[59] By then, Baltimore's roster was talented—Robinson was at third, Triandos behind the plate, and a bright young staff; "The Baby Birds," sportswriters nicknamed them: Chick Estrada, 18–11; Milt Pappas, 15–11, "Fat Jack" Fisher, 12–11; Steve Barber, 10–7; Hal Brown, 12–5. Knuckleballer Hoyt Wilhelm anchored the bullpen.[60]

That year, 1960, saw the mighty Bombers nail down the pennant with a 15-game win streak at the end of the season. But the Orioles impressed several sportswriters, who praised Richards. Jerome Holtzman tabbed the skipper, "Baltimore's most-quoted sage since H.L. Mencken," while Roy Terrell called hin, "A cold man, and a hard one," who when he relaxed "the imperious reserve that cloaks him" was capable of charming "a ballplayer right out of his spikes."[61] Things looked great in Baltimore, and the team's marketing slogan was "It can be done in '61." New arrival Jim Gentile took over at first, giving Richards the slugger he longed for, as he told scribes, "All this team really needs is that one big man. A monster who can hit 40 home runs and bat in 130."[62] Gentile obliged, batting .302, with 46 homers and 141 RBIs. The Orioles finished 95–67, their best record yet. Although the Yankees won 109 and the Tigers 101, putting Baltimore in third place as Richards went home to the Lone Star state, Oriole fans at last had a winner on their hands.

Richards was not in Baltimore to reap the harvest he sowed. In fact, his sharp persona made his Texas homecoming brief. By 1966, he was off to Atlanta with the relocated Braves. Later, it was on to the White Sox. When sportswriters sought to describe him, they usually resorted to adjectives bringing up his western, cowboy nature. This was accurate so far as it went; he really was a taciturn man from the plains. But Richards' organizational acumen, while anchored in baseball principles, also mirrored effective management principles being put in place at a variety of enterprises at that time in American business. Like many executives, Richards understood that systematizing training, fixing in place an organizational philosophy to which all members should adhere, breeds product coherence, which in turn boosts a brand. Over the years, as baseball people discussed "the Oriole Way," they often located its core in the "perfect practice makes perfect" ethos of the Ripken family. Richards set up the structure that produced teams that played and won by actualizing that bit of baseball truth. Perhaps Richards' personality was too severe for him to receive the rewards directly, but his successors in Baltimore grew closer and closer to collecting. 1962 saw a step backwards on the field, with roster losses to the Army (Barber and infielder Ron Hansen) and a 77–85 finish under new skipper Billy Hitchcock. The next season put the Birds on the top side of .500, as they went 86–76. Both were seasons of Yankee dominance, so there was no pressure in the standings. The 1964 season, however, was the team's best yet. The Yankees took the pennant, edging out the White Sox, but the third-place Orioles—this time under Hank Bauer—kept pace nearly all season long, finishing up at 97–65. Brooks Robinson won the MVP, the first modern Oriole to win a major player award. For his part, Bauer, whose frown could freeze from a distance, landed on the cover of *Time*, as the team captured its first share of national attention.[63] 1965 was the Year of the Twins in the American League, as Minnesota went 102–60. The White Sox followed at 95–67. But third place, 94–68, was no disaster. The Orioles were young, their everyday lineup strong, their pitching staff poised for dominance. They were on the brink of greatness. One of the best trades in baseball history would put them there.

Soaring Birds, 1966–1978

One misguided comment can obscure the work of a lifetime. Cincinnati GM Bill DeWitt was a baseball lifer. He was at the helm in St. Louis when the Browns won their only pennant, in 1944. He served as assistant GM in New York during the Bombers' 1950s dominance. He helped to turn around the Tigers, and won a pennant in 1961 with the Reds, before becoming team owner. DeWitt had plenty of reasons to trust his judgment when the Reds landed Oriole starter Milt Pappas, along with Dick Simpson and Jack Baldschun, on December 9, 1965. Pappas was fresh off a 13–9 season with a 2.60 ERA, and at a mere 26, heading into the traditional pitching prime years. In exchange, DeWitt parted with star outfielder Frank Robinson. Another Reds casualty was popular manager Dick Sisler. On his way out the door, Sisler pronounced himself astonished that DeWitt moved the All-Star outfielder. "I was a lot more surprised when they let Frank go than when they dropped me," he said. "He was a leader. You don't replace that kind that easily."[64]

Robinson, a 10-year veteran with a 1961 MVP to his credit, was "an old 30," DeWitt observed to skeptical writers, who publicized his unfortunate phrase. He said that Pappas could anchor the Reds' staff for years. Pappas voiced disappointment at leaving Baltimore, but Robinson was furious at being traded by the Reds.[65] New Orioles owner Jerry Hoffberger, president of Maryland-based National Brewery, restored the original link between beer and baseball in Baltimore. Hoffberger, who eschewed the limelight, was an astute businessman pursuing majority team ownership since 1963. On May 26, 1965, he was announced as the new owner.[66] Hoffberger hired Harry Dalton as GM, and Dalton pulled off the trade. Dalton, who built the team's fertile farm system, was a product of Richards' organizational philosophy. Dalton—described by the *Sporting News* in 1961 as "alert, quick, intelligent … with a fantastic memory for names and figures, sound baseball judgement, and a seemingly limitless capacity for work"[67]— knew the organization from bottom to top. He thrived under Hoffberger's leadership method, which was to hire good baseball people and let them do their jobs, pending results. "When Jerry gave me the job… he said, 'I've only got one piece of advice for you: as long as you make more right decisions than wrong ones, you'll never have any trouble.'"[68] Trading for Robinson certainly was a right decision. He immediately became one of the best Orioles ever. Plus, in the words of manager Bauer, Robinson was "The missing cog…. He had something to prove."[69] Robinson echoed the sentiment. "The trade gave me a little extra incentive," he admitted. "I had to prove them wrong. I had to prove myself."[70]

The outfielder wasted no time, homering in the first three games of 1966. On Mother's Day, he clubbed the only home run ever to clear Memorial Stadium, a blast so memorable that it was memorialized by a flag over the left-field bleachers that simply read, "HERE." For the next three decades, home fans relished explaining the banner's significance to curious visitors. Robinson's torrid pace never slackened; he won the 1966 Triple Crown, hitting .316 with 49 home runs and 122 RBI. His slugging average, .637, had him .99 ahead of runner-up Harmon Killebrew. The Orioles followed Robinson's lead all the way to the pennant, going 97–63, well ahead of the second place Twins. It was doubly significant because, given Baltimore's segregated past, having a black player as unquestioned team leader—with the same last name as fan favorite Brooks—set a note of public racial comity. The Colts were emblematic of improvements in local race relations during the 1950s and 1960s, while the Orioles were viewed suspiciously on that score. But the installation of Frank Robinson meant that the Orioles were suddenly a symbol for social betterment in a city that sorely needed that. The two Robinsons were often photographed together, and there were japes about using the players' uniform numbers to tell them apart. Newspaper photos and mild humor were hardly revolutionary, but these were years in Maryland, and the United States, where any signs of racial ease were cherished against the backdrop of national controversy. Part of the formula for the Robinson partnership was Brooks' innate decency. In Frank's own words, the native Arkansan was personally welcoming and conspicuously conscientious on racial matters. "I suspect Brooks was a key reason why, for the first time in my 14 years of professional baseball, black players and white players had drinks and meals together when we were on the road," he said.[71]

That surmise was set against earlier memories of playing exhibition games in Baltimore during the late 1950s, when Jim Crow kept the Reds in separate hotels and restaurants. But instead of a hostile reception, Robinson found himself set at ease. At first, there was difficulty in finding a house, since real estate agents were hesitant to deal with a black family. But, according to Robinson, Hoffberger took the lead in overriding such hidebound prejudice.[72] No stranger to racism, of course, the new Orioles outfielder appreciated an owner willing to act against it. "Once we moved in it worked out beautifully and that made it much easier on me to perform my job out on the field. I didn't have to worry about my family and I was able to concentrate fully on baseball."[73] Other Orioles would credit Hoffberger's performance on this score as contributing to the team's tight-knit atmosphere, which helped to breed success. Hoffberger, whose long record of philanthropy was, if anything, more locally important than his team ownership, would credit his Jewish upbringing and commitment to social justice. His aim was to help Baltimore overcome its sad racial past through aggressive defense of Robinson's rights off the field and leadership on the team. Robinson understood. "He wouldn't come over and slap you on the back and say, 'Nice game winning home-run.... The first words out of his mouth were, 'How are you? How's your family? Is there anything I can do for you?' And that ... was the greatest significance.... I looked up to him not only as the owner of the ballclub but as a friend of mine."[74]

To this day, the full impact of Frank Robinson's arrival and immediate leadership role on the Orioles has not been fully recognized by media outside of Baltimore. Coming as it did during the switch into integration, the timing could not have been more crucial, nor the situation more fraught. Robinson's class and talent gave the franchise an instant public relations advantage. The irony was that, in his earlier years, Robinson had the reputation of playing angry, a loaded phrase when leveled at a black player. "There's something about the way he stands at the plate," Phillies' ace

Robin Roberts—who pitched with Baltimore from 1962 to 1965—observed. "He sort of bristles. He wants to hurt you. And he usually does."[75] Outfielder Eddie Kasko allowed that, prior to arriving in Cincinnati, he loathed Robinson. "Before coming to the Reds, I played two years against Robinson and I hated him.... He just has the attitude of a guy you want to beat. He challenges you all the time."[76]

In Baltimore, his game lost none of its fury, but Robinson's personality revealed humor and joy in winning. He led the team's Kangaroo Court, handing out fines for on-field mistakes. His commitment to victory made him a natural fit with the Oriole Way, and he became a fierce advocate of strong fundamentals. His

Arriving from Cincinnati in 1966, outfielder and future Hall of Famer Frank Robinson was a team leader who stressed fundamentals and supported the Oriole Way. He won the 1966 Triple Crown as well as the MVP, and he was the first African American superstar in formerly segregated Baltimore.

rise to team leadership was organic, based upon his own drive and work habits. Don Baylor, whose major league career began as an Oriole and who rose through the team's minor league system during its best years, explained it. "When I first came to the major leagues, Frank *was* the Baltimore Orioles. Everybody, including Brooks, flocked to Frank.... How to run the bases, how to play certain stadium walls, how to hit, or whatever. And the way he played the game was the way it should be played.... If you couldn't learn from watching him, you couldn't learn anything. Frank did not solicit the leadership role.... Yet guys gravitated to Frank because he had charisma. He was the manager on the field."[77] Baylor also admired Robinson's stint as Kangaroo Court judge. "He held court after every victory at home," the younger outfielder recalled. "He closed the clubhouse door for fifteen minutes, letting players relax.... Then, came judgement day. Frank's system was a funny, caustic reminder that the game should be played correctly—or else."[78] It was partly due to Robinson's prodigious intelligence—the game held few mysteries for him, which allowed him to prosper later as a manager—that he swiftly grasped the Oriole Way in its entirety and set about shoring it up.

Robinson also revealed a sense of humor, at least to his teammates, that eased his entry into team leadership When beefy Boog Powell nicknamed the newcomer "Pencils" because of his long, slender legs, Robinson tagged the first baseman with the appellation, "Crisco." "What I was telling Boog was that he was fat," the outfielder laughingly admitted.[79] He enjoyed clubhouse practical jokes, scaring Luis Aparacio with false warnings about snakes, or giving hotfoots. "The joking never stopped," Robinson recalled.[80] But the joking was designed to relieve the tension that came from high expectations for baseball performance, reflecting the tone set by Bauer. Robinson liked his new manager, who blended a gruff Marine Corps veteran exterior with a professional concern for his players' welfare.

When Baltimore swept defending champion Los Angeles in the World Series, it seemed a monumental upset. The Dodgers, with Sandy Koufax, Don Drysdale, and Claude Osteen, had strong pitching and were used to winning big games. But in the Series it was the Orioles starters who had shone, allowing only two earned runs over thirty-six innings.

The Birds were a more balanced team than the Dodgers, too. They led the American League in most offensive categories and had good depth, with competent subs like outfielder Curt Blefary coming off the bench. They played stellar defense, with Aparacio and Brooks Robinson winning Gold Gloves that year and Boog Powell, Dave Johnson, and Paul Blair winning them in the future. Bauer, whose 14-season playing career included nine World Series appearances with the Yankees, was hardly overwhelmed by the pressures of the Fall Classic or the Dodger mystique. Robinson was deeply familiar with the Dodger staff. And if the Orioles' pitching staff was not as famous as the Dodgers', it was nevertheless extremely tough. Dave McNally (13–6, 3.17), was the ace, with Steve Barber (10–5, 2.30), Wally Bunker (10–6, 4.29), and the lanky 21-year-old Jim Palmer rounding out the staff. Palmer, 15–10 with a 3.46 ERA during the regular season, would outduel Koufax in a Game 2 gem, winning 6–0 and becoming the youngest starter ever to toss a World Series shutout. Meanwhile, the bullpen was scintillating, with relievers Eddie Fisher, Dick Hall, Stu Miller, and Moe Drabowsky ending threats all season long. Drabowsky's lengthy Game 1 appearance in relief of McNally saw the relief ace set a record with 11 strikeouts, including six straight. The scores—5–2, 6–0, 1–0, 1–0—made the Orioles' pitching performance abundantly clear. The Baltimore ERA for the Series was 0.50, and Los Angeles mustered only a .142 batting average.

Few could have foreseen it, but the Orioles had the pieces in place for a dynastic run. While some stars of the 1966 team would soon move on, including Aparacio, Barber, Bunker, and Miller, their replacements—players like Gold Glove shortstop Mark Belanger and starting pitcher Mike Cuellar—filled in or actually improved the team. Cuellar, for example, was a Cuban lefthander with a fine screwball who split the Cy Young Award with Tiger Denny McLain in 1969. Also, young players like Powell moved into their prime. Powell was a bona fide slugger, 6'5" and at least his listed 265 pounds. Despite his size, however, he was a magnificent fielder, especially once he moved to first. He feuded with Bauer about his weight, which Earl Weaver never bothered about.[81] But there was no second-guessing Powell's performance as a Gold Glover and MVP winner. He was an Oriole from 1961 through 1974.

There were three more pennants and another World Series win in store for the Orioles of 1966–1971. Nineteen sixty-six brought their first World Series win, 1969 an upset five-game loss to the Mets, 1970 a five-game win over the Reds, and 1971 a nail-biting seven-game loss to the Pirates. This iteration of the Orioles firmly marked the team as a major baseball power. They ranked with the best teams of their era, such as Cincinnati's Big Red Machine and Oakland's Swingin' A's. Through it all, the Oriole Way preached sound fundamentals, strong pitching and defense, and good power on the field. Off, the team soared with notably excellent scouting and player development. When the occasion warranted, as it did with Robinson in 1966, and less positively in 1972, when the Orioles moved him to the Dodgers for a slew of prospects, the front office was willing to make trades as well.

But the sunny future was not yet known when the team tailed off in 1967, with arm woes derailing the starters en route to a 76–85 mark. It was a letdown. A slow start in 1968 doomed Bauer, who was replaced with the first-base coach, a short, feisty, chain-smoker named Earl Weaver. By his own admission, Weaver, who climbed every rung of the minor leagues before arriving in the bigs as a member of Bauer's staff, found the prospect of managing a star-laden team simultaneously thrilling and sobering. "There was no problem with managing the ball club," he would relate. "It was just, how good is the ball club going to be? Or how good am I going to be?"[82]

From 1961 to 1974, Boog Powell was a fixture at first base. His stellar fielding earned him four Gold Gloves, and his slugging led to a Most Valuable Player Award in 1970.

Born in St. Louis, where his father ran a laundry that cleaned the uniforms of the Browns and Cardinals, Weaver hung around those locker rooms as a boy, imbibing the atmosphere, collecting autographs and worshipfully observing the ballplayers.[83] That boyhood fixed his lifelong passion for the game. Weaver was a career minor league infielder who found a niche as a manager, rising in the Orioles' system. Before AAA Rochester, Weaver managed in the Class D Georgia-Florida League, at Fitzgerald; then up through Dublin, Georgia; Aberdeen, South Dakota; Fox Cities, Wisconsin; and Elmira, New York. Winning three championships and finishing second three times during his 11-year ascent, Weaver was well known and trusted by the team's front office, a mentor to many on the roster, and a natural choice for a franchise that believed it was on the right track but needed an infusion of vigor. One of Weaver's most obvious traits was a lack of concern with appearances. To him, the game was all-consuming, his involvement with it total. Because of this naked commitment, he would become a special favorite with famous writers who adored the game and saw in it the stakes, values and adventure which make baseball the richest sport in literary terms. Weaver's manifest intelligence matched that of the authors, while his eagerness to discuss the game at length anyone e interested made him a compelling interview for smitten wordsmiths. Roger Angell wrote, "Weaver doesn't give a damn what anybody will think later, which makes him a pearl among managers and men."[84]

Introducing the 5'4" manager, Dalton was blunt. "In short, I consider Earl Weaver a winner. He is very aggressive, He is a battler for the team, for his organization, and for what he thinks is right on the ball club."[85] Weaver thought strong starting pitching, consistent defense, and power at the plate were right. Taking over for Bauer during the middle of the 1968 season, with the Orioles hardly sinking at 43–37, Weaver went 48–34 the rest of the way. He knew many of the players already, and scout Jim Russo detected signs of what became Weaver's signature, a deep awareness of possibilities on the diamond and the ability to manage contingently—that is, to make a series of interlocking decisions arranged so as to arrive at advantageous matchups and situations. To do that required penetrating vision. "Earl took to managing from the very first game. He had a feel for it. He could visualize an entire ballgame and put each thing that happened in its proper perspective. He always had in the back of his mind what he would want to do in the seventh, eighth, or ninth inning when he was playing the second inning. He also knew what he would do if the other guy did something."[86]

Many books would be written featuring details on Weaver's approach to the game, including three titles by Weaver himself. Certain phrases, such as "Pitching, defense, and three-run homers," or "On offense, your most precious possessions are your 27 outs," or, "If you play for one run, that's all you'll get," summed up his outlook. But rejecting small ball tactics like the bunt or hit-and-run, both of which Weaver deplored, was not the crucial aspect of his managing. Instead, his pioneering use of statistics allowed him to relentlessly pursue favorable matchups. In an era before laptops, his box of index cards might have been the game's best informational treasure trove. His mastery of players' situational records allowed him to make full use of his bench, so that substitutions and platoons became signatures for Weaver teams. For example, if the skipper knew that pinch hitter Chico Salmon matched up well against a certain pitcher, he would not hesitate to bat him, even in place of a slugger like Powell.

An emphasis on defensive fundamentals paid dividends in 1969, when four Orioles won Gold Gloves. **From Left: Brooks Robinson (3B), Mark Belanger (SS), Davey Johnson (2B) and Paul Blair (CF).**

So Weaver's formulae rested upon the foundation of knowledge, well before analytics came into vogue.

The 1969 season saw his methods jibe with the team's obvious talent, as the Orioles rolled to a 109–53 record. The new divisional alignment meant that they were AL East champions, headed to the playoffs, where they swept the overmatched Twins. It seemed a foregone conclusion that they would roll over the plucky "Amazin's," the upstart Mets, who reinvigorated New York's National League tradition that year. But closer examination should have bred caution, for the Mets were hardly a fluke. Their pitching staff, led by Tom Seaver (25–7, 2.21) and Jerry Koosman (17–9. 2.28), was first-rate. They also had a young spot starter named Nolan Ryan. Their lineup, while not as power-laden as the one the Orioles' boasted, was filled with strong role players, like Tommy Agee, Cleon Jones, and Jerry Grote. After the Orioles won Game 1, the Mets never looked back, winning the next four, sending New York fans into paroxysms of joy, and New York writers to their publishers. Nineteen sixty-nine was an *annus horribilis* for Baltimore fans, who found their favorite teams, the Colts and Orioles, improbably cast as heavy favorites against endearing underdogs from New York. Even the NBA Bullets lost to the Knicks that year in the playoffs. So conclusive was the New York annihilation of Baltimore sports hopes that *Mad* magazine wrote a parody song, "The Road to Baltimore," about woeful upsets. Weaver's Orioles promptly rebounded. The 1970 squad again cruised, going 108–54. McNally, Cuellar, and Palmer each won 20 games, and Powell took home the MVP after clubbing 35 homers and walking 104 times. When a resentful opponent pointed out that the Orioles were not supermen, Frank Robinson, Paul Blair, and Moe Drabowsky laughingly mugged for the cameras, opening their jerseys to reveal Superman tee-shirts underneath.[87] In the playoffs the O's faced the Twins, again, who were swept, again. The high point of the playoffs came when Cuellar belted a grand slam in Game 1. McNallly then hit a grand slam of his own during Game 3 of the World Series, against Cincinnati. The Orioles won the Series in five, alleviating the gnawing pain that had dogged them since being upset the year before. The Series' hallmark was the amazing fielding display put on by Brooks Robinson. Time and again, he robbed the Reds, prompting Lee May to dub him "the Human Vacuum Cleaner."[88] Robinson also cleaned up at the plate in that Fall Classic, hitting .429 en route to winning the World Series MVP Award.

Baltimore won another AL East title in 1971, courtesy of a starting rotation that featured four 20-game winners: McNally, Cuellar, Palmer, and newcomer Pat Dobson. Then came another playoff sweep—this time over a talented young Oakland team—and a World Series against Pittsburgh. In a fretful classic, the Pirates won in seven games. Starters Steve Blass and Nelson Briles, helped by young reliever Bruce Kison, pitched just well enough to prevail. The loss marked the end of the Orioles' solid six-year run.

Now it was Baltimore that decided to move Frank Robinson, seeking to cash in on what they could get for their 36-year-old star. Frank Cashen, who moved into the top chair after Harry Dalton departed for the Angels, engineered a deal with the Dodgers that netted four young players, including starting pitcher Doyle Alexander.[89] Shocking as the trade was, the Orioles front office was convinced that Rochester rookie Don Baylor, a hard-hitting outfielder, would soon fill Robinson's shoes. The 1972 team was younger, courtesy of that blockbuster deal with the Dodgers, but finished 80–74, good for third behind the Tigers and Red Sox. The biggest problem with the Birds was anemic hitting, which led to plenty of close losses. Another strange development for Orioles fans—and fans of every other team—was a 154-game season, courtesy of a player strike that delayed Opening Day for nearly two weeks.

In 1966, Nineteen-year-old Jim Palmer went 15–10 during the regular season and shut out the Dodgers in Game Two of the World Series. He went on to win three Cy Young awards and 268 games over 19 seasons, all with Baltimore. Palmer was elected to the Hall of Fame in 1990.

Fiery Earl Weaver arrived to manage the Orioles in 1968. Obsessed with optimizing match-ups, he pioneered the use of statistics to determine in-game moves.Weaver managed in Baltimore for 17 years and was inducted into the Hall of Fame in 1996.

Other off-field currents also affected the Orioles trajectory in the early Seventies. The Colts, who shared Memorial Stadium, had mirrored the Orioles by losing to a New York underdog in 1969's Super Bowl III, then recovering their composure to gain a measure of solace by winning Super Bowl V. This meant that 1970 marked a double-championship season for Maryland fans, who perhaps grew too accustomed to such rare accomplishments by their favorite teams. Colt owner Carroll Rosenbloom, a product of the generous and influential Jewish philanthropic community that did more than any other group to build Baltimore's civic and cultural institutions during the 20th Century, was dissatisfied. A magnate with diversified holdings, he had interest in show business, adding movie production to his portfolio.

After his divorce from his first wife, which took a decade to finalize, Rosenbloom was free to marry Georgia, an actress. She was unaffiliated with Baltimore, while he wanted the city to build him a new stadium. When local authorities balked, Rosenbloom looked to Los Angeles, a better venue for his new wife's acting ambitions. In an unusual arrangement, he solicited a new buyer for the Rams, an Illinois businessman, Robert Irsay. Irsay's purchase of the team sailed through NFL ownership circles, whereupon Rosenbloom and the new owner swapped franchises. Baltimore was surprised to find that their hometown owner, Rosenbloom, had decamped to California, leaving them with a newcomer. The city and its fans would get to know Irsay all too well. Almost at once, Colt demands for a new grew louder and more insistent. After investigating, civic leaders put forth a tentative plan to build a multi-purpose dome. Eventually, the cost estimates proved too daunting and the plan was scrapped.[90]

The Orioles were keen observers. Nobody could have foreseen it at the time, but the failure to build a multipurpose dome in Baltimore during the 1970, first seen as a failure, spared fans from a dreary 1970s version of the Seattle's Kingdome or Montreal's Olympique.[91] The Orioles played consistently well, thanks to their systematic philosophy and practice. But it was clear that the sports environment was changing everywhere, not just in Baltimore.

Weaver, who was shaped by, and helped to shape, the Orioles Way, was confident enough to recognize the wisdom of having excellent coaches. George Bamberger, Billy Hunter, George Staller, Jim Frey, Joe Altobelli, Cal Ripken, Sr., and Ray Miller were just a few of the coaches who filled out his staff over the years. Several went on to managerial careers of their own, as less-well-run teams looked to import a bit of the Oriole formula to upgrade their own teams.

Another part of Weaver's career—the one most visible to out-of-town fans—was his fraught relations with umpires. Weaver fussed, feuded, screamed, and protested often. His in-game histrionics delighted Baltimore fans, who stood to applaud particularly memorable performances. Taking a base and refusing to surrender it, tearing up a rule book, tossing his cap, all the while letting loose a steady stream of high-grade profanity, made Weaver fun for fans. Players also enjoyed these displays, especially since the inevitable ejection took pressure off of them, making Weaver the temporary focus. But umpires were less amused, and Weaver's protests led to sustained feuds, especially as quiet men in blue like Nestor Chylack gave way to a new generation of voluble umps, like Ron Luciano, Ken Kaiser, and Marty Springstead. These three were among Weaver's bitterest enemies. The situation only compounded itself, as the manager accused certain umpires of harboring a grudge against him, and therefore his team, while the umpires, less and less inclined to turn away and remain invisible, enjoyed arguing back to their sawed-off tormentor. But the difference between Weaver and other high-octane managers like contemporary Billy Martin was that the Orioles skipper's displays were strictly in-game affairs, driven by competitive fire. He was arrested for drinking and driving after dining out with his wife, and that was troubling; but he never come across as personally unhinged, a point sportswriters made often when they described his lengthy, often meditative post-game disquisitions. In fact, during those post-game baseball talks, with the anger of the in-game moment passed, he sometimes seemed abashed, if still stubbornly convinced of his point. In fact, the only "out of game" stories about Weaver that made the rounds dealt with his appealingly innocent hobby: a tomato-growing contest waged every season against groundskeeper Pat Santarone, beyond Memorial Stadium's outfield wall. The mercurial side of Weaver showed itself entirely within the context of baseball games, and came to be seen by admiring fans as an amusing and performative aspect of his zeal to win. If he shredded a rule book and tossed the scraps like confetti, or uprooted a base and refused to give it back, fans in the stands and players in both dugouts roared with laughter. Mature umpires usually allowed him to complete his little comic pageants before ejecting him. Some of the newer umps, however, saw no humor in his showmanship.

Luciano was a particular foe, and Weaver's disdain for the charismatic umpire was fully reciprocated. "I hate Earl Weaver with a passion," Luciano once said. "I met Weaver in my second year in baseball. I threw him out that first game and three nights after that. Our relationship has gone downhill ever since. He's about three-foot-one. I tell him to get his nose off my kneecap and I call him Mickey Rooney."[92] The capacity of each to irritate the other was so well-known that Ray Miller, Weaver's pitching coach during the late 1970s and early 1980s, was not above a bit of subterfuge to minimize the chances of a Luciano blowup and Weaver ejection. According to Luciano, Miller worried lest the back-and-forth screaming distract his pitcher, and would therefore tell the ump during mound visits that he was "going back to the dugout and tell that little !@#$% to stay off your back." In the dugout, however, the peace-making coach would tell his manager, "The pitcher's okay. And I told Luciano off. That big &%$$#'ll call a better game now. Just give him a few pitches."[93]

One aspect of Weaver's career was paradoxical, in that it involved the media yet received insufficient attention from observers chronicling his career. This was his excellent relations with writers and broadcasters covering the club. Simply put, Weaver loved talking baseball, and had no beef with reporters. If a writer was willing to pull up a chair in the office after a game while Weaver decompressed with a salted beer and cigarettes, that scribe could engage in plenty of baseball talk, including detailed explanations of why certain parts of the previous game went the way they did. In Baltimore, Weaver had a notably strong pool of reporters with whom he could speak. The *Sun* had morning and evening editions, blessed with several career press members the caliber of Bob Maisel (son of minor league Oriole star Fritz Maisel) and Alan Goldstein, along with columnists like Bill Tanton and Phil Jackman. Their editorial excellence extended into football, too, with Vito Stellino, Cameron Snyder, and Jon Morgan. The two *Sun* papers devoted abundant coverage to the Orioles all season. So did the Hearst-owned *News-American*, whose leading sports page luminary was John Steadman, most passionate of Baltimore sportswriters. Baltimore's weekly *Afro-American* featured local legend Sam Lacy, the longest-serving sportswriter in the city's history and a fearless spokesman for civil rights. Starting in the early 1970s, the situation in Washington, D.C., meant that Weaver also had a bumper crop of excellent writers disenfranchised by that city's loss of the Senators. Among these were Thomas Boswell, of the *Washington Post*, who would become one of the foremost baseball writers of his generation.

By his own account, Boswell loved covering the Orioles because of the team's quiet excellence, Memorial Stadium's mild and positive aura, and Weaver's fascinating approach to the game. "The modest, make-do Orioles, the team that won more games than anybody since 1957," the *Post* writer called them in the early 1980s.[94] "Why are there so few cliques?" Boswell wondered admiringly about Weaver's team. "Why do most of the players live in Baltimore in the off-season, not Southern California? Why is race seldom an issue? How can rookies feel welcome almost immediately, even become team leaders? Why is the locker room so relaxed after a loss?"[95] Answering his own questions, Boswell cited "Baltimore intelligence" and the Oriole Way. For his part, Boswell was more than just a common beat reporter, but rather a developing author of rare gifts who could lay fair claim to being the most perceptive and talented baseball writer of his generation. Having studied Weaver at close perspective for many years, Boswell eventually wrote a column terming him "the best manager there is."[96]

Boswell was a writer of enormous literary skills; he happened to specialize in sports and cover the Orioles. Weaver became one of the young writer's preferred subjects, and the resultant reportage forms one of the best, in-depth profiles of the Oriole manager. It also reveals Boswell's insatiable appetite for ever-increasing amounts of baseball knowledge. Weaver, for whom baseball was every bit as fascinating, was hardly a soft touch for reporters, and his salty language meant that he was happy to insult them with terms such as "second-guessing idiots."[97]

But Weaver was secure enough to enjoy swapping barbs with reporters. He laughed out loud when Peter Pascarelli, formerly of the *News-American* and later based in Philadelphia, imitated the manager's gravelly voice and tough talk: "That's the way we like it. Tough as nails," Pascarelli mimicked. Weaver, hardly upset, laughed so hard he nearly choked on his post-game sandwich.[98] But immersed in a similar quest for deeper baseball wisdom, Weaver recognized kindred spirits, and he welcomed Boswell into what amounted to tutorials for the sharp, deep-thinking writer.

Boswell was subjected to rookie hazing like any young player would have been. Weaver's humor tended less to insults than to put-ons, as when he advised Boswell how much Palmer loved discussing fundamentals: "Be sure to talk to Jim," he urged the *Post* reporter, collecting information for a sustained piece on the Oriole Way. "God, don't talk to me about fundamentals," Palmer responded when Boswell followed Weaver's advice and queried the star pitcher. But tellingly, despite his self-declared exasperation with the subject—"So dull, so dull. I hate fundamentals. Cursed Oriole fundamentals.... I've been doing them since 1964. I do them in my sleep."[99]—his passion simply confirmed that he was, in fact, fully immersed in the Oriole Way of doing things on the diamond. Rather than playing a cruel trick on the Washington journalist, what Weaver did in this instance was to glean that Boswell craved baseball acumen, a state of mind the manager obviously respected. The Orioles with whom Boswell spoke all provided helpful details, which helped Boswell to identify the centrality of fundamentals in Spring Training, and to explain this otherwise hidden aspect of the team's culture to his many readers. During the early 1980s, Boswell's closeness to the team meant that Weaver and Baltimore players were subjects of some of the best American sportswriting, featuring not just in numerous articles and columns but in Boswell's several elegant and thoughtful baseball books.

One such book was endorsed by perhaps the only other active writer who could claim equal status as an intellectual covering the game. This was another *Post* figure: editorial columnist, author, and noted fan George Will. Will, temperamentally miles away from Weaver, nevertheless resembled the manager in his understanding of Boswell as a true student of the game. The editorialist praised Boswell as "the thinking person's writer about the thinking person's game,"[100] which was a title many observers might have bestowed on Will himself. It remains a significant, if little remarked-upon indicator of Weaver's appeal that both intellectuals were won over as profound admirers by years of close observation of the Orioles manager's approach to the game.

A noted Cub fan, baseball devotee Will succumbed to the charms of the Orioles, whose winning ways, proximity, and hospitality made them the pundit's second-favorite team. It also helped that Will's son, Jonathan, became an enthusiastic Baltimore fan and frequent attendee.[101] Will observed how convenient Memorial Stadium was from Washington, and he was not wrong. The route: head out on Connecticut or Wisconsin avenues; go north on I-95 or the B-W Parkway; exit at Russell Street or MLK in downtown Baltimore; up Charles or Howard; left on 33rd, then look for parking. Depending on traffic, it took about one hour from the Connecticut Avenue exit on the Capital Beltway to get to the brick ballpark in Waverly. The result was that Baltimore suddenly had the very favorable attention of some of the nation's best high-profile baseball writers, and also of fans who could reach Baltimore with relative ease from the city and its suburbs in Maryland and Northern Virginia. The reason for new metro region fan attention, of course, was the decline and death of the Washington Senators. Washingtonians never stopped wanting a new home team, but that did not mean they needed to starve themselves of baseball. In the pages of the *Post*, and on local television and radio, the Orioles offered an attractive stopgap.

The Senators had their roots in the 19th century, and an early, sometimes uneasy relationship with the Orioles of that era. As the 20th century wore on, despite the well-worn bromide, "First in war, first in peace, last in the American League," the Nats did experience success, winning the World Series in 1924, pennants in 1925 and 1933, contending in 1945. They had star power, with Hall of Famers like Walter Johnson, Joe Cronin, and Goose Goslin. Most of all, they nurtured their tradition as the capital city's team. Presidents from Robert Taft onward appeared on Opening Day, throwing ceremonial first pitches to begin each season. This was a revered baseball rite. But owner Calvin Griffith allowed himself to be swept up by the winds that rearranged the game's landscape during the 1950s. He moved the franchise to Minnesota, where they became the Twins, after the 1960 season. Partly to avoid congressional displeasure, the American League replaced Griffith's team with an expansion franchise, also called the Senators, in 1961.[102]

There were no lost seasons but Washington fans grimaced when their homegrown favorites, like Harmon Killebrew, won the 1965 pennant as Twins. D.C. was stuck with a struggling expansion outfit. The new Senators moved out of Griffith and into Robert F. Kennedy Stadium. But the ownership was not deep-pocketed, and their bargain-conscious methods ensured losing baseball.[103] In 1968, they sold to Robert Short, a trucking executive with ties to the Democratic Party. Uneasy fans realized that Short, former owner of the NBA Minneapolis Lakers, moved that team to Los Angeles. Manager Ted Williams coaxed the 1969 Senators to an 86–76 finish, relying on a healthy mix of stars like Frank Howard, rising prospects like Mike Epstein, steady performers like Del Unser, and reliable starting pitchers like Dick Bosman and Joe Coleman. But the thrill was evanescent. Short—who, according to radio announcer Shelby Whitfield, spent only borrowed money on the team[104]—demanded strange changes to the roster. It was he who hired Williams, a brilliant coup. But he also traded Coleman, reliever Jim Hannan, and infield stalwarts Aurelio Rodriguez and Eddie Brinkman to Detroit for Denny McLain in 1970. Such moves fed fan cynicism and intensified speculation that Short had bought the team to move them, which he did, after 1971.[105] Short fended off last-ditch attempts by such luminaries as super lawyer and Redskins president Edward Bennett Williams, to broker a last-minute Senator-saving deal. The team moved to Texas for 1972, becoming the Rangers. Fans stormed the field during the last Senator game, bringing protest culture to major league baseball. When Short accompanied his Rangers to Baltimore for a series with the Orioles in 1973, angry Senator fans showed up with a hanging effigy. One fan got close enough to pour beer over Short's head.[106]

Soon, the quiet Baltimore franchise found itself well known and somewhat chic, by virtue of the capital's attentions. The annual congressional Democrat-Republican game relocated up the parkway. Eventually, presidents found their way to Baltimore, the new home for Opening Day. Fans, too. What they found was winning baseball in a relaxed venue at an affordable price.

1

SETTING THE STAGE (1973–1979)

The 1973 season, the dawn of the DH era, proved a year of Oriole transition. Mainstays Brooks and Boog were still there, but on the down-swing. Promising youngsters like Baylor and speedy outfielder Al Bumbry arrived from Rochester. The pitching staff remained anchored by the McNally-Cuellar-Palmer trio. But Palmer, long the junior partner, was now the staff ace, one of the best pitchers of his generation. The season saw the team pull away in the AL East, courtesy of a 14-game winning streak in August and September. It also saw a new style for a Weaver team, more reliant on speed than power. Skeptics who disagreed with Weaver's disdain for one-run-at-a-time baseball often observed that waiting for home runs was easy when Frank Robinson and Boog Powell batted in your lineup. But 1973 showed that Weaver could adjust to his talent, and the basepaths lit up. In a *Sports Illustrated* article late in the season, William Legget joked that the Orioles were suddenly more like sandpipers, running all the time. In 1971, the writer recalled, Baltimore won with only four players stealing as many as 10 bases. But in 1973, he noted, steal totals were spread across the lineup and as many as eight Orioles might finish with double-figure stolen bases. The article praised Palmer, took due notice of the team's perpetually stellar defense, and credited Weaver with handling the talent on hand.[1]

The Orioles won the East, Bumbry took home Rookie of the Year, and a five-game playoff loss to Oakland did nothing to dampen optimism. Young second baseman Bobby Grich had a strong season at the plate and in the field, and the Orioles' pipeline pushed other top-level prospects up toward the majors. The team also looked outside of the organization for missing pieces, bringing in veterans like Tommy Davis, who fit comfortably into the new DH role.

In 1974 the long-dormant Red Sox stirred, as did the Yankees, who began their Bronx Zoo renaissance. The Orioles fended off both rivals, as Cuellar won 20 again and new starter Ross Grimsley notched 18 wins. Oakland, however, took three out of four games in the AL Championship Series, winning the pennant.

In 1975, Palmer won his second Cy Young Award on the strength of a 23–11 record and a 2.09 ERA. The Orioles chased the Red Sox all season, finishing second ahead of the Yankees. That season was notable for Cashen's bold trades. He picked up Lee May, who promptly drove in 99 runs, and also swung a deal with the Expos for Mike Torrez and right fielder Ken Singleton. All three became Orioles standouts. May provided power at DH for the remainder of the decade and no small amount of clubhouse authority, somewhat restoring the atmosphere established by Frank Robinson.[2] Torrez would go 20–9 in 1975, and Singleton settled into right field where his reliable fielding, big bat, and steady demeanor made him a mainstay for the next 10 seasons.

The off-season was dominated by the Players' Association's battle for free agency. One of the lead cases was that of former Oriole Dave McNally, whom the Expos took in return for Torrez and Singleton.[3] Along with Andy Messersmith, McNally challenged his obligation to pitch unsigned for the Expos, arguing for his release into free agency.

The McNally-Messersmith case formed a bookend to the earlier, celebrated Curt Flood case. Flood challenged baseball's monopoly status and anti-trust violations, while the two pitchers, who failed to reach agreement on new deals, were forced to pitch without contracts. This attracted the gimlet eye of Marvin Miller, the indefatigable executive director of the Players' Association. Believing resolutely in both the justice and feasibility of his cause, Miller organized the players and kept pressure on the owners. Some Orioles, such as Brooks Robinson, were noted supporters of Miller, and he mentioned them gratefully in his memoirs. Contesting the idea that a ballplayer remained under invisible obligation to his most recent club, Miller won the case and helped to usher in the modern free-agency era.[4] In Miller, the most intransigent owners finally met their match, and the power balance in Major League Baseball swung away from executive boardrooms and towards players and agents.

Fans wondered what it would mean for their favorite team, especially after years of doom-mongering from owners desperate not to lose the now-defunct reserve clause. Oriole fans worried that Baltimore might not be a glamor destination. But the front office had long kept the team competitive by being adaptive and smart, so there was no sure reason to assume the worst. The new era announced itself in Baltimore in a big, big way in 1976. That was a season of two huge trades, each of which helped set the stage for Orioles Magic. The 1976 Orioles had a new GM, bespectacled Hank Peters. Peters stunned baseball and Baltimore a week before Opening Day 1976, announcing a trade with Oakland. The A's, whose owner, Charlie O. Finley, hated the upward salary pressure of free agency, would get Baylor, Torrez, and reliever Paul Mitchell in exchange for starting pitcher Ken Holtzman and superstar outfielder Reggie Jackson. Strictly in baseball terms, the blockbuster had much to recommend it for Baltimore, although Baylor— raised in the Oriole Way—was a rare talent. But Jackson was clearly Cooperstown-bound. He was also a one-season wonder in Baltimore, because Reggie wasted no time making it plain that he was there for a short duration. The star had his eyes on a more lucrative deal in a larger market, and the Yankees had their eyes on him. A one-month holdout to start 1976 exasperated Baltimore fans. His eventual season totals (.277/.351/.502, with 27 home runs and 28 stolen bases) were excellent as usual, but fan ambivalence about his imminent free agency made him a controversial Oriole. Wherever Reggie went, press attention followed. Ron Shapiro, a Baltimore lawyer and player representative, explained that Jackson was just not a Baltimore fit. "Observing Reggie was like observing an island," he opined. "He just didn't tie in with the land around."[5] Jackson became "The Straw That Stirs the Drink" in the Bronx Zoo, carving out an imperishable legacy as "Mr. October."

Another swap that did more to reshape the Orioles and their future. On June 15, Peters swung a trade with the Yankees, who took pitchers Holtzman, Alexander, Grant Jackson, and veteran catcher Elrod Hendricks for pitchers Tippy Martinez, Scott McGregor, Rudy May, Dave Pagan, and catcher Rick Dempsey.[6] The Birds finished 10½ games behind the pennant-winning Yankees, yet in landing Dempsey and McGregor, they added two young stalwarts. At the same time, as Brooks Robinson approached retirement, Doug DeCinces stepped in as his successor. It proved a hard role. When Grich left during the off-season for Southern California, signing with the Angels, Oriole fans learned another lesson about how free agency could work. But they also saw a lineup that was younger and talented. with plenty more on the way. The Red Wings pipeline still yielded plenty. A hard-hitting first baseman, Eddie Murray, sailed through AA Charlotte and AAA Rochester in 1976, readying himself for the big club in 1977. All that newcomer Murray did was win the BBWAA Rookie of the Year Award, en route to tying Lee May for the club lead in homers. A young starting pitcher from Nicaragua, Dennis Martinez, was the next great pitching prospect. He proved ready to join the rotation, going 14–8 with a 4.10 ERA. As usual, the alert front office picked up useful role players, such as veteran outfielder John Lowenstein, who became a perpetual platoon player as Weaver tirelessly sifted through his statistics, shifted his lineup, and moved players where they could help earn a win. The 1977 season was, by general acclaim, one of Weaver's best as a manager. Nine rookies moved up to the majors that year, making up for losses to free agency. The Orioles' lineup was more makeshift than star-laden. Rookie second baseman Rich Dauer struggled at the plate, with just one hit in his first 41 at-bats: "0 for April, 1 for May," wrote one wag. But he steadied at the plate under the protective gaze of mentors like Lee May. While he shared keystone time with Billy Smith, by season's end the position belonged to him. Dauer's average was a respectable .243, and his fielding percentage, .982, meant that weeks went by without any errors at second base.

The Orioles of 1977 did not resemble the 1966–1971 Birds. A better comparison was with the rising Baby Birds of the early sixties. Singleton's .328 set a new team batting record, and Palmer—the biggest star left over from the glory years—went 20–11. But it was players like Lowenstein, and fellow outfielder Pat Kelly, whom Weaver managed adroitly. Kelly, a sound player, was also a religious man, responsible

The first Nicaraguan major leaguer, right-hander Dennis Martinez was a mainstay in the Orioles rotation from 1976 to 1986. He later pitched for Montreal, Cleveland, Seattle, and Atlanta, retiring after a 23-year career in which he won 245 games.

for one of Weaver's great lines. When the manager expressed impatience with too much piety, Kelly asked Weaver, "Don't you want me to walk with the Lord?" "Pat," Weaver answered, "I'd rather have you walk with the bases loaded." It was all in fun, and the team was close. The Orioles hung in with the powerful Yankees and challenging Red Sox all season long, eventually finishing as runner-up to the pennant-bound Bombers, 97–64.

Two happenings stood out. "Thanks, Brooks Day," held on September 18, gave a full house the chance to rock Memorial Stadium with cheers for the beloved, now retired, third baseman. And

The Orioles picked up Rick Dempsey from the Yankees in 1976. He became one of baseball's best defensive catchers and in 1983 was named MVP of the World Series. Dempsey's rain-delay pantomimes were legendary.

Weaver, in one of his most memorable on-field outbursts, forfeited a game in Toronto when umpires refused to remove a rolled up tarp left behind

in right-field foul territory. Forfeits are extremely rare, yet Weaver pulled his team, he said, out of concern for player safety. Whatever else the forfeit did, it fixed attention and pressure firmly on the manager, allowing the players to chase the Yankees with less pressure on themselves. Attendance at Memorial was solidifying. The team was up-front

First baseman Eddie Murray won the AL Rookie of the Year Award in 1977 and went on to star for the Orioles through 1988. One of the all-time great switch-hitters, he was elected to the Hall of Fame in 2003, his first year on the ballot.

Lefthanded starter Scott McGregor came from New York in the same 1976 trade that netted battery mate Dempsey. A staff anchor, he won the deciding games in the 1979 playoffs and 1983 World Series.

in its stated desire to improve those figures. "A Million or More in '74" was the first marketing slogan to concentrate on attendance numbers. That year, they fell just short, but starting in 1975, they would not fall below the million mark again.

In 1978, the Orioles had another quiet, strong season, going 90–71. This was good only for fourth place. But all the new parts were well tuned. The pitching staff enjoyed balance between Palmer's veteran leadership and rising hurlers like Martinez and McGregor. The bullpen featured a curly-haired stopper, Don Stanhouse, tabbed "Stan the Man Unusual," but whom Weaver called "Full Pack" because the slow-working pitcher's pace meant the manager could polish off lots of cigarettes in the breeze way during save situations. The rest of baseball marveled at the epic pennant chase between the Yankees and the Red Sox. The most important even for the Orioles in 1978 did not reveal itself as memorable until years later. It came in the June amateur draft, when Baltimore used one of its extra second round picks to sign Cal Ripken, Jr., the son of stalwart coach Cal Ripken, Sr.[7] Meanwhile, the Orioles franchise could look with some satisfaction on its Baltimore achievements. Since 1954, they were 2,157–1,814, with four pennants and two World Series titles, plus a slew of player awards. There was some nervousness in the face of rumors that Hoffberger wanted to sell. Oriole Advocates and other local business leaders put out the word that the asking price was approximately $12 million. Washington, D.C. was without a team to call its own, and there was discussion of building a new ballpark between the two cities, perhaps in Laurel, Maryland. Some had the Orioles moving to the nation's capital, as the NBA Bullets had done. What nobody could imagine was that some of the storied franchise's greatest moments lay just ahead.

1979: The Magic Begins

It was in June 1979 that the phrase "Orioles Magic" was first heard, and the era that it refers to ran through 1983's World Series win over Philadelphia. The five magical seasons included one world championship, two league championships, three division titles, and yearly contention. Peter Gammons recalls these Orioles as one of the last fun teams in major league baseball. The "magic" is shorthand for a talented team that played loose and showed a propensity for comebacks. Belief meant no opposing lead was safe, that the Orioles were always ready to rally and win. In 1979, fans and players kept this faith from mid-summer through October's taut World Series defeat against the Pirates.

There was another kind of suspense permeating that 1979 season. This originated off the field, sparked by owner Hoffberger's determination to unload the team. For fans and civic leaders, there was anxiety about what this meant for the franchise's future in Baltimore. Washington-based fans wondered if the Orioles, who offered the jilted capital region a nearby team to enjoy, might move down I-95. Many observers thought the Orioles should claim both cities by moving to a new ballpark in between; Columbia, perhaps, or Landover. Since major league franchises rarely come up for sale, rumors and reportage drew wide attention. Fans in the mid–Atlantic knew that having a major league team in their hometown was never guaranteed. The record showed that once a city fell out of a major league, it had trouble getting readmitted. Fears were intensified by the instability of the NFL Colts.

Fans in the know saw that the Orioles would need a certain series of events to fall into place if the team's future was to unfold in Baltimore. This awareness was put into sharp focus by the sad state of the Colts. By 1979, they were entering the final, demoralizing phase of the Irsay years. The embattled owner's relationship with press and fans was past repair. Irsay wanted a new stadium, and shifted between shopping for other cities and trying to convince Maryland that his franchise deserved a new facility. The football team suffered on the field, while the chemistry between owner, fans, politicians, and press grew toxic. Irsay's alcohol-fueled antics became Baltimore's primary off-field sports story. Until, that is, the Orioles intruded.

Even before pitchers and catchers reported to spring-training headquarters in Miami, the Orioles made front-page news in 1979. Shirley Povich, revered baseball scribe and dean of the *Post* sports page, first wrote of the rumored sale on January 17, 1979. According to Povich, a Detroit-based consortium was on the verge of striking a deal to purchase the Orioles. The group included nobody from Baltimore. It was headed by former Treasury Secretary William Simon, and made no guarantees about keeping the team in Baltimore. "Deal for Orioles Is Seen Imminent, Barring Hitch, Simon Has Deal," ran the headline. Povich's article read as if based on a warning leak from someone close to the heart of the deal. An unnamed source added an interesting admonition against late changes of heart by Orioles ownership, based upon alleged "previous pullouts in the past, when, with the club seemingly on the verge of being sold, Hoffberger ended negotiations."[8] Povich's report stated that Hoffberger was under pressure from family members and stockholders to sell the team and recoup past expenditures. The question of civic obligation was met with bitterness from the current owner, according to an *Evening Sun* report. "I'm tired of hearing of my responsibilities [to Baltimore], Hoffberger's quote ran. "I've busted my _____ for 20 years with this club and I'm fed up."[9] Povich quoted Simon as interested in playing games in Washington. The article cited the irony behind Baltimore fans and power brokers urging Hoffberger to reconsider, when they were reluctant to buy season tickets, assist with financial support, or back a city bond issue to help the club.

"The same guys who won't buy tickets are now asking why I don't keep the club here," Hoffberger was quoted as saying. According to Povich's source, Hoffberger was about to embark on a pilgrimage to Israel and wanted the deal done before he left.[10]

Over the next month, Povich's reporting was augmented by *Post* colleagues. There were more accounts of Hoffberger's supposed diffidence when it came to pulling the trigger, including stories which said that what he truly wanted was to sell a major interest in the franchise to obtain cash support, yet retain a leadership role. To the mix were added conflicting accounts from Annapolis, where Baltimore legislators now talked up possible state aid to the baseball team. Governor Harry Hughes, an Eastern Shore politician aware of the rest of the state's aversion to Baltimore-focused spending, tried to hew a middle path. The situation seemed problematic.

On February 6, Nancy Scannell reported in the *Post* that Simon was pulling his bid. "Mr. Hoffberger wants to play both ends against the middle," Scannell quoted Simon as saying. "Well, he can forget this end. I think at this point and at this time the game is over. He has damaged the merchandise and acted in bad faith. I think I've been played dirty pool everywhere to Sunday."[11] Povich confirmed that Simon pulled out in anger. Describing Simon as "In a sulphurous cloud of disgust," Povich quoted him: "I've never seen such duplicity in my life.... Hoffberger played both ends against the middle.... Well, the game is over." Adding shock value was the contention—detailed with specifics—that Hoffberger had dangled the Orioles for years, tantalizing multiple would-be buyers. The article listed previous "unwary bidders responding to the 'for sale' sign on Hoffberger's Baltimore Orioles," naming Bill Veeck and Hall of Famer Hank Greenberg. It would have been poetic redress if Veeck—pushed out before the Browns' 1954 move to Baltimore—took over the Orioles. Povich pointed out that Veeck, who had a Maryland residence, cooperated with partner Greenberg on a deal to buy the team in 1975, only to see Hoffberger back out after negotiations at Veeck's Easton retreat. Veeck said it was Hoffberger who approached him to initiate a sale. Three other aspirants—former General Motors president Ed Cole, Pennsylvania coal magnate Ken Pollack, and Washington Board of Trade boss R. Robert Linowes—all told similar stories. Each recounted attempts to close a deal, belief that a sale was imminent, and surprise at Hoffberger's late-stage disavowals. Linowes wryly commented on Simon's disappointment. "Well," he said, "It looks like another bidder bit the dust. I found Hoffberger unconscionable in his dealings. He called me. I didn't call him."[12] Povich reported that only Washington businessman Joseph Danzansky, whose efforts to buy the San Diego Padres in 1974 came so near success that Topps issued baseball cards reading "Washington National League," resisted Hoffberger's siren song.

A flurry of related news in Washington and Baltimore made Hoffberger sound like either a baseball Lorelei luring aspirant buyers to grief, or a deeply ambivalent Baltimorean who liked owning an excellent baseball team but was frustrated by the market. No doubt there were elements of truth both ways. Witty and erudite, Povich turned to Alexander Pope's "Moral Essays on Knowledge and Character of Men" to explain Hoffberger: "Alas, in truth, the man but changed his mindPerhaps was sick, in love, or had not dined."[13]

What none of the reporters knew yet was that major league franchises, whose prices had been relatively stable for years, stood on the verge of a major increase in value, thanks to upcoming developments including cable television, a stadium construction bonanza, and better marketing and merchandising.[14] Soon, franchises would routinely sell for more than the rumored $12 million Hoffberger wanted from Simon. But the boom days of the 1980s under Peter Ueberroth were around the future's bend. In 1979, baseball's near-term prospects looked rocky. The waning Kuhn years were marked by disputatious labor relations, plus acrimony between rich owners able to plunge into free agency and less well-heeled bosses who watched their teams' costs. Hoffberger was correct—Maryland politicians were not ready to swing behind the concept of using the public purse to help sports teams. In the Old Line State, that would not change until the Colts moved to Indianapolis in 1984.

Mayor William Donald Schaefer paid close attention. Ever alert for threats to civic institutions, Schaefer, gaining a national reputation as a tireless advocate for Baltimore, was not a rabid sports fan. But he believed in the intangible benefits sports accorded to the city he cherished. He contemplated ways to assist the Orioles in upping their civic profile and building partnerships to boost ticket sales. He knew that Annapolis would act only after Baltimore did whatever it could. So he explored ways to push civic efforts to buck up the team. These bore fruit later in 1979. But as spring training loomed, Baltimore's major league club straddled two shaky perches: tentatively at home in Baltimore while trying to maintain an old management formula in a new free-agency era.

Such was the outlook of Sun sports editor Bob Maisel, when he wrote "Renegotiation Is Name of Game." The piece appeared when the team reported to camp on February 22. Using Boston's renegotiations with star

Carl Yastrzemski as an example, Maisel described a new business environment in which players, benefitting from labor gains, were no longer bound by outmoded deals. The Orioles, Maisel intimated, had managed to avoid contentious arbitration. But they were about to navigate difficult contractual waters. Hank Peters confirmed the changing circumstances, saying the upcoming season would determine if the Oriole Way could still succeed.[15]

Maisel recognized the potential that an Orioles sale to out-of-towners might lead to a capital relocation, just like with the NBA Bullets. Abe Pollin moved that team from downtown Baltimore to Landover, near the Capital Beltway, in 1973. They remained in Maryland, but revamped themselves as a D.C.-area team. That looked like a potential Oriole model. Maisel also discerned an awakened spirit among Baltimore civic leadership in response to the stories. One source for a positive Baltimore angle was Jim Palmer, whom Maisel and others quoted. Palmer described the city as a pleasant place for ballplayers in which to play and live. Maisel interviewed the ace hurler at the downtown Morris Mechanic Theater, while both attended the premier of an homage to Eubie Blake, the city's great jazz pianist.[16] Maisel also quoted national television reporter Jim McKay, a passionate Marylander. Pitcher Scott McGregor chimed in, too. "I really enjoy this town," he said, adding that it made him forget his native California. "They don't believe me, but it's true." McGregor, the subject of trade talks, made it clear that he wanted to remain a Baltimore Oriole. Maisel noted approvingly that Schaefer presided over a meeting that included the team's ticket manager, Bud Freeman. "Activity has picked up since the meeting," Freeman explained, "Some businesses have called to double and triple their season tickets, as they said they would.... I'd say the campaign is off to a good start."[17] By "campaign," Freeman meant the drive to involve local businesses directly in driving up gate support. The story emphasized Schaefer's effort to alert Baltimore's civic leaders that they needed to step up and support the club.

This was a challenge. Politically, Maryland was only beginning to grapple with the issue of making friendly financial arrangements for teams. The very idea astonished some politicians, especially beyond Baltimore. State representatives and senators from Montgomery County, the Eastern Shore, and western Maryland were publicly doubtful, if not axiomatically opposed. There would need to be some aggressive horse-trading in the state capital if the idea was to advance. That would take time and powerful executive leadership. For now, bills introduced in Annapolis saw the state legislature react with suspicion. The Maryland Senate considered a bill to provide a $2.5 million loan to the Orioles. Governor Harry Hughes signaled his approval, but the bill failed on the floor.[18] Baltimore City was where Schaefer had sway, thanks to his successful campaign for the downtown refurbishment exemplified by the new, much-praised Inner Harbor development. The mayor set forth instituting steps to bind team and town together. The most important in 1979 was the Orioles Advocates, a unique non-profit corporation dedicated to promoting and stimulating interest in baseball and the franchise. Formalized in September, the group of 75 came from a cross-section of the local business community and took the lead in shoring up ticket sales and community relations.[19]

A precursor to the Advocates, and a proactive civic initiative, came in March. Schaefer lent his own press secretary, Christopher C. Hartman, to the Orioles. Hartman helped with season ticket sales. Formerly executive vice president of the Chamber of Commerce, and staff director of the new Keep the Orioles Committee, Hartman joined a ticket office further augmented by staffers donated from the Greater Baltimore Committee. These were tangible signs that civic leadership recognized the need to buttress the Orioles' position before a sale. Among other efforts were a 24-hour answering service for ticket orders, printing and distribution of 500,000 schedules with order forms attached, and an agreement to deduct from payroll any money spent by municipal employees on tickets. It was time, Hartman said, to boost Oriole attendance to a new level. No longer should the season total hover just north or south of 1 million. "If we can assure attendance of 1.5 million," he said, "Whoever finally buys the Orioles won't have any reason to move the team."[20] Results from the ticket drive were immediate. Another Schaefer appointee, F. Barton Harvey, said the top 100 businesses in Greater Baltimore would be targeted, and expected to purchase packages. These included Chesapeake & Potomac Telephone, Bethlehem Steel, Baltimore Gas & Electric, and the Sunpapers. Most had increased their ticket buys "dramatically," Harvey boasted, adding that smaller businesses would be the next focus of organized sales pressure.[21] Obviously, with the mayor's public blessings, businesses were expected to pony up. Schaefer was a real old-time mayor, who knew how to reward, cajole, or punish. The campaign's nakedness attracted national attention. In the *Sporting News, Sun* reporter Jim Henneman reported that the near-sale to Simon, with its condition of playing 13 games in Washington's RFK Stadium, was seen by Baltimore leaders as the first step to permanent loss of the team.[22]

All the off-season back-and-forth regarding boardroom dealings was viewed darkly by Oriole players—especially those living in and around

Baltimore. Mark Belanger, peer-less shortstop and player union activist, was downbeat about the prospect of playing 13 games a year at RFK. "With travel time, it would mean not getting home until maybe 2½ hours after the game," he calculated. "And if you have to play a game the next day it would be even worse." Belanger promised to take the matter up with the players' union. Starting pitcher Mike Flanagan was no less hostile. "We're on the road half the time as it is," the lefthander pointed out. A clubhouse leader, Flanagan also promised that, until the D.C. issue became actuality, he would ignore it. Rich Dauer's main concern was keeping the team in Baltimore. He had just spent his first off-season there instead of return-

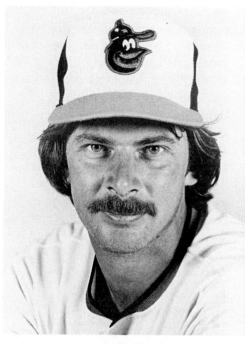

Lefty Mike Flanagan started for the Orioles from 1975 to 1987, winning the Cy Young Award in 1979. His dry sense of humor made him a clubhouse favorite.

ing to his native Southern California, and said, "I love it here. I can't believe how many great people I've met.... I have really enjoyed the winter here. I bought a townhouse. I'm doing things I've never done before and I love it."[23]

Pro-Baltimore feelings were thus on the rise. When batterymen reported to Miami on February 22, followed by the full squad on February 25, attentions would shift from sales and rumors of sales to players and preparations. But there was reason to believe that, back in wintry Baltimore, the Orioles were on the verge of better local backing. A chord was struck. After years of taking the team's stability for granted, Baltimore once again faced a chance of losing its big league status. Once struck, that chord resonated across the region and roster. Meanwhile, hopes on the field were strong, and rightly so.

The Orioles were hardly the underdog in 1979. But the question was whether they could keep pace with or overtake the Yankees and Red Sox. The 1978 New York-Boston battle was an all-time thriller; both teams looked ready to renew the battle. Questioned by Ken Nigro, Peters pronounced himself optimistic that the Orioles would also be a factor, thanks to an influx of role players. The previous three years, free-agency losses—Jackson, Grich, starting pitchers Wayne Garland and Ross Grimsley—hurt system depth, Peters admitted. But now, the GM bragged, depth was a strength. "We've got 37 players on the roster and every one of them is a bona fide major leaguer or guys considered to be fine prospects." Among the additions were an incoming pitcher, former White Sox righthander Steve Stone, with 27 wins under his belt the previous two seasons. While Stone lent his strong arm to a talented staff, new arrival John Lowenstein promised flexibility. The handyman could play outfield and infield as well as pinch hit, offering the platoon-loving Weaver a bundle of options. Another key move was re-signing former Rookie of the Year center fielder Al Bumbry.[24]

Surveying the roster under Miami's sun, Weaver was at turns thoughtful and optimistic. His talks with reporters revealed his conviction that the team was lucky and smart. "We survived a crisis in the history of this club without ever falling from contention," said Weaver. "Face it, we were depleted. We got nothin' for Reggie Jackson, Bobby Grich, Wayne Garland and Ross Grimsley. Eddie Murray was nothin' but a stroke of lightning for this club. Garland left, but we had to make room for Flanagan, anyway. Now that looks awful good. Then Rudy May [was traded] and Grimsley went out the window, but McGregor and Martinez stepped in and maybe, in the long run, we're better off that way."[25]

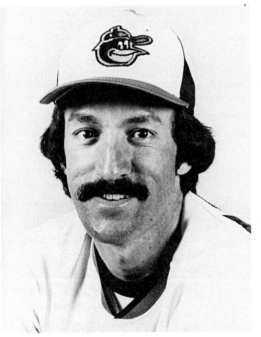

Baltimore picked up John Lowenstein in 1979. Part of a left-field platoon with Gary Roenicke and Benny Ayala, he was also known as the clubhouse philosopher.

Writing for *Street & Smith's*, Richard Dozer took due notice of these moves, still tabbing the Birds for fourth.

The Yankees, Red Sox, and Brewers looked loaded, he thought, while Baltimore's modest alterations were insufficient to overtake the top tier. On the other hand, Dozer admitted, 25 years into this version of the franchise, the Orioles were not to be taken lightly. "Baltimore must be doing something right," he wrote.[26] Perceptively, Dozer noted that swingman Sammy Stewart might play a valuable role. The 24-year old right hander went 13–10 at Rochester in 1978 before making his Oriole debut in September, once fanning seven in a row to set a major league rookie record. Stewart could start or pitch long relief. Among other strengths Dozer picked out were the power and stabilizing character of Lee May, the utility of pinch hitter Terry Crowley, and a host of great gloves up from Rochester, including Dauer and DeCinces. At the *Sporting News*, prognosticators termed the team a "Mystery Contestant," admitting that the Yankees and Red Sox would receive more favor, but also warning that no one should undervalue Baltimore.[27] Of all the forecasters, the most astute turned out to be none other than Yankee great and former Oriole Reggie Jackson. Never shy, always insightful, the Yankee outfielder opined, "Baltimore could just be the team we have to beat. Everybody knows what Boston can do and cannot do. But nobody knows how good this Orioles team can be."[28]

Two imperatives emerged during exhibition season. The first was to avoid a recent penchant for slow starts after Opening Day: 1–4 in 1977, 0–5 in 1978. The second was to hammer home good old Oriole fundamentals. To ensure that lessons were learned, Weaver imported Frank Robinson, who spent the previous year managing Rochester, as his "Communications Specialist—Defensive Coordinator."[29] Oriole players simply called Robinson "Coach." Whatever they called him, they also listened carefully when he preached the Oriole way: how outfielders should talk to each other, cover ground, and catch flies. Here again, the Oriole Way made itself felt through repetition, repetition, repetition. Robinson, one of the method's most assiduous advocates, made observations like, "We score a lot of runners from third base on infield grounders with one out. That's because we're aggressive and practice it. The runner's front foot should hit the ground in a running stride just as the pitch crosses the plate. That's what everybody practices in BP."[30] The players, newcomers and old hands alike, listened.

A third storyline of that spring training was Jim Palmer; specifically, the state of his arm and head. Palmer was well-familiar with the dangers of arm trouble. Early injuries nearly derailed his career. Boswell delighted in writing about this ambiguous star, in whom strands of generosity and self-interest, moodiness and level-headedness, civic-mindedness and self-involvement all mixed together. To Boswell, the clash of visible attributes made Palmer—at all times palpably intelligent and devoted to baseball minutiae—a fascinating study and a thoroughly admirable pitcher and man. To others, the sight of the handsome 6'3" star posing for magazine ads in his famous Jockey Shorts was provocative, a breach of old-fashioned baseball protocol. While complainers debated the propriety of the ads, Boswell took them as a sign of the seventies, pointing out that the dutiful Palmer was the most reliable model the underwear company ever used. Palmer was dependable on the mound or in his briefs. "You tell Palmer when and where to be, and he's there," said an amazed corporate official. "That's one of the reasons we made him the company's spokesman."[31]

In like manner, when it came to mound work, Palmer wound up right where the Orioles and Weaver wanted him, but not without delivering critiques along the way. Weaver was used to his anchor's worries over potential arm trouble and had a unique explanation. Where others saw hypochondria, Weaver saw concern. "Jim has kept himself in such perfect physical condition that he's scared to death of every little ache and pain. Everybody else walks around every day with a sore toe, a stiff neck, or something, and learns to live with it. Palmer thinks he's not supposed to have pain."[32]

Palmer, tall and tanned, was frankly ambivalent about his short, chain-smoking manager. He likened their relationship to "a marriage where each partner knows exactly what to say to make the other one mad," and reporters such as Boswell merrily covered the bickering of Baltimore's odd couple.[33] Palmer knew enough to figure out that Weaver's needling stemmed from the manager's conviction that his ace gave the Orioles the best chance to win. "The only thing I ever asked from Earl was that he treat me the way I would have treated him," the pitcher claimed, before admitting that there were other, higher considerations. "Of course, that's just not Earl. That doesn't mean I would rather have had Earl be compassionate and thoughtful than be a winner."[34] Both were competitors of the fiercest kind, style differences notwithstanding. Palmer understood that Weaver's perpetual lack of satisfaction was a result of the manager's deep belief that number 22 was his team's strongest on-field asset. Weaver's faith meant that, in the heat of a season, he considered a Palmer with arm twinges superior to any alternative. Palmer, good looks matched by his sharp baseball mind, understood the nature of their relationship. He called Weaver's motivation style, "Positive-Negative," meaning that "Earl would always tell you what not to do, how not to screw up, tell you all the things you were already doing wrong, or order you to do fewer things wrong.

And he thought that would somehow motivate you to do better."[35] Like many of the comments each made about the other, that was a backhanded compliment. Buried in the observation were the notions that Weaver was difficult, that a top-level performer like Palmer "got" him and could handle him, but that praise-oriented "Negative-Positive" might make younger or more insecure players less nervous.

He liked talking about his manager. Later that season, when *Time* ran an article about Weaver's methods and success, Palmer served as one of the magazine's most loquacious sources. There was nothing ambivalent about the pitcher's explanation that, at the core of all the manager's antics and habits was the fact that Weaver was put on earth to win.[36] The Oriole manager would be pushed off the *Time* cover by Egyptian President Anwar Sadat and Israeli Prime Minister Menahem Begin, but the adulatory article added to the manager's mystique. Palmer had erudition and elegance to spare. Weaver was peppery, and obsessed with winning. The relationship between the two was, at a glance, a plain mismatch. But each fed a deep need in the other. Tellingly, Palmer would later write a book about their relationship, *Together We Were Eleven Foot Nine.* Some readers thought it critical, but the book explained how their enmeshment enabled victory. Weaver, by then in retirement, made no bones about the soft spot he held for his best starting pitcher. "I probably talk to Jim more than anyone else on my teams," he admitted.[37]

A quiet optimism pervaded sunny Miami, not diminished by a 10–14 Grapefruit League record. The hardest knock came when the team released popular veteran catcher Elrod Hendricks on March 26 (a blow lessened when the Orioles re-signed Hendricks in September). On Opening Day, Palmer started on the mound, with this lineup behind him:

CF	Al Bumbry	DH	Lee May
SS	Mark Belanger	LF	Gary Roenicke
RF	Ken Singleton	2B	Rich Dauer
1B	Eddie Murray	C	Rick Dempsey
3B	Doug DeCinces		

This remained largely the look of the team all season, except that Kiko Garcia wound up playing more games at shortstop than Belanger. Lowenstein platooned with Roenicke, and Pat Kelly saw outfield duties too, while Mike Flanagan, Dennis Martinez, Steve Stone, and Scott McGregor rounded out the rotation. Sammy Stewart served as a spot starter/long reliever, with Tim Stoddard, Don Stanhouse, and Tippy Martinez handling late-inning duties. A 5–3 Opening Day win over Chicago had fans hoping

for a quick start, but the team promptly stumbled, sitting at 3–7 after 10
games, thanks to a skid that reached six against the Yankees and Brewers.
Reporters noticed no consternation in the clubhouse even after those
losses to divisional rivals. On April 19 against the Yankees, Baltimore
kicked off a nine-game win streak. That was ended by a loss to the A's on
April 28, but a six-game win streak immediately followed. At April's end,
they were 14–9; one month into the season, May 7, the Orioles were a
comfy 18–9. Their mound strength and opportunistic hitting led the way.
They moved into first place on June 5 and stayed there for the rest of the
season.

June turned out to be the most memorable month in Oriole history,
partly because of on-field heroics, partly because of clubhouse antics, and
partly because of what happened in the stands. The latter was the first
noticeable development.

Prior to 1979, Memorial Stadium was a notably easygoing baseball
venue. "The World's Largest Insane Asylum" label was appended during
the late 1950s strictly for football and the Colts. That team was in extremis
by the late 70s,[38] whereas Oriole fortunes were bright, so much of the
exhibitionistic passion transferred to the baseball club. Oriole attendance
was usually modest, if consistent, and regular fans had the sense of being
in on a nice secret: watching baseball played by an excellent team with a
penchant for doing things the right way, but never having to scramble for
tickets. If the Orioles were known for quiet excellence, their fans were
known for quiet satisfaction.

That changed in 1979, partly because of a cab driver from Dundalk.
"Wild Bill" Hagy, who sported beard, beer belly, cutoffs, and cowboy hat,
made his perch in the upper right field deck, Section 34, along with a crew
of blue-collar friends. Hagy, who had attended games for years, imported
the idea of spelling out O-R-I-O-L-E-S, as fans had long shouted C-O-L-
T-S. Hagy added a contortionist's touch by twisting his ample frame into
the shape of each letter (a move debuted at Colt games by superfan
Leonard "Big Wheel" Burrier) while his friends shouted along. Soon, the
entire stadium joined in, and a Baltimore baseball tradition was born. It
began with an appeal delivered by Hagy, and sometimes by the crowd: a
prolonged "Ohhhh..." And that love of the "O" planted itself in the national
anthem, since fans yelled "OH! Say does that Star-Spangled Banner yet
wave ..." Rather than trying to stymie this non-scripted display of enthusiasm, Oriole management embraced it. If someone complained about
desecrating the anthem, they were told it was written in Baltimore to begin
with. Bob Maisel called Hagy "A working guy who liked to go to ball games,

sit in the upper deck, drink beer, and lead cheers," and asked the Orioles what they thought of their loudest fan. "We've done very little for him," explained PR man Bob Brown. "Two years ago, when he came to the games all the time and tried so hard to get some excitement going in his section, we approached him about letting him in free, but he said he'd rather do it his way. He had his followers buy their own tickets."[39]

Hagy led his cheer at tense moments, sometimes from the top of the dugout. It was all in fun, although the newly intense atmosphere took some visitors by surprise. That July, a Detroit fan wrote to the *Sporting News* complaining about being harassed at Memorial Stadium. The paper carried a "Flash" notice in late August that the scene at Baltimore games was marked by too much "general rowdiness."[40] 33rd Street certainly was more raucous than before. But onlookers like Maisel denied that there were behavioral problems beyond high spirits. "They haven't resorted to violence or made spectacles of themselves by running onto the field," he pointed out in defense of Hagy and the new stadium vibe.[41]

Rowdy though it was, there was no exclusionary atmosphere in Section 34. Newcomers were welcome, so plenty of fans made a point of sitting near Hagy at least once, shaking his hand, buying beers for his crew, and tapping into the magical atmosphere. Beer played big part in the Section 34 fun. Relaxed stadium rules meant it was okay to bring in filled containers through a special entrance, so there was never a suds shortage. Other corners of the stadium had their own mini-cultures, such as the lower-deck bleachers, Section 13, down the left-field foul line. There, fans could chat over a short fence with the Orioles bullpen staff, or crack wise at visiting left fielders. Oakland's Rickey Henderson was a favorite target, but also held in affection, because he bantered back. Once, when fans challenged him to steal a base off Dempsey, he promised to do so. Later, having stolen the promised base, he returned to his post and bowed to Section 13, which responded with applause. The Memorial Stadium crowd was mixed socially, economically, and racially, involved but easy-going, and prone to off-kilter displays of glee. It was surely Baltimore's leading place for social mixing. Security was mild, and it was easy to wander from section to section, so the feel was that of a large outdoor party. Besides Hagy, other fans made themselves known through performance or eccentricities. One was Pat Walker, a senior citizen in a homemade Oriole uniform who roamed the stands playing a bugle. Another was Arthur Linde, a Washingtonian who made himself conspicuous in Section 13 by wearing a suit jacket, tie, dress socks, wing tips—and gym shorts. Oddball behavior at Memorial was frequent and encouraged, but never harsh. There were bed sheet signs hung in the outfield and along the upper deck: "Tippy's Tweeters," for fans fond of Tippy Martinez; "Garcia's Gang," put up by young women taken with the handsome shortstop; "Weaver's Believers." There were also chants to augment Hagy's O-R-I-O-L-E-S routine. Among the favorites were "Come on Al, hit a home run now!" (which rhymes in a Baltimore accent), "Come on John Lowenstein, hit the Busch beer sign!" and "Come on Ken, put it in the bullpen!" Memorial Stadium became something it had only ever been for football: a difficult place for opposing teams and a hotbed of vociferous ardor for the home club.

There was another side to Memorial Stadium which fit into the fan-driven atmosphere epitomized by Wild Bill. This was the choice of background and between-innings music. The loudspeakers had long featured a bugle call, met by fans with "Charge!" whenever game action tightened. Often it repeated again and again. Added to the overall aural experience was what Boswell admired as the major leagues' best popular music soundtrack. The franchise laid aside the organ and old-timer's tunes, opting instead for relatively modern music that was—like Baltimore fans—racially and culturally mixed. According to Bob Brown, PR Director from 1968–1989, the idea was Frank Cashen's, before the GM left for the Angels' helm in 1971. "Let's play something a little different," Cashen suggested.[42] So the team opted for a repertoire of broad appeal, with numbers intended for each fan group. Among the favorites were the wistful "Downtown," released by Petula Clark in 1964, the soul classic "Yester-Me, Yester-You, Yesterday," sung by Stevie Wonder in 1969, and, above all, "Thank God I'm a Country Boy," recorded by John Denver in 1975. The last song became a particular anthem and the regular seventh-inning stretch song. According to Charles Steinberg, a public relations executive with the Orioles who moved on to the Padres, it became a local tradition, held dear because only Baltimoreans knew about it. "It gave Oriole fans a distinctive way to celebrate the seventh-inning stretch. Oriole fans had this collective family secret. We knew that when you came to an Orioles game, you'd hear 'Country Boy,' and it was unlike any ballpark experience any other city was having."[43] Whether the songs were intense or soothing, funky or amusing, all fans grew accustomed to hearing them and associated their favorites with particular moments. Bob Seger's "Old Time Rock-and-Roll" would become popular, with Rick Dempsey and Eddie Murray filming a video to the tune. Many in the stands took the entire fan culture experience for granted; one long, comforting expression of Memorial Stadium, Baltimore, and home. By 1979, these practices had been in place long enough that fans expected and revered them, often without quite knowing why.

In the 1979 clubhouse, two antics involving Weaver made their way into Oriole lore. The first occurred on Father's Day, Sunday, June 17, in Minneapolis. It turned into one of the most memorable Palmer-Weaver donnybrooks, much to the delight of the team, which snickered as the pair pecked at each other. Palmer had given an interview to the *St. Paul Pioneer-Press* in which he expressed disgruntlement over his contract and came off as less-than-enthused with Oriole management and his future in Baltimore. The article appeared after a series of complaints from the starting pitcher, who had pulled himself from a couple of starts and gone 16 days without pitching. He complained about what Ken Nigro called "alleged pain with his back, or his forearm, or his elbow, depending on what month it is."[44] Weaver riposted right away that Palmer had agreed to his $265,000 salary—admittedly less than what he could fetch on the open market—and suggested that if the pitcher craved a big payday, he should just wait until 1981, when his option was up. Angrily, the manager taped a copy of the article to Palmer's locker, scrawling a message: "HAPPY FATHER'S DAY. NOW GROW UP!"[45]

Writers and players alike enjoyed the ensuing controversy, egging the two on. Palmer affected nonchalance, but pointed to future problems with free agency in order to justify his criticism. "I'm sure Earl had more important things to worry about," the pitcher said. "If he wants to get aggravated, fine." But, Palmer added, "I'm just like the rest of the guys here. They're all going to leave so they can get more money."[46] Weaver's aggravation was no doubt worsened by Palmer's additional remark to reporters that the pitcher, who was already fashioning his broadcasting career, hoped to be in the booth for the 1979 World Series. Weaver, who wanted him on the mound for that event, was disgusted. His complaint against Palmer was mingled with implied recognition of the pitcher's value. "Jim can broadcast the second, third, fifth, and sixth games of the World Series, but he's pitching the first, fourth, and seventh for me."[47] For good measure, the manager made a comparison to his other Hall of Fame stars. "Brooks never gave me any gray hairs and Frank never gave me any. It's always Jim."[48]

Perhaps the most important thing about this spat was that it never bothered the rest of the team. In fact, since clubhouse chemistry was positive in 1979, other players laughed it off, as they did all of Weaver's tantrums. ""We've heard all this before," one unnamed player told a beat writer. "Jim ought to make copies of the story and distribute them to every city we visit."[49] In fact, as everyone knew, the 1979 roster had several players hoping for bigger future paydays, but none of them expressed any public dissatisfaction with their contracts during the season. On the contrary, reporters from every AL city noted a looseness in the Baltimore lineup; a relaxed confidence which befitted a team winning and having a good time. Weaver's tightly wound temperament and reliable blow-ups merely induced laughter and mimicry from Oriole players. Weaver, for his part, was secure enough not to mind the mockery, so long as the players performed during games.

A huge walk-up boosted the crowd to 47,539 on June 8, "Tankard Night." Such a figure was previously rare. It was a harbinger of summer popularity, for the team would break its all-time attendance record by August.[50]

The Weaver performance that drew the most glee across the nation was one of his most epic on-field protests. This happened in Cleveland, on June 18. Larry Barnett was the crew chief when the Oriole skipper raced out to protest what he thought was a mistaken non-call of catcher's interference. Barnett, remembered for his non-call when Boston's Carlton Fisk collided with Cincinnati's Ed Armbrister in the 1975 World Series, tried to warn Weaver off, but the manager would not be stayed. He took out a rule book, pointed to the relevant page, and then, upon meeting with inevitable disagreement, shredded the book into confetti, which he tossed aloft.[51] Tribe fans roared with mingled disapproval and laughter, for it was a theater of baseball absurdity. *Post* writer and Pulitzer Prize-winning critic Jonathan Yardley—an Orioles fan who knew performing magic when he saw it—termed the entire stunt "Ultimate baseball, inexpressible happiness."[52]

The same date as his bravura performance in Cleveland, Weaver was the subject of a fawning story in *Sports Illustrated*. His photo graced the cover, beside the caption, "Baltimore's Resident Genius." The article noted the success of Baltimore's cost-conscious decision-making, congratulating the front office on its ability to forge a winner without relying on sheer cash power. Writer Douglas S. Looney also took note of the uncommon team spirit. For example, when Rick Dempsey was pulled from the starting lineup in a game against the Rangers, the catcher did not sulk, but instead climbed atop the bullpen bench waving a rally towel, joining Hagy and bringing all in Memorial Stadium to their feet. The writer looked to several team sources for explanations of the Oriole way. "We're typical Baltimore people," explained one official. "We think small." Coach Jim Frey stressed the team's competitive drive: "We're trying to win more games than anybody else." But it was the front office and Weaver who received most of the credit in this article. Dempsey, whose distinct lack of diffidence made him a frequent Weaver target, put it this way: "He puts us down and that makes us perform better to show him he's wrong. When you have been under the pressure of Earl Weaver, that's more pressure than other teams can give you." Singleton added that Weaver always believed the team should win, no matter what happened in New York, Boston, or elsewhere in baseball. Quoting his manager, the right fielder said, "If we play the way we should, we'll win."[53]

The signature moment of the 1979 season—the in-game occurrence that birthed "Orioles Magic," and became the most celebrated regular-season memory for a generation of fans—unfolded in Memorial Stadium on June 22. The mood surrounding the team was upbeat: they were the hottest in baseball, anticipating a large weekend crowd happy about Oriole success and interested in seeing new Detroit manager Sparky Anderson, in Baltimore for the first time since the 1970 World Series.[54] GM Peters and other officials pointed out to reporters that the team was on track for its best seasonal attendance ever, and the Maryland Transit Authority laid on extra buses to handle the throng.

Fresh from a 7–1 road trip, the Orioles faced the Tigers that June 22 to open a four-game series. It was one of those normal summer nights which outsiders find so trying an aspect of tidewater life: stifling hot, dripping humidity, nary a breeze—the prismatic dampness refracting the stadium lights as the entire sky assumed a twinkling pink-orange hue. Visitors often asked about this optical effect, but for Baltimoreans, it was too normal to notice. With two outs in the bottom of the ninth, the Birds trailed by two. None of the 35,000-plus in attendance had any thoughts about beating traffic. Garcia led off and flied out, but Singleton followed with a homer to draw the Orioles within a run. Murray singled, but was stuck on first base when Roenicke popped to the second baseman. With two outs, DeCinces dug in at the plate. With powerful Lee May on deck, Tiger reliever Dave Tobik went slowly, choosing his pitches with care, working the count to 1–1. The stadium bugle call blared incessantly; only Oriole fans could have found the sound anything other than mind-numbing. The crowd buzzed in anticipation of something special; optimism crackled across the stands. Night games were when old Memorial Stadium came alive, since the darkness forgave the unaffected ballpark's lack of glamor. Here was a classic, suspenseful baseball moment, outcome on the cusp, fans far beyond an otherwise humdrum midsummer Maryland night. In the radio booth, Bill O'Donnell, longtime partner to the famous Chuck Thompson, who rotated out of the booth into TV coverage, called the scene with Charley Eckman, a voluble Baltimore favorite at WFBR-AM,

Orioles Magic started on June 22, 1979, when Baltimore rallied at home to beat Detroit, 6-5. Baltimore won the AL East, defeating the Angels in the playoffs before losing to Pittsburgh in a tough seven-game World Series.

the new flagship station. They wrung out every drop of sweaty drama. O'Donnell's word pictures set the stage while DeCinces awaited Tobik's 1–1 pitch.

When DeCinces lashed his game-winning home run, the entire stadium erupted with a paroxysm of joy, and the Orioles bench cleared to welcome the runs at the plate as if the pennant was clinched. But the craziest scene transpired in the WFBR booth. O'Donnell was hardly sedate, but still the consummate radio professional. He allowed the noise of the stadium to come through, the tension to mount second-by-second. When DeCinces earlier fouled back a 1–0 pitch, O'Donnell made it clear merely with emphasis that the batter's *"big rip"* meant he was swinging for the fences. It was the irrepressible Eckman who provided the volatility which made the radio home run call a classic. "Here's a fly ball to deep left field," O'Donnell began, his voice rising with blissful possibility, "It might be—" "Get outta here! Get outta here!" interjected Eckman at the top of his lungs. "Gone!" called O'Donnell, "Home run! Home run! Home run! The Orioles win it! ... The Orioles have won the ballgame in 1979 style!" Eckman's words were thenceforth indecipherable, merely audible expressions of joy. One phrase fans could understand was, "Going crazy!"[55]

Eckman, a radio jack-of-all-trades whose own background was in basketball and the race track, later admitted to tossing professionalism aside. "I got caught up in the excitement," he said. "Chuck Thompson loved it, but Bill O'Donnell would have preferred that I do what the Swiss do. Stay quietly neutral."[56] For weeks after, fans phoned in requesting that WFBR replay the home run call. It was the station's best bit for the rest of the summer, amplifying the advent of Oriole Magic.

Astute observers knew that, while late-game plate heroics at the plate were fantastic, this game was also won thanks to a superb joint relief effort by swingman Stewart and closer Tippy Martinez. Stewart came in for Flanagan when the latter had a rare ineffective start, allowing the Tigers to race to a 6–1 lead. Stewart and Martinez shut the Tigers down the rest of the way, allowing the comeback. DeCinces, of course, received a curtain call, the first in his career. It was cathartic for him since he bore the onus of replacing Brooks Robinson; some fans never forgave him for inheriting third base. Singleton, whose 15th homer to dead center started the rally, offered his own gleeful explanation for the wonderful comeback. "Tonight wasn't a miracle," the team leader announced after the game, "but somebody up there sure is helping us. I want Him to know that we appreciate it."[57] Weaver put the comeback more prosaically, reminding reporters of his own unshakeable faith—in home run power. "As long as we can send batters to the plate in the ninth who can hit home runs, we can do it. We have that extra few who can hit the ball, and there will be more of this."[58]

Weaver was already considered a baseball prophet by many. It did not hurt his reputation when, the very next night, Murray clinched another comeback victory. With an equally large crowd chanting "Ed-die! Ed-die!" the peerless first baseman homered twice, his clout in the bottom of the ninth giving Baltimore an 8–6 win. That was the first of a twin bill. The nightcap held more excitement, as the Orioles came back in the ninth, again off the unfortunate Tobik, to win 6–5. Three comebacks in two nights convinced fans and players alike that something unusually good was underway. A loss on Sunday barely dampened spirits, for it came on "Silver Sunday," the team's official celebration of the 25th year since moving from St. Louis. Guests included Paul Richards, Lee MacPhail, Frank Cashen, and many favorite former players. Associations dated back not just to 1954, but to the 19th century's original Orioles, offering a historical imprimatur to whatever was stirring the 1979 team.[59]

The assembled celebrants included Tiger broadcaster Ernie Harwell, who worked in Baltimore prior to his legendary Detroit career. As *Sun* columnist Bob Maisel put it, "Everywhere I've gone the last couple of days,

When Murray batted at home, fans chanted "Ed-die! Ed-die! Ed-die!" Murray emerged as a true star during the Orioles Magic years.

the one remark I've heard more than any other is, 'There's never been anything like this for baseball around here.' Ernie Harwell said it, George Kell said it, a man who lives near the stadium said it. Everybody is saying it and it is true. The way this Oriole team has been playing, and the way the people have responded to it, is something to see: a completely unique experience."[60] Whatever that was, whether or not it was magic, it was powerful enough for the team to run through June with a 23–6 record.

June's magical elements did not escape Boswell's appreciation. But as games were won, the *Post* also monitored an upsurge in speculation about returning baseball to Washington, or nearby. Local super-lawyer Edward Bennett Williams, long a fixture in the NFL Redskins' management structure, was reportedly interested in a National League team for the capital. Dave Kindred speculated that Williams might be behind talk about a two-team expansion to the District and Denver; that the prominent attorney was dickering with Hoffberger over the Orioles' territorial rights to Washington; that new Redskin majority owner Jack Kent Cooke was ready to run his team without the help of Williams, who thus needed a new franchise of his own. Kindred even allowed that some people felt Williams might want to buy and move the Orioles.[61] At the same time, reporter Scannell uncovered a plan by area businessmen to build a stadium complex in Columbia, halfway between Baltimore and Washington, presumably suitable for some combination of the Orioles, Colts and Redskins, or any other team.[62]

One significant article capturing the new mood surrounding the Orioles showed up, not in the sports pages, but in the Style section of the *Post*. It stressed the bargain-priced fun of a baseball outing to nearby Baltimore. Entertainment writer Susan Dooley said it was time to move past crying over the departed Senators and embrace the good times at Memorial Stadium. "Taking a party to Memorial Stadium for an afternoon or evening of baseball is one of the area's last good buys," she enthused, quoting with wonder the low ticket prices: $1.75 for kids and seniors, $2.50 for adults in general admission; $3.50 for reserved seats; $5.25 in the mezzanine or terrace boxes; $6.50 for the best box seats. "There is even a bus to take you to the Sunday games," she added, pointing out that Washingtonians could hop aboard at the Beltway Plaza Shopping Center, at $4.00 per round trip.[63] Such stories made it plain that capital-area residents willing to extend their horizons 40 miles north could do so without much cost or trouble. There was baseball nearby, and it was cheap, enjoyable, and excellent.

Once Washington-area fans got there, they found a team tough to resist, said the perceptive Boswell, who correctly intuited the Orioles coming together as a squad destined for big things. Just days after the comebacks against Detroit, Boswell spoke with Hank Peters, who expressed dismay at the recent Yankee move to reacquire Bobby Murcer for $1 million per season. "What a typical Yankee power play," the angry GM said, adding that the Yankee outfielder would make more than any Oriole that season. "You mean to tell me that our values in this game haven't gotten warped?"[64] But instead of swallowing Peters' self-pitying small-market lament, Boswell interpreted it as just another example of Oriole smarts. "The time has come to stop feeling sorry for the Birds," he wrote. "Their record—50–24, the best in baseball—is no fairy tale."[65] He added that the team was powerfully built for long-haul success, even though its roster mainstays attracted few oohs and ahs beyond the crabcake belt. The team's grasp on first place was neither quixotic wonder nor fluke. Oriole players were confident, comfortable, and on top of things. "There is not a barbarian in the lot. Civility and intelligence are two of the most widely unreported qualities in sports," Boswell wrote, quoting Singleton for support. The outfielder noted that more players brought books on flights than tape players; that Stone was a published poet; that Lowenstein, whose lapidary wit enhanced an outgoing personality, was the team's "lay anthropologist." Peters explained to Boswell the front office's intention to bring in players who fit together smoothly and bought into the team's way of doing things. Peters did not use the expression, but he was talking about the Oriole Way, and Boswell told readers that the effect was a winning team comprising bright, friendly, contented players who wanted to master the game while beating their opponents. He openly mocked the idea that Palmer, or any other player, was truly discontent. Boswell pointed out that Weaver's worries about chemistry centered on press coverage of the biggest loudmouth on the Orioles: himself.[66] Here, typically, Weaver's joke underlined his penchant for letting his own irascibility soak up pressures that might otherwise slosh onto his players. That was a rationale behind his anti-umpire conniptions, so at odds with his balanced, if cheerfully profane, conversations with the press.

Continuing to analyze the team's systematic excellence, Boswell inquired further. The normally restrained Peters was clearly impressed by the winning streaks and comebacks. "That's removed my last doubt," he admitted. "This team is built to win the close games, because the majority of your season is one and two-run games. And now we're doing it. For the first time, I am sure that our players are convinced they can win everything, right through to the World Series."[67]

Peters' willingness to admit the obvious on the record—the Orioles were good and getting better, their success the intended result of a deliberate organizational formula—dovetailed with dawning awareness around the region that Memorial Stadium was the place to be. This, Boswell correctly noted, was a watershed moment after which the team's culture would not be the same. "Fandom is on the verge of discovering the Birds. Quaint and quiet Memorial Stadium is becoming jammed with noise and naive fans who mistake every routine fly ball for a homer and roar their lungs out." Peters called the crowds "unexpected and inspirational, adding, "You wouldn't think that after 25 years a town would show a new pattern of attendance, but we love it. You can see that some of our players hardly know what to make of it.... It unquestionably wins you games. While it's new, the players get fired up and it carries them."[68] Altogether, the signals were clear. While the Colts spun into self-parody, with Irsay openly dangling the team and misbehaving in public; while Washington fans were emerging from the initial shock of the Senators' heist and remembering how much they liked baseball; while Baltimore fans were waking up to the reality that the Orioles were as good as the good old days; and while everyone marveled at how cheap and accessible and easy the Memorial Stadium experience was ... while all that was happening, the franchise officially admitted to itself that it was excellent and expected to continue winning throughout 1979.

The only smudge on a glowing orange-and-black horizon that All-Star break was the snub of Singleton by voters. Despite his club-leading statistics—.319 batting average, 15 home runs, 47 RBIs, 49 walks—he finished just 15th among 27 outfielders on the ballot. But writers like Ken Nigro, at the *Sporting News*, interpreted this instance as a representation of the team at large. The quiet outfielder's numbers were great, but his subtle approach to the game and calm demeanor led fans to overlook him in their quest for charismatic stars. Ever-loyal to his players, Weaver lobbied successfully for Singleton to be added to the AL team. "I'm not one to criticize the fans, because they are the managers of the All-Star Game," Weaver contended. "He deserves to be on the team. He should be on it on any criteria you can name."[69]

Heading into the break that July, the Orioles clearly benefitted from what some called Weaver's adroit use of "irregulars." A host of players had productive numbers, but every player was productive in some specific context. The major change from Opening Day was that shortstop Belanger, battling injuries, yielded everyday duties to young Kiko Garcia, whose .262 average at the halfway point justified the move. The rest of the team had good halfway stats. Lowenstein was at .293, Roenicke, .295. Starting centerfielder Bumbry hit .282, while substitute Pat Kelly's .313 bat gave Weaver even more outfield options. Among infielders, only DeCinces struggled somewhat at the plate, hitting .237, but gaining after his comeback dramatics. Dauer's average stood at a respectable .266, Murray's at .274 and designated hitter Lee May batted .287. Adding to the flexibility was the fact that Murray and Singleton were switch hitters. So, while the Orioles sat tenth in AL batting, team average .269, they were second to the Red Sox in home runs, with 84. Given that most of the players were also quality fielders, Weaver's multiplicity of options as a game wore on was more clearly than ever a Baltimore strength. His starting pitchers— Palmer, Flanagan, Stone, Martinez, McGregor—were all effective, while the bullpen was as deep as the outfield. His earlier top teams, the pennant-winners of 1969–1971, were more star-studded, while the 1979 team was more of a mix between a few top talents and a host of role players.

The option-laden roster went a long way to explaining why Weaver's charges, winners of 22 of 25 entering the All-Star break, owned two-game lead over second-place Boston.

As the second half of the season started, the question was, would the Orioles keep their lead? Weaver, used to desperately chasing down division leaders, made it clear that he liked playing in front. "Sure it's hard to stay on top all the way, but what is harder is to get behind and try to catch the guys in front." But lest readers think him sanguine about that lead, Weaver grew hot when it was pointed out that a .500 record would probably suffice to clinch the division. "Don't ever say all we have to do is play .500 ball," he bristled to a reporter. "It's the worst thing you can say. We're better than that." Weaver added that he knew exactly who trailed Baltimore by how many games, with an exact knowledge of the number of upcoming head-to-head matchups.[70]

As August wore on, the team continued to win, its comfortable margin in the East extending. The rest of baseball began commenting upon the Orioles' smooth path to a divisional crown. Toronto Blue Jays president Peter Bavasi was frank in his admiration for the team's combination of thrift and sagacity. "The Orioles are not prone to panic, they're imaginative, and they're creative," he enthused. "They have a certain management style with a certain sense of vision. They have had to be frugal but they've been successful. An awful lot of clubs spend a lot of money to get to the position where the Orioles perennially find themselves. We have emulated the style of the Baltimore organization."[71]

A prominent *Sporting News* article by Nigro in late August contrasted the Orioles with other teams, finding their style and methods refreshing. While some self-conscious organizations such as the Dodgers could come off as arrogant or stuffy, the writer argued, the Birds were always informal and accessible, handing out their players' phone numbers, encouraging openness to the press, eschewing cloak-and-dagger secrecy. "There's certainly not a lot of formality with us," Peters admitted, while Nigro pointed out how the GM stuck to the model established by predecessors Cashen, Dalton, and MacPhail. Looking for clues, the reporter found some in the team headquarters. "Part of that informality can be traced to the very location of the Oriole offices," he argued, seeing windowless rooms in the "back catacombs" of Memorial Stadium, modestly furnished, next to the clubhouse. "It is not unusual to see two or three players wandering through and shooting the breeze with some of the employees in mid-afternoon.... Peters and other club officials can zip right over to the clubhouse in a matter of seconds."[72]

Nigro went on to further explicate the Baltimore model for his national readers, who might not have been familiar with the 1979 squad, given that it did not appear on national television until July 30. Two emphases in particular attracted his attention. The first was a long-standing policy of avoiding players with problematic personalities, while actively courting those who would fit in with the atmosphere. This, Nigro reasoned, fostered organizational consistency, since the franchise had no intention of shifting itself to fit the vagaries of a particular player. Peters was quick to explain that the team was not exclusive, and felt that saying "no" to some talents was more than offset by the habitual improvement of newcomers who relished the Oriole Way. Another area of team excellence, Nigro revealed, was scouting and player development. Jim Russo, special assistant to Peters, received plaudits here, since, as super scout, he monitored players in both leagues, preparing exhaustive dossiers, utilizing advanced statistics, and ensuring that, before they traded for or signed a player, management already knew him well. Backing up his insight into this little-known but always crucial area of major league success, Russo noted that in 1978, the Orioles devoted $1.8 million—a full quarter of their operating budget—to player development.[73] The pith of Nigro's piece, which also explored how much coaching talent the Orioles had produced over the years, much of it lost when other teams went looking for good managerial prospects, was that "The organization is a seemingly indestructible force."[74] But Nigro also noticed a danger sign: to his eyes, it looked like the top levels of the farm system were less productive than in bumper years. He wondered whether this was a sign that the system had lost some of its momentum. Peters denied it and termed the team ready for any future earthquakes that might shake Major League Baseball's structure.

It was no coincidence that Nigro's massive piece on Orioles management techniques appeared that August, because the man who sat atop the organization, Jerry Hoffberger, had at last unloaded his property. The Orioles' sale to Edward Bennett Williams was announced that month. Hoffberger had only made the news when complaining about the burdens of owning a major league ballclub. But Williams—whose client list included such famous figures as Jimmy Hoffa, Frank Sinatra, Senator Joe McCarthy, Sam Giancana, and Joe Costello, was very, very different. Whereas Hoffberger was a Baltimore fixture, Williams was a D.C. star who craved, and earned, the limelight in a city with plenty of powerful figures. The meaning of his purchase, in terms of the team, its future, and even its location, was hard to figure. One initial point of discussion was the price: $12 million.

It seemed reasonable, even generous, at the time, but in retrospect, it is clear that Williams made a great bargain, since baseball's economics were headed skyward. For his part, Hoffberger came to regret his loss of the team, trying unsuccessfully in future years to buy the Orioles back. The moral was that major league teams are rare assets.

Hoffberger had controlled the team since 1965, heading the organization with baseball's best overall record for 14 years. For the last six of those years, the brewery magnate fed rumors that he was tiring of running the team. His hands-off style—he kept no office at Memorial Stadium—made him the very model of the owner who delegates authority, as Brooks Robinson noted. "Hoffberger has stayed out of the way, which is good," the retired third baseman told reporters. "He turned the club over to a baseball guy and I've always felt it was a real plus for him to do that, even though he was the owner. It was the baseball guys who went out and got a guy like John Lowenstein because they knew he would fit in."[75]

Briefly classifying a forceful figure like Williams would be difficult, but one might observe that he was the opposite of Robinson's description of Hoffberger. It was hard for anyone to imagine that the high-rolling attorney had purchased the Orioles merely to hide in the background. He was a headliner, part of the permanent ruling class that provided the nation's capital a continuity that outlasts any presidential administration. Among his colleagues and social peers were Kay Graham, publisher of the *Post;* Joe Califano, a legal partner who became Jimmy Carter's Secretary of Health, Education, and Welfare; Henry Kissinger, former Secretary of State; Pamela Harriman, wife of Averill, social doyenne and Democratic power-broker; R.W. Apple, star *New York Times* reporter; Thurgood Marshall, Baltimore-reared Supreme Court Justice; and Marvin Davis, Reagan-friendly oil main. His peers ranged across politics, business, media, entertainment. Nobody in the nation's capital—or the nation at large—could boast of being so important that they had no time for Williams, and in Washington, such influence is the main measure of status. Although Williams' background was in Democratic politics, he was part of the capital ascendancy that viewed itself as the landlord class of Washington, D.C., with Presidents and their courtiers merely renting White House space.

Crucial to Williams' identity was his track record as a defender of high-profile, sometimes very controversial, clients. Williams excelled in the demanding environment of a courtroom, which he sometimes called "the goldfish bowl," an environment with no place to hide, where verdicts provide a bottom-line index of winners and losers. Not only did he never shy away from competition even against long odds; he relished it. That and his rare skills made him a very desirable attorney for those in dire straits. His fees were as lucrative as his clients were rich, but Williams never lost his orientation towards the outcast or the little guy. This might have been a result of his humble upbringing in Depression-era Hartford, Connecticut, where his father worked in a department store and was sometimes unemployed. Wealthy as well as powerful, Williams was also a man of internal substance. Devoutly Catholic, he was a Holy Cross undergraduate and Georgetown Law product who began attending daily mass when he first battled cancer in 1977. At Georgetown's Holy Trinity Church, he was a regular lay reader at least twice per week, notably kind and welcoming to fellow parishioners, generous with charity. At 59, he was known to be antsy after years of intense legal laboring, and often mused with *Post* editor Ben Bradlee, a personal friend, about how rewarding it might be to spend the balance of his years engaged in pro bono work.[76]

That August, he remained Chief Operating Officer of the Redskins, far and away Washington's most preferred cultural asset. But that team's new owner, Jack Kent Cooke, himself a very active man, was eager to take the levers of his NFL team. This left Williams in need of another sports operation. It was Cooke, having partnered with Simon in an earlier attempt to land the Orioles, who led Williams to Hoffberger. While Simon found Hoffberger's coyness unendurable, and Cooke happily concentrated on the Redskins, Williams kept his connections to Baltimore alive. Ultimately he swung the deal, offering Hoffberger the inducement of a sinecure as team president.[77] Hoffberger would have been well-advised to ponder how much power and tenure such a position really held.

In any case, Baltimore fans soon started worrying that the D.C. titan had not purchased the team because he loved crabs or the Chesapeake Bay. Washingtonians likewise speculated that Williams would soon find the commute to Baltimore far more grating than a brief limousine ride to RFK Stadium. Williams would surely relish being the hero who restored baseball to the nation's capital, ran one line of speculation. His assumption of ownership constituted the sort of seismic shift that might shake the team right into a new city. But two signs augured that Williams' purchase was more than a white-collar snatch-and-grab. First was his own clear admonition: "I want to say to you it is my intention to keep the Baltimore Orioles in Baltimore. I did not buy the Baltimore Orioles to move them. I bought them to play in Baltimore and so long as the people of Baltimore support the Orioles, they will stay here. That is my pledge."[78]

While lawyer-words can be slippery, such was not Williams' style.

His personal life and behavior were uncontroversial. It was his penchant for defending wealthy and notorious clients that raised eyebrows. But Williams, whose courtroom performances were marked by rare skill at relating to juries, had the common touch. That was why he spoke about the fate of the team being in the hands of the fans. Since the fans of Baltimore were already being lionized for showing up in record numbers and supporting the Orioles in unprecedented fashion, there was no obvious excuse to look southward to D.C., beyond the latter's status as deserving a baseball team. In fact, Nigro wrote in the *Sporting News* that Baltimore was now discernibly a baseball town, and that, "Attending an Oriole game has rivaled going to the race track as the thing for a Baltimorean to do."[79] Even Wild Bill Hagy weighed in when a *Post* reporter asked him about the likelihood of the team moving. Pronouncing himself certain they would remain in Baltimore, and that Williams had too much sense to shift even a few games to RFK, the cheerleader asserted, "Edward Bennett Williams saw a good thing happening here. There's a lot of money and people coming into the stadium and the city's being built up. He saw something in Baltimore everyone else already saw and he's going to stay here."[80]

Williams' first high-profile decision came at the end of August, when he discounted the proposal broached during the Simon negotiations to have the Orioles play up to 13 games per year in Washington. Advocates saw this as a great way to audition the capital for a franchise shift.Others thought it would at least encourage Washingtonians to embrace the team, while still others hoped it might mark the nation's capital as Oriole territory. But Williams announced that the 1980 season would see all 81 home games in Baltimore, a move applauded by the *Sun*, which editorialized, "Now, it is up to sports fans of Baltimore to demonstrate that this season's large attendance is no fluke, and that they are going to give the Orioles the kind of support a team of championship caliber deserves."[81]

It was apparent that Washington fans made up part of the upsurge in Oriole attendance. Estimates ranged as high as 25–33 per cent of folks clicking the turnstiles on 33rd Street came from Washington or thereabouts. This meant that the relative proximity of Memorial Stadium already offered some satisfaction to fans from the metro area. The second sign of plausibility for Baltimore hopes to retain the team was September's public welcome for the Oriole Advocates, under the ramrod-like pressure of Mayor Schaefer. Schaefer, architect of Baltimore's much-ballyhooed downtown renaissance, was audacious when it came to making his city's case. He clearly intended to decisively demonstrate to Williams—and to everybody else—that Maryland's largest city would hold on to its winning baseball team. The shadow entity in the background of all this was the Colts. The Redskins stood on the edge of perhaps the most illustrious period in franchise history, with playoffs and Super Bowl championships in their near future. But the Colts were in a death spiral. Irsay had alienated Baltimore's fans and leaders, embarrassed the NFL, and left the likelihood of a franchise shift higher, not least because the bibulous owner kept talking to reporters about moving when in his cups.

Williams dearly loved the royal court environment of the owner's box at RFK, with its never-ending procession of luminaries coming to pay homage to the boss of the capital's most popular team. But that would now be Cooke's prerogative, so Memorial Stadium needed to become Williams' new palace. He attended his first game there as owner one week after buying the club, reiterating he had not bought the club to move it, and that fans were certainly supporting the team magnificently. If the stadium was farther from downtown Washington, it offered a major compensation: baseball has 81 home games per year, 162 per season; football merely eight at home and 16 in a regular season. It did not hurt that Williams had grown up loving the game, declaring enthusiastically to a law school friend, "This is *the* sport!"[82]

That same week, baseball was numbed by the loss of Yankee catcher and popular star Thurman Munson, killed in a plane crash. This tragedy came as the Yankees set themselves up for a four-game series with the runaway Birds. New York—indeed, the entire major leagues—were shaken by Munson's tragic accident, and so it came as no surprise when the Yankees failed to play their way back into contention.

Falling Just Short: The Postseason

The Orioles cruised to the division crown, having the luxury of setting up their playoff rotation during the last two weeks of September. As the postseason neared, *Sun* writer and historian Theo Lippman, Jr., was moved to observe that the upcoming opponent, the California Angels, were owned by cowboy crooner and movie star Gene Autry. Autry's friend, Lippman added, was Richard Nixon. The retired, resigned president was an avid Angel backer, attending 20 games in 1979, and jesting that he might travel to Baltimore to scout the Orioles. "It wouldn't be the first time Nixon visited our fair city," the writer added. "He was at the opening day game in 1954 when the present Orioles franchise arrived. He was Vice President then, and threw out the first pitch."[83] But at least one man was looking forward. Edward Bennett Williams bought a full-page ad in the *Sun* special playoff section, congratulating the team on the regular season and the fans for breaking attendance records. He urged everyone to come back next season for a repeat performance—in Baltimore.

1979 marked a full decade of Championship Series playoffs, and the 88–74 Angels, having won the West over pursuers Kansas City and Texas, were clearly a threat to Oriole pennant aspirations. Their manager was Jim Fregosi, and their lineup featured former Baltimore players Bobby Grich (.294, 30, 101) at second base and Don Baylor (296, 36, 139) in left field. First baseman Rod Carew, the future Hall of Famer, led off, with tough outs like right fielder Dan Ford (.290, 21, 101), third baseman Carney Lansford (.287, 19, 79), and catcher Brian Downing (.326, 12, 75) threatening down the order. Off the bench, solid veterans Joe Rudi (.242, 11, 61) and Bert Campaneris provided depth and postseason experience, along with bad memories for Baltimore fans recalling 1973 and 1974, as both Rudi and Campaneris had starred for the championship A's. The rotation was equally strong. Nolan Ryan (16–14, 3.59) was the marquee starter but Dave Frost (16–10, 3.58) and Jim Barr (10–12, 4.20) were also capable, while Mike Clear (11–5, 3.63) and Don Aase (9–10, 4.82) could pitch effectively out of the bullpen.

But by this point, the appeal of the Orioles was so great that Boswell— among the first to figure out that the 1979 team had a fetching blend of skill, unity, and character—wrote only partially in jest that, while the Angels were "Fine fellows and all that.... If they beat the Orioles, it will be a revolting development to anyone with a broad sense of baseball tradition. In fact, it will be foul play, a raw deal, and a kick in the shins to everybody's white-haired mother."[84] What lent the morality-play angle to Boswell's analysis and that of many other writers was the way that Baltimore's frugal-but-savvy approach served as an antidote to the free-agency spendthrift approach adopted by California and other squads, like the Yankees. If Baltimore could win on the cheap by playing it smart and building a truly interconnecting team rather than by signing stars, then perhaps there was hope for other franchises in this mercenary era. The *Post* columnist noted one potential danger: if the series went five, the Angels would get three games at home, and the Orioles' lack of team speed might be exposed on Anaheim's fast artificial turf. Such worries aside, Baltimore was loose going into the playoffs. Palmer found time for his never-tired routine about Weaver. Discussing whether or not he would be able to sleep well before his game 1 start against Nolan Ryan, Palmer said, "I had trouble sleeping the other night. I was dreaming of spiders. I usually go to bed about 1 a.m. Now, Earl, he goes to bed at 9:30—p.m., not a.m. I guess I could always give Earl a call if I have insomnia. And he'd hang up on me."[85]

Comfortingly for Baltimore fans and players, the playoffs began October 3 with another dose of Orioles Magic. Palmer and Ryan started, the former pitching nine innings, the latter relieved in the eighth. Knotted at 3–3 heading into the 10th, it was time for Weaver to make the kinds of moves that made him famous. DeCinces led off the Birds' side of the extra frame with a single, Dauer bunted him to second, and pinch hitter Terry Crowley popped up before reliever John Montague intentionally walked-Bumbry. There were two on and two out when John Lowenstein batted for Belanger. Montague worked to an 0–2 count while Memorial Stadium simultaneously squirmed and screamed. Lowenstein knocked the next pitch far into the night, a three-run walkoff homer. The team raced from the edge of the dugout to welcome "Brother Lo" to the plate, while fans gleefully concluded that Orioles Magic worked in the postseason, too.

It was coincidental, yet meaningful for the larger Baltimore sports context, that the first playoff game and its dose of late-inning glee coincided with something very different on the gridiron. *Post* columnist Ken Denlinger, noting the coincidence that on the very day, the Colts lost their fifth straight, wrote, "The darling Birds sit on the loftiest perch in baseball.The despised Colts cannot even play a game without stirring bile." Denlinger went on to point out that, two years ago, the Colts seemed on the rise, with an AFC East crown to their credit, while the Orioles struggled at the gate. Now, the roles were reversed, and unlikely to change back. Why? The newspaperman saw a simple reason to trust that Baltimore's baseball team was on top to stay: "The Orioles' new owner, Edward Bennett Williams, is the essence of intelligence and urbanity. The Colts' owner, Robert Irsay, is a bumbling clod who made a fortune in air conditioning and a fool of himself in sports."[86] Denlinger was right. The only recourse for Colt fans was despair, and a restorative dose of Orioles baseball.

More excitement came the next night, in a game both wild and tense. Paced by another three-run homer, this one in the second by Murray with Garcia and Singleton aboard, the Orioles cruised to an 8–1 lead and seemed to have the game in hand. Angel starter Frost could not make it past the first; he gave way to Clear. But in the eighth, Orioles starter Flanagan tired, so Weaver called in Stanhouse, who this night truly lived up to his nickname, "Full Pack." The Angels scored three before Stanhouse extricated himself from the eighth. When Stanhouse walked former Bird Larry Harlow on four pitches to start the ninth, Weaver raced to the mound. "He looked at me kinda funny," the reliever—who plainly relished his capacity to torture his manager—told reporters in the clubhouse after the game, "I looked down at him and said, 'Earl, I'm throwing my strikes.' And he said, 'Do we have a chance to win this game?'"[87] They did, but it was hard. Stanhouse faced eight batters, and by the time he intentionally walked Baylor, there were two outs while the bases were jammed. The wild-haired righty coaxed a Downing bouncer to third, resulting in a game-ending force play and a 9–8 Oriole win.

Povich was there from the *Post*, and, befitting his status as dean of Washington sportswriting, he took care to observe Williams as the top of the ninth unfolded over 42 minutes. After Downing's bouncer to DeCinces, the owner looked, an amused Povich decided, "newly convinced he had made a heckuva deal."[88] Meanwhile, Weaver looked as though he had lived through World War III, according to the *Sun's* Nigro. The gassed manager wasted no time in tossing a veiled barb at Stanhouse, while assuring everyone within hearing that he would turn to his closer again without hesitation: "We might have learned a valuable lesson today," he rasped to the reporters assembled around him. "I didn't, because I've seen this happen before."[89] But near-thing though it was, the win sent the teams to Anaheim with the Orioles up 2–0, a commanding advantage in a best-of-five series.

The Angels came out desperate in Game 3, and played their best game. Frank Tanana started for California, while Denny Martinez took the mound for Baltimore. Tanana gave way to bullpen ace Don Aase in the sixth; Martinez to Stanhouse in the ninth. It was a game of scratching out single runs, until the last inning. The Orioles clung to a 3–2 lead when a Rod Carew double prompted Weaver's first call to the bullpen with one down in the ninth. Stanhouse walked Downing, Grich reached base on an error. Then, Harlow's double gave the Angels their first win in the series, and the former Oriole a measure of revenge against his old team. But that was the Angels' last moment of glory. Game 4 was a laugher, an 8–0 complete-game shutout by McGregor. Kelly, in at DH, tagged a three-run homer in the seventh to put the game out of reach, while McGregor scattered six hits. For the first time since 1971, Weaver's Orioles were pennant-winners. They would face the NL champion Pittsburgh Pirates, who easily swept the Reds in their championship series,, in the Fall Classic.

With that playoff sweep on top of their 98–64 record, these Pirates were tough from top to bottom. Pittsburgh was then in the midst of a sports renaissance, with the Steelers perennial Super Bowl contenders and the Pirates obviously excellent. Fans in Baltimore recognized holdovers like Willie "Pops" Stargell and Bruce Kison, both of whom helped beat the Orioles in the 1971 Classic. But these Pirates were flush with younger talent, including a pitching staff led by top hurlers such as Bert Blyleven (12–5, 3.61), Jim Bibby (12–4, 2.80), John Candelaria (14–9, 3.22), and, out of the bullpen, rail-thin submarine-style Kent Tekulve (10–8, 2.75). Their lineup was similarly powerful, with team leader and first baseman Stargell pacing the squad (.281, 32, 82). Accompanying the future Hall of Famer in the Pirate attack was right fielder Dave Parker (.310, 25, 94), third baseman Bill Madlock (.328, 8, 44), center fielder Omar Moreno (.282, 8, 69), second baseman Phil Garner (.293, 11, 59) and left fielder Bill Robinson (.264, 24, 75). There was not a single hole in the batting order. Defensively, the Pirates were just as stellar. Moreno devoured everything hit his way, catcher Ed Ott was sure-handed, and Garner played second with real abandon, justifying his nickname, "Scrap Iron." Capable subs included Manny Sanguillen, Steve Nicosia, Mike Easler, and John Milner. Manager Chuck Tanner had taken over when the legendary Danny Murtaugh died after the 1976 campaign. On top of all their talent, the Pirates had their own kind of charisma, fully a match for Orioles Magic. Their theme song, "We Are Family," by the Pointer Sisters, always brought the fans at Three Rivers to their feet along with the players and players' wives, who danced, laughed, and enjoyed their victories to a disco beat. Among the players' wives, the lead cheerleader was Omar Moreno's wife, who accompanied her singing with a cowbell. The cacophony at Three Rivers Stadium certainly matched that at Memorial.

The Series opened in Baltimore on October 10, one day late thanks to an unrelenting cold rain. Commissioner Kuhn made the call to postpone a Series opener for the first time in major league history. But the heroics of Pat Santarone's grounds crew had the field something close to playable by the next night, although *Sports Illustrated* reporter Ron Fimrite, noting the turf upturned by the recent Colts-Jets game, described the outfield as "Pure Chesapeake Bay mud."[90] Unfazed by the conditions, the Orioles burst out for five runs in the first, knocking out Kison and holding on behind Flanagan for a 5–4 win. The Orioles' starter, a New Hampshire native, had no problem pitching in the cold, but did admit, "When I woke up this morning, I thought I'd slept too long and it was December."[91]

Blyleven rescued the Pirates in the next game, helped by relievers Don Robinson and Tekulve. Crucial was the performance of pinch hitter Sanguillen, another Buc whose 1971 heroics brought back bad Baltimore memories. He did it to the Orioles again, this time singling off Stanhouse with a 1–2 count and two outs in the ninth to drive Ott home with what turned out to be the winning run. Murray moved to cut off Singleton's throw home from right field in one of the game's more pivotal moments. "I thought the throw was off line," the first baseman explained after the game, with Weaver backing him up. Tanner, not the type to show up another team, was equivocal: "You'll never know," he said. "If the ball had hit the mud out there, it might have stuck." Singleton felt his throw was hard enough to nab Ott, who claimed that a benchmate asked him, "Can you believe they cut that ball off?"[92]

The Orioles broke the one-all knot on October 12 when they slammed their way to an 8–4 victory in Game 3. Garcia was their hero at the plate, going 4-for-4 with a double and triple, accompanied by Ayala's two-run homer. A rainstorm in the third inning delayed play for over an hour, but starter McGregor's changing speeds kept Pirate batters off-balance all night. Afterwards, the slender lefthander observed, "I guess I pitch pretty well after rain delays. We get enough of those in Baltimore."[93] The next game, another slugfest, saw the Orioles pound their way to a 9–6 win, giving them a comfortable lead in the Series, needing just one more victory to clinch the championship. The game was redolent with all the signs of Orioles Magic, since the Birds came back in a monster eighth inning rally, scoring six to erase a 6–3 Pirate lead. Lowenstein and Terry Crowley were this night's heroes. Down 4–3 in the third, Crowley predicted, "It'll be you, me, and Kelly." He was not wrong, although Kelly's pinch hit was not that consequential. Lowenstein came up big in the eighth, batting for platoon mate Roenicke and doubling to right, making the score 6–5 Pittsburgh. The next pinch hitter, Billy Smith, drew an intentional walk to set up a double play with the bases loaded. Then Tekulve took Crowley to a 2–2 count before the pinch-hitting specialist laced his own double to right, scoring two and sending the Orioles on their way to the win. Pitcher Tim Stoddard—a 6'7" former North Carolina State basketball star, but hardly used to batting—kept the rally going. Playing one of his mysterious angles, Weaver let the towering reliever bat and Stoddard, using Lowenstein's bat and Singleton's helmet, jumped on the first pitch from Tekulve, slapping the ball past Madlock for an insurance run. Played on another chill, blustery night, Game 4 was the longest nine-inning contest in World Series history.[94] With a series of managerial moves paying off so richly, Orioles players and fans felt their Magic was working, and were confident that a three-games-to-one lead was unassailable.

This Bucs squad was too experienced, too loose, and too mentally tough to be rocked by one game, no matter how dramatic. They reasserted themselves promptly in Game 5, pasting three Baltimore relievers for five runs on the way to a 7–1 win. Rooker and Blyleven kept the Oriole bats in check all night. Game 6 saw more of the same, with John Candelaria and Tekulve combining for a 4–0 shutout and Moreno accounting for three of the ten hits off Palmer. October 17 brought Game 7, and Oriole fans hoped that their favorites' bats would heat up along with the Baltimore weather, suddenly balmy. But it was not to be. A Stargell home run off McGregor left Singleton hanging on the fence as the rightfielder watched the ball soar past in the sixth inning for a 2-1 Pirates lead. In words that sounded eerily familiar to the Orioles, after Pittsburgh's 4–1 clincher, a teary Pops explained his team's approach: "We're not trying to be sassy or fancy, but we depended on each of the 25 men. There was a closeness. We worked hard, and we scratched and clawed together.... We go out to have fun.... Right now, I'm one very proud individual."[95]

It was a crushing loss, with the scant consolation that President Jimmy Carter, who visited both locker rooms, graciously congratulated both teams, adding, "I hope the Orioles will stay in Baltimore."[96] While Palmer looked on in mild bemusement at the Secret Service agents, Weaver thanked the President. "Thanks," said the manager. Asked about meeting Carter, the manager politely said, "It makes it a little easier."[97]

Less comforting was the presence of ABC sportscaster Howard Cosell, part of the national broadcast crew. Baltimore fans well remembered his barb just the previous season, when, during a Monday Night Baseball broadcast, the Memorial Stadium lights went dark, causing a long delay. "This would never have happened in a major league city," Cosell remarked. Perhaps mindful of the need to repair his local image, Cosell was nothing but gracious when drunken fans shouted insults while he traversed the parking lot: "It was an unfortunate incident that happened in a great city like Baltimore."[98] *Sun* writer C. Fraser Smith summed up Baltimore's mood best, when he described "a pall of bittersweet gloom ... like a funeral wreath" falling over the home fans.[99]

But as they drifted off into the night, facing the sad but unalterable truth that Orioles Magic proved less powerful than We Are Family mojo, there were a few reasons for fans with perspective to moderate their misery. Jarring as the Series loss was, Baltimore had just gone through one of the most memorable and enjoyable seasons in its long baseball history. Besides a pennant and host of unlikely comebacks that created the Orioles Magic phenomenon, there was the happy fact that the 1,680,561 attendance set a franchise record. The Official World Series Program carried an article about the sudden rise in Memorial Stadium crowd numbers. "Why does a club with a steady predictable attendance pattern for 25 years suddenly break out of that pattern with a year almost 40 percent higher than its previous all-time high? Every Baltimorean has his own answer, but clearly the underdog Birds' hot start in spring and summer-long exciting play were the biggest keys."[100] The uncredited article went on to cite other factors, including the newly aggressive marketing of WFBR-AM Radio and WMAR-TV, Wild Bill Hagy, clever giveaways, and increased coverage and presence in Washington, D.C. The question was, "Is 1979 the touchstone of a new attendance era or merely an aberrant [sic] once in a quarter-century freak?"[101] The fans heading home, temporarily forlorn, carried the answer to that fateful question.

The off-season allowed for more measured assessment of the previous season. *Sun* columnist Bob Maisel reviewed all the events, deciding "Maybe the most amazing development was the love affair which grew between the fans and the team. In the process, these fans just might have revolutionized baseball rooting."[102] At the Cy Young Award event, Flanagan defiantly insisted that he pitched for the best team in the majors. Player agent Ron Shapiro predicted a winter of massive demand for Oriole appearances. "When you make it into the World Series, everyone wants a piece of you," he said. According to Shapiro, stars such as Singleton and Murray, and colorful players like Dempsey, were only at the beginning of a PR bonanza.[103] He suggested that the Orioles' roster possessed few players who would mishandle their new pennant-winning celebrity, pointing out how many on the team made their home in Baltimore year-round. The team's talent base was young and intact, so there was little reason to fear that their accomplishments that season were a fluke. Shapiro was correct.

2

A STONE'S THROW (1980)

Losing the World Series stung, but looking ahead to 1980, Orioles fans saw little reason to assume that their favorite team's fortunes would reverse. Football lent perspective to the baseball team's accomplishments, since the 1979 Colts had a dismal campaign, staggering to a 5–11 mark that included two five-game losing streaks. Irsay's standing in Baltimore continued its unabated decline, especially when he fired head coach Ted Marchibroda, with whom fans sympathized. Another football event also cast the Orioles into sharp refraction. This was the ongoing argument between Edward Bennett Williams and NFL commissioner Pete Rozelle. The NFL's leader had no intention of changing his league's rule against owning a franchise in another sport. But the policy had a moot aspect in this case, since Williams was more and more a lame duck as president of the Redskins. In November 1979, and again in January 1980, the *Post* reported that Jack Kent Cooke, who owned 86 percent of team shares, intended to become the Redskins' chief operating officer, leaving no place in Washington for Williams.[1] Baltimore onlookers had mixed reactions. On the one hand, being phased out of the NFL might make Williams long for his stature as a Washington sports power-broker, ramping up Orioles-to-D.C. speculation. On the other hand, the super-lawyer was now free to concentrate on his baseball team. Baltimore power brokers could count on access to Williams as they worked to shore up the team's status in Maryland. With the Colts, dealing with Irsay was well-nigh impossible. Here again, the Oriole situation was bright by comparison.

Ken Nigro was one of several writers who commented on what looked like a paradigm shift in Baltimore, a shift that might enhance the city's chances of keeping the Birds. He wrote about it in a *Sporting News* piece in January. "For as long as anyone can remember, Baltimore has always been a Colts town," he wrote. "Baseball was a second-class citizen, and no

matter how many magic moves Earl Weaver made, the Orioles ranked a
distant second.... But now, a new era has dawned.... Baseball fever is taking
over."[2] The reporter cited hot ticket sales during the off-season to buttress
his claim. In the previous winter, the team reported $1,350, 000 in ticket
sales, their best ever. But by New Year's Day 1980, they had already smashed
that mark by $500,000. Nigro pointed to the "Designated Hitters" and
Orioles Advocates, the two civic groups tasked by Schaefer with boosting
ticket sales. Copying the successful model of the Kansas City Lancers,
who backed the Royals in like fashion, the Advocates and Designated Hitters were drumming up business primarily in greater Baltimore, providing
valuable evidence of community support that did not even include the
estimated 10–20 percent of fans coming up from the capital region.[3] For
the first time, team officials dared to speculate that total attendance would
approach the heretofore unimaginable 2 million mark. That numerical
aspiration took hold among fans, and would eventually culminate in a
"Thanks A Million.... No, Thanks *Two* Million" 1983 ad campaign.

In Annapolis, Governor Harry Hughes promised to support a plan
to provide the Orioles with state-backed low-interest loans as an inducement to explore new stadium possibilities in Maryland.[4] Two bills backing
bonds in that direction showed Williams that the sometimes slow-moving
machinery of Maryland state politics was gearing up on his team's behalf.
Hughes, a courtly and mild-mannered politician whom even foes admitted
was a gentleman, was not above gently suggesting on the record that a
public promise by Williams to keep the Orioles in Maryland would smooth
plans to pay for improvements at Memorial Stadium. This idea might also
serve, the thinking went, to mollify the discontented Irsay. While the football owner's statements on the subject were hard to follow, Williams said
all the right things, including his by-now ritual pledge that as long as Baltimore supported the Orioles, the team would not go away. Even talk about
locating a future ballpark in Columbia, the pioneering planned community
built between Washington and Baltimore, did not rile city politicians,
since it brought legislators from other parts of Maryland onto the pro-
aid-to-the-Orioles bandwagon.[5] The politics were tricky: if suburban legislators near Washington supported helping the team because they felt
baseball might wind up in their neighborhoods, then at least they would
have given their approval to the concept of state aid to sports franchises.
Schaefer and others could use that later, when the time for choosing stadium locations arrived. They were playing a long game.

In the meantime, the Birds continued effective community relations.
One visible success was Orioles Basketball. They fielded a basketball team

that played charity pick-up games against local celebrities and other assorted squads. The basketball Orioles were helped on the court by the under-the-rim presence of 6'7" Stoddard, who started at power forward for North Carolina State when the Wolfpack won the 1974 NCAA championship. In the wake of Stanhouse's departure via free agency, Stoddard— or "Bigfoot"—was expected to become the late-innings relief ace in 1980. Whenever he led the Oriole hoopsters on to local courts, such as the hardwood at Johns Hopkins, close to Memorial Stadium, Bigfoot spent plenty of time hobnobbing with the fans, as did the other players.

Stoddard's mound mate McGregor attracted local attention for coaching basketball at Gilman, a Baltimore prep school, and enrolling in teaching classes at Towson State University. He also announced his personal New Year's resolution for 1980: "To throw one less pitch to Willie Stargell."[6] Not too far away, in Pennsylvania, Pat Kelly and his NFL star brother, Leroy, opened up a Burger King franchise. Jim Palmer and Steve Stone stayed in Baltimore, keeping in shape by playing racquetball at area gyms. Singleton and Weaver were guests of honor at a local Tops in Sports banquet. Stories like these made it clear that plenty of Orioles enjoyed being in Baltimore year-round. There was some of the same spirit of local involvement that the old Colts epitomized.[7] Ten Orioles went to Hawaii for the SuperTeams competition, competing head-to-head against the Pirates in made-for-TV events such as swimming, cycling, and the obstacle course. They bested the Series champs, five events to two, but Weaver and the coaching staff had plenty to grumble about when the ten showed up at Spring Training sore and tired after losing in the finals to football's Los Angeles Rams.[8]

The team's 1980 media guide featured Oriole players doing the "O-R-I-O-L-E-S" body letters, Wild Bill–style. Certainly the most widely heard part of the team's off-season was the March 1 release of a promotional song: "Orioles Magic—Feel It Happen," a catchy ready-made tune by Perfect Pitch, Inc., which became a radio staple the very day the 45-rpm record appeared. Besides codifying the fateful term "Orioles Magic," the song gave shout-outs to the manager ("When Weaver moves/When we score the runs,/Nothing could be more exciting/ Nothing could be more fun!") and doted on the connection between fans and team ("There's a love affair/Between you and the team;/You're the reason we win when we win/And you know what the Magic means").[9] Playing the song at Memorial Stadium reified and institutionalized the idea of Orioles Magic as the paradigm for that era. Heading to Miami for Spring Training, it looked like the Orioles' sunny fortunes would continue.

Although he went home to New England that winter, New Hampshire native Flanagan, 28, received plenty of favorable attention after winning the Cy Young Award. His dry wit made him a preferred interview, and similarly delighted his teammates. Singleton described him as, "Sort of sneaky crazy like the guys on "Saturday Night Live." He's calm and invisible and lays back and then, for about 10 seconds, he's hilarious."[10] Part of the southpaw's clubhouse routine was awarding nicknames, such as "Cy Old" to Palmer, or "Inspector Rousseau" to superscout Jim Russo. Others were "Cy Future" for McGregor, and "Son of Sam Stewart" for Sammy Stewart. "Maybe it's the way I grew up but I was always a fly on the wall," Flanagan admitted. "Someone has to initiate something, then I comment."[11] He did an imitation of an angry Weaver that reliably brought down the clubhouse. Flanagan got his baseball drive from his father, who was once a minor-league pitcher in the Red Sox system. His humor came from his mother, a regional cult figure thanks to her penchant for calling radio talk shows across New England, enlivening them with her own droll takes on issues of the day. It was his own penchant for wry observation that made Flanagan a particularly funny needler of Weaver. But the manager never minded, which was easy to understand. Weaver was too happy with Flanagan's mound performance: 15–10 in 1977, 19–15 in 1978, 23–9 in 1979.

On the field, the 1980 team would largely resemble the 1979 version, although some roster changes were in store. Billy Smith, whose role was now strictly utility infielder with Dauer's firm claim on second base, cut against his "Easy Billy" nickname and expressed anger after losing at salary arbitration. "If they don't think that much of me, why don't they trade me?" he demanded, introducing an unusual note of discord into the clubhouse.[12] Smith would be released, replaced by catcher-third baseman Floyd "Sugar Bear" Rayford, who did not mind being a utility player and became a fan favorite. Of more serious concern was the state of the minor league system. A dismal 1979 Rochester Red Wings squad caused worry that the pipeline might be running dry, but Peters was reassuring. "We're coming on again," said the man in charge of perpetuating the Oriole Way. "We had a talent gap when the class of '76 graduated. We knew that class would be followed by nothing because we had nothing."[13] Peters was right about the classic 1976 Red Wing crop, which yielded Flanagan, Murray, Dauer, Dennis Martinez, McGregor, Garcia, and catcher Dave Skaggs. Since that group, only Sammy Stewart and Dave Ford had made it to the big club. But Peters, who said that the pressures of the Seattle-Toronto expansion draft and an admittedly poor decision to join the Central Scouting Bureau caused problems, saw a better future for Rochester and, ultimately,

Baltimore. Two of the up-and-coming talents he praised were Drungo Hazewood and Cal Ripken, Jr. "The thing I like about Cal is that he's a low-ball hitter who can hit for power, and you don't see that often," said coach and Instructional League manager Jimmy Williams. "The ball jumps off his bat."[14] Ripken was tabbed a member of the Rochester class of 1982.

Talking up the minor leaguers who should come aboard when current stalwarts like Dauer and McGregor were eligible for free agency was one way for Peters to signal that the Orioles understood the nature of the game in a new period. Owner Williams joined his GM in sending such signals, soothing the nerves of those who feared that free-agency baseball was beyond Baltimore's means, or that it might mean turning away from the traditional formula of putting player development first. The Orioles, said Williams, were not the Yankees. But neither were they unable to figure out ways to hold on to their talent. "Steinbrenner's got a $5 million television contract and we've got a $1 million contract," he observed—no doubt missing the NFL, where teams shared TV revenues equally. "But that's what makes it challenging. WE can beat this guy with our town. We've got something he doesn't have.... In my judgment, we have to be ready to keep people like Murray and the pitching staff. We know we'll have to pay them."[15] Williams' theme was picked up by New York columnist Dick Young, who took a biting Big Apple outlook. "I get a laugh out of commentators who compare the $21.1 million price of the Mets with the recent sales of the Red Sox for $15 million and the Orioles for $12 million," he sneered. "Fred Wilpon and his pals were buying the New York market. There's a slight difference between a TV commercial in Baltimore or Boston, as compared with New York."[16]

The team planned a unique goodwill trip to Nicaragua, led by Dennis Martinez, where they would play against locals. John Lowenstein delivered a cryptic utterance beforehand: "I know one thing," said the clubhouse philosopher. "If they hold an embassy party for us, I'm not going."[17] The two-day jaunt to the recently war-torn country was a novelty made possible because of Martinez's great popularity at home. It was a split squad that traveled to play two games in Granada, the pitcher's hometown. The Orioles were the favorite big league club there. Citizens were just beginning to recover from years of civil war and adjust to the eight-month-old Sandinista regime. Of course, Martinez was their superstar. Elrod Hendricks, back in the Oriole fold as bullpen coach, diplomatically observed, "Hopefully, this trip will spread goodwill between our countries. You don't know how poor a country is until you actually see it, but the warmth of the people still showed through. They love baseball ... and they know all the players. They used to be all Yankee fans in Nicaragua, but with Dennis an Oriole, they root for us now."[18] The fans loved the Orioles even more after the trip, which dominated Nicaraguan media. Baltimore won friends by tying one game (limited to nine innings) and losing the second. Probably the national reaction was summed up by the young Sandinista soldier working as a security guard, wearing his army uniform and toting an Uzi while shaking his head in amazement at the spectacle of the Orioles taking the field. "The big league. I never thought I'd live to see them here," murmured the revolutionary-*cum*-baseball fan.[19] All agreed that the team's visit did plenty to improve touchy relations between Managua and Washington.

Besides the trip, most of the early talk in Miami concentrated on the DH position. May and Kelly were expected to share some duties there, but DeCinces—whose back was a concern—also figured into the conversation, as did Lowenstein. Roenicke was expected to see more playing time in left field, where a platoon offered the best chance to fix the batting hole left since Frank Robinson's departure. Garcia—described by reporters as "lackadaisical" —was slated to be the everyday shortstop, although Belanger remained in the wings.[20] Of course the starting rotation was expected to be strong, led by Cy Young winner Flanagan (23–9 in 1979); a fully healthy Palmer (10–6); a rested Dennis Martinez (15–16), who played no winter ball after a campaign in which he pitched 18 complete games; McGregor (13–6); and Stone (11–7). What nobody could have foreseen was that Stone, expected to round out the rotation as the fifth starter, would be the staff ace, tossing one of the best seasons ever by an Oriole pitcher.

Nothing that happened in Miami Stadium, the 10th Avenue relic that was the Orioles' Spring Training home since 1959, occasioned nearly as much debate as what transpired in a series of boardroom meetings between the players' union and the owners. Ongoing labor tensions led major leaguers to boycott several exhibition games, throwing the usual March routine into chaos and threatening the start of the regular season. Marvin Miller ascribed the hard-line stance taken by ownership as an attempt to roll back the gains of free agency, citing Kuhn's declaration to him that "The owners need a victory."[21] The Players' Association chief was unsympathetic, pointing out the game's exponential revenue growth, thanks to booming attendance, concession sales, and media income. He especially disdained ownership's claim that free agency imperiled competitive balance. The owners hoped for a structured pay scale and an end to salary arbitration, as well as a recalibrated compensation sharing from media rights and other sources. Rather than allow inroads against their recent gains, the players voted on April 1 to boycott the final week of Spring Training games before returning to the field return for Opening Day, but to reserve May 23—the start of Memorial Day weekend—as a possible strike date if the owners continued to impede negotiations for a new basic agreement.[22]

With exhibition games on hold, Oriole players held informal workouts at Biscayne College. Sparsely attended, these sessions were slipshod enough to send Weaver into his first 1980 tirade. "This is the most worthless thing I've ever seen," he complained to reporters. "I guess it's as good as it can be, but I would be ashamed of holding another workout like this. There's nothing to do. Anything to break the monotony would have been appreciated. At least we know batting practice is supposed to be boring, but when you stand around in BP you stand around with a purpose."[23] At the same time, though, Weaver took up for free agency. "I've always been happy about free agency in every respect," said the manager who'd lost Reggie Jackson, Bobby Grich, Wayne Garland, Ross Grimsley, and, most recently, Don Stanhouse. "What I think free agency has shown is there's going to be more balance in baseball for ever and ever. The days of the Yankees winning nine pennants in 10 years are gone."[24] He also opined on the merits of salary arbitration, approving that players no longer came to camp angry after being forced to take whatever the club offered. Weaver speculated that there should be a better system to compensate teams losing players to free agency, an idea that left player representative DeCinces cold. The third baseman said, "You get no compensation where it would affect the word 'free' in free agent."[25] But DeCinces and other Orioles likely also noticed how unusual it was for a manager to publicly adopt a pro-player position. Ownership's chief negotiator, Ray Grebey, icily said, "I'm surprised Earl commented publicly on it. I don't have any comment at all."[26]

It took a few days for the frigid labor climate of Spring 1980 to warm, but eventually owners and players agreed to keep talking about their points of disagreement. The problems would crop up more disruptively in 1981, but Opening Day remained on schedule. As their opener in Chicago approached, the Orioles voiced their sentiment that pre-season predictions of a Yankees-Red Sox divisional race failed to credit the 1979 pennant winners. Singleton was peeved. "People are still picking us to finish third or fourth this year. They never catch on. We don't play in New York or Boston, so that means we must not be very good. Well, let's just do it to them again. Let's sneak up on them and whup them all. Maybe a couple of world championships would open some eyes, because for the next couple of years, this is going to be a real tough team to beat."[27] Canvassing all 201 members of the Baseball Writers' Association of America, the *Sporting News* found that the Orioles actually remained the favorites in the AL East, slightly ahead of the resurgent Yankees. But to those who did think the team was destined to fade, Weaver had a ready response. "There was no magic last season," he insisted. "No trickery and no chicanery. We just had talent. And we've got the same talent back this year."[28]

Not surprisingly, it was the always-perspicacious Boswell who put the Orioles' prospects into proper perspective. His writing from Miami stressed that pennants might be won in September, but February, March, and April were months of fundamentals. Commenting on their best record in baseball over the previous two decades—Baltimore was 501 games over .500, 43½ games ahead of Cincinnati, the second-best team of the past 20 years—Boswell was forthright about the reason: "Fundamentals are the Orioles' edge."[29] Singleton explained his own take on fundamentals to the admiring writer. "What is a baseball fundamental?" the right fielder and Most Valuable Oriole from 1979 asked rhetorically. "It's any baseball act that is so simple that the man in the stands thinks, 'I could do that. Why can't those big leaguers?'"[30] His paean to the Oriole Way included obligatory mentions of the organizational book on how to play the game. By this time, the book had become mythic, which was why pitching coach Miller swore, "That book is under lock and key in my home. Nobody gets it away from me."[31] But of course Miller, as well as Boswell and many Oriole players, knew that the "book" itself was simply an artifact emerging from the Paul Richards-established vertical organization of baseball methods. Seen in that light, Spring Training 1980 was merely one in a long series of consistent preparatory sessions, each one regularized, always marked by franchise-wide commitment to teaching and learning a host of in-game scenarios, making correct decisions reflexive rather than reflective. There is no time to think in the middle of a double-play or run-down. Players must react. Part of what made Boswell such a superlative baseball writer was his deep understanding of the effect the Oriole Way had on the team. He credited it with building "a sense of composure and mutual trust."[32]

Boswell was absolutely right, but the Orioles did little to show it by tottering through the month of April. Their slow start had by now become a virtual ritual, notwithstanding Weaver's various schemes to forestall it. In fact, he resorted to a bit of philosophizing in the season's first week, as he admitted his puzzlement after losing three to the White Sox. "What defines a start? This year we're 1–3. Last year we went 3–8 but we were in first place by May 1 … I've always been satisfied with the 25 men I left Florida with, but that's because you can't project the future."[33]

In another interview at the start of the season, Weaver could not avoid revealing how galling he found the 1979 World Series loss. "We had our best pitchers coming up in rotation," he recollected, "What it was was that the Pirates got their job done, we didn't." But the skipper was also looking forward. "What we have to worry about now is, can we win 102 games again? Would 102 have been enough last year if the Yankees hadn't taken some pretty stiff shots?"[34] For a man who professed not to believe in projections, Weaver's numbers turned out to be startlingly accurate. The Orioles' 7–11 April was typically poor. Yet even more problematic than a losing month was a sudden pitching emergency. Martinez, with high hopes for his rested arm after not pitching winter ball, had a new change-up and seemed set for a big season. But the Nicaraguan came up short with shoulder trouble right at the start, as well a biceps tear. His move to the disabled list elevated Stone to fourth in the starting rotation. Coming off a strong spring, Stone looked up for the challenge, pronouncing himself willing to trust all his pitches rather than rely on hard stuff. "The harder I threw, the worse I got," he remembered about 1979.[35]

Doldrums starting the regular season frustrated many newer fans, so much so that *Sun* columnist Bob Maisel detected a hint of panic in the stands. "It is understandable why people are frustrated about the … sputtering start," he wrote near the end of April. "It isn't just the losses that have people scratching their heads, but the way the Orioles are losing. They are losing the 1-run games and they are losing games in which they hold late leads, neither of which they did very often last year."[36] Among the trouble signs, Maisel identified the 37-year-old Lee May's slow bat. But Maisel advised fans to take their cue from Weaver, who refused to panic. The season was long, he said, and there was time for the Orioles to improve. But their hopes took another blow when McGregor joined Martinez with arm trouble of his own. Trainer Ralph Salvon attributed it to his habit of throwing across his body, but also predicted that the young star would not go on the disabled list. The team's options on the mound included using Stewart as starter, and moving Stone still higher in the rotation.

Things turned brighter in May and part of the reason was Dempsey's hot bat. The catcher credited hitting coach Frank Robinson as well as an off-season weight training program. "All I've tried to do is get Rick to slow his body down, so he can use his hands," Robinson explained. "You have to get the body out of the way, so you can use your hands. You don't generate power with your body, but with bat speed, and you get that from your hands and arms."[37] But he was less certain about how to help the struggling May, who suddenly looked his age. Nor did Robinson have instant cures for other players struggling to produce. "If I knew what was wrong, I'd correct it," Robinson explained. "I do what I can, I talk to the players and try to make suggestions. But really, all you can do is just keep waiting until they start doing what they're supposed to do."[38] In the GM's office, Peters too expressed frustration, delivering a veiled threat to the punchless Birds. "It's reached the point where our bats are embarrassing us," he admitted, hinting at roster changes.[39] The whole team scored just 74 runs in April, over 18 games. The staff kept them afloat because it gave up only 77 runs. But while waiting for the collective batting funk to end, Weaver showed a touch of whimsy, inviting his perennial foil, umpire Marty Springstead, as guest on the pre-game WFBR-AM show, "The Manager's Corner." The two completed the interview without any audible rancor.

May proved friendlier to the team than April, as the Orioles found their footing, going 15–13. This left them just shy of .500 at the end of a month in which baseball's biggest story was the looming Memorial Day-weekend strike deadline. Every Oriole interviewed expressed strong support for the union's position. Singleton, usually very mild in demeanor, pronounced himself "kind of militant on this," adding that, "In '72, the older guys did it for us and now we've got to do it for the guys in the future. There's no sense backing down and giving back what we've already got." Belanger said, "If we took a vote right now, 26 guys would say they don't want to strike. But 26 would say they will."[40] On May 22, with the deadline a day away, Boswell quoted the downcast Williams, plainly distressed to see such a standoff menace his first full season as team owner. "I have a sense of failure just being part of this," he admitted quietly as the Orioles beat Detroit 5–1 behind McGregor. "I just feel irritation," players rep DeCinces said. "Nobody knows how long this strike is going to take," Singleton warned, "But if a strike is what the owners want, then that's what they're going to get. It's going to cost them and cost them big."[41]

Boswell and other students of the game understood that conducting labor negotiations during the season brought political brinksmanship into the minds of fans who only wanted balls, strikes, wins, and losses. Tiger manager Sparky Anderson put it well. "I used to think that we lived in a special world—almost blessed by the innocence of playing a kid's game. I thought we were a little different, even a little better, though not through any merit of our own, but just 'cause we were part of the game. But now,

I guess maybe we're just like everybody else."[42] With stress felt across the entire sport, it was not surprising that the imminent strike, then its last-minute deferment as owners and players agreed to a mediated stopgap agreement, dominated attention as May wore on. Fans and players alike were hesitant to commit themselves to a season that might be cut short. When Memorial Day weekend brought news that the season would continue, there was a visible lightening in the Oriole clubhouse, and the team went 6–3 to close out the month. Part of the reason might have been that the players—who made Baltimore one of the strongest pro-union teams in the majors—felt reasonably comfortable with their ownership and management. Weaver had voiced his pro-free agency stance, while Williams was willing to extend DeCinces—a player representative for the entire American League—with a new three-year contract even before the strike was so narrowly averted. His legal skills held him in good stead, as Williams became a voice for temperate ownership positions. "You have to take the recrimination out of negotiations," he told Boswell, who broke the story that the Orioles owner, along with Peter O'Malley of the Dodgers and John McMullen of the Astros, had coalesced as a compromise cohort. "It does no good to curse Marvin Miller. He has always been a ground breaker—the man out front. Your goal cannot be defeating him, because you don't beat a good man. But you can reason with him and compromise."[43]

Williams took pains to differentiate between football, which faced its own upcoming labor meltdown, and baseball. In the former, it was possible to simply shut down an entire franchise by not playing or practicing. Everything could go on hold; expenses would be minimal. But baseball was far too multivalent, with far-flung minor leagues and constant scouting. These would continue during any stoppage, and require funds to operate. It was also possible, Williams worried, for sports fans to develop new habits. He pointed to the end of preseason sellouts at RFK after the NFL's strike. As he mulled things over, Williams was presiding over a shift in Baltimore sports patronage to the advantage of his team. Most of all, what came through in Boswell's story was Williams' unparalleled comfort with the give-and-take of negotiations. Williams was the last owner who would sacrifice the game's well-being simply to signal that the owners were determined. His entire professional life had taught him that winning a negotiation did not mean annihilating the other side.

The game on May 23 brought back memories of the previous season's magic. With 16,000-plus fans in the stadium, and Singleton's game-winning two-run homer in the bottom of the eighth both delivered the win and seemed to end his slump. As usual, Wild Bill Hagy did his thing in Section 34. Also, Stone pitched a three-hitter through eight innings, despite struggling with subpar stuff. That the righthander scuffled a bit made pitching coach Miller all the more pleased. "It's special when a curve ball pitcher has no curve and lasts through the eighth," he enthused. "There's a lotta thought about location going on out there." Palmer chimed in during the clubhouse interview, revealing that he had tipped off Stone about fastball-hitter Tim Corcoran. "So he threw him 13 straight hooks," Palmer said. "Finally, he adjusted and lined one off Stone's glove!" As the players dissolved in relaxed laughter, Mark Belanger's 10-year old son, Robbie, a constant and welcome presence in the locker room, read his own game account out loud, concluding, "Great Game, Steve!" to universal approval. Surveying the scene, Terry Crowley succinctly observed: "Like the O's of old."[44]

There was a baseball gem buried in Palmer's comments. Stone *was* throwing lots of curves. He was trusting his best pitch, sometimes throwing as many as 75 in a single game.[45] Of course, so many breaking balls were stressful on Stone's arm, but it was a calculated risk. As injuries to others moved him up in the rotation, his effectiveness only increased. Going 2–2 with a 4.50 ERA in April, Stone improved to 4–1 and 3.05 in May, then 5–0, 2.47 for June. He wound up a cinch for the All-Star Game. Stone formed part of a good one-two punch with Stoddard, who saved Stone's first five victories. While Stone asserted himself as the *de facto* stopper, the Orioles themselves heated up, going 17–9 in June. They fattened up as the schedule grew kind, pitting them against the struggling Tigers, Indians, Mariners, Angels, and Twins, as well as the overperforming Blue Jays and A's. Spotting that break in the schedule, Ken Denlinger predicted that, if the 1980 Orioles were to make a move upwards, it needed to happen then. Failure to "claw into this feast," he wrote, might mean big trouble by the All–Star break.[46]

They did precisely what Denlinger said, and the Orioles also witnessed another comforting team ritual: a Palmer-Weaver dust-up. On May 27, in a 10–6 loss to Cleveland, Weaver pulled Palmer when the Tribe rallied from a 3–0 deficit with four runs in the fifth inning. Palmer, visibly frustrated, hands on hips, glared at his manager before the two had sharp words. "I didn't want to come out," the starter admitted after the game. "When I saw him coming I couldn't believe it. I was in shock." Asked if there was a confrontation, Palmer nodded. "Yeah, there was. I don't remember what was said. I thought he made the wrong move. He did make the wrong move, we lost the game." But Weaver, speaking to intrepid reporter John Feinstein, was self-deprecatory. "I don't remember saying nothing out there," he claimed. "Jim wanted to stay in the game, I know that. He wanted to win. They all want to win. Right now, I wish I had left him in."[47] It did seem like old times.

One of the unheralded stars of the team's June hot streak was substitute catcher Dan Graham, a rookie who spelled Dempsey as the latter's bat cooled down. Graham specialized in hitting righthanders, and got off to a good major league debut, going 9-for-16 in his first few games. Weaver, delighted to have lineup choices, promised to try his new find against Ranger hurler Gaylord Perry. "I want to see if he can hit a low spitter," wisecracked the manager. Flanagan made a point of welcoming Graham, the latest in a series of valuable role-players, by crediting his game-calling skills. Dempsey had no complaints, so the injection of a new ingredient into the 1980 formula went smoothly, as usual.[48] Other players also sharpened their edge. For example, Bumbry, who had battled nagging leg pains, burst out in late May, garnering AL Player of the Week honors and pushing his batting average all the way to .356 before coming back to earth.

On June 19, in a home game against the A's, with the Orioles in fourth but riding a four-game winning streak, pinch hitter John Lowenstein kept a rally going with a run-tying single off Rick Langford in the bottom of the seventh. Next, running the bases, he took a thrown ball to the back of his neck and head. This allowed Bumbry to score the go-ahead run on the live ball, punching Lowenstein's ticket into Orioles Magic lore. Trainer Ralph Salvon and the medical team raced out as Lowenstein lay prostrate where he fell on the basepath. They placed the motionless Bird into a stretcher and carried him off the field, while fans excited over the rally wondered at its price. A hush came over the crowd. Then, the supine Brother Lo raised his arm aloft and punched the sky, giving a #1 sign. Memorial Stadium erupted.

Part of the Orioles' improvement tallied with the fact that 1980 brought a balanced schedule. Whereas the previous two seasons saw the team play many early home games—when they traditionally drew fewer fans—the new year put them on the road early, giving them more home match-ups later. Peters had complained about the two prior seasons, but acknowledged that 1980 was friendlier. "There are some fine weekends which are helping," he noted. Bob Holbrook, in charge of creating the AL schedule, agreed. "This year, the Orioles are heavy at home when they want to be heavy. They have more home dates from the end of June until Labor Day than any other team in the league."[49] What that meant in effect was that the Orioles were at home for 11 of the season's final 16 weekends, including two four-game series with the Yankees and Red Sox, great for attendance as well as divisional gains. They also played at home on Memorial Day, July 4, and Labor Day, giving them the chance to keep moving their attendance figures northward. Through June 5, after their first 24 home games, they were already up 16,012 over their 1979 figures, with a total of 411, 246.[50] Hotter weather and summer vacation were sure to keep those numbers climbing higher. Winning would also help, as the team finally surmounted .500 for good during June's second week.

A comic incident on July 1 provided some relief from pressures of their battles against mediocrity. Before a healthy Canada Day crowd at Toronto's Exhibition Stadium, a grouchy Weaver headed to the mound to confer with Palmer. While the two consulted at length, fans began clapping rhythmically. Weaver seemed not to notice, but, on his way back to the dugout, he stopped, cupped his hands to his mouth and shouted, "Shut up!" And, as he later chuckled, "I'll be durned if the whole ball park didn't shut up, just like you'd turned off a switch. We almost died laughing."[51]

While all the forecasts were rosy, the Orioles continued to struggle into July. They trailed division-leading New York by 11 on July 15. Their record that month was 16–11, but they still trailed the Yankees and Brewers, with the Red Sox also in the mix. Weaver tore into his team prior to the All-Star Break. "I counted 42 errors, physical and mental, in the game," he ranted after a bad 7–5 road loss to Seattle. He cast enough blame to go around. "Everybody's making them and they're piling up. One of the big things is getting doubled off base on a line drive. Nine times this year we've had guys doubled off," he complained. But with just over half the season left, Weaver denied panicking. He pulled out an old reference to make his point. In 1975, as they chased the Red Sox, Weaver exulted that the Orioles had "climbed out of more coffins than Bela Lugosi." This time, he said, "I'm not using that old Bela Lugosi line this early."[52] Weaver understood that, with Martinez still on the Disabled List, along with Roenicke; with Lowenstein and Garcia just off the DL; with minor injuries and some bad luck—such as a potential game-winner by Singleton that hit a Kingdome speaker, becoming into a double instead of a home run, there was time left to recover. But not very much time, especially since the loaded Yankees were playing well and showing no signs of relinquishing their lead.

Stone and others performed well enough that the summer situation, while frustrating, was not dire. The righthander started the All-Star Game that July, and kept on rolling after. Wins against the Royals on July 12 and the Brewers on July 16 made his record a glittering 14–3. The Orioles won five of their last six in July, then started August with a blistering ten-game winning streak. A three-game sweep in New York beginning on August 8 was the crucial component of their hot spell, and the finale of that game gave Baltimore fans reasons to believe the magic was back to stay. The game was a sellout, 54,123 packing into Yankee Stadium to see if Dick Howser's Bombers could stave off the fast-rising challengers. Behind ace Tommy John, New York led 5–4 as the Orioles came to the plate in the top of the ninth with their 8–9–1 batters. Recent Rochester product Lenn Sakata, a versatile infielder with pop in his bat, started the inning with a triple. While he lingered on third, Weaver began pulling levers, pinch hitting May for Belanger. May lined out, then Dauer, also pinch-hitting, flied out. With two outs and the tying run still 90 feet away, Dempsey—who had homered in the seventh—rapped a single to center, scoring Sakata. Weaver promptly inserted Garcia as a pinch runner for Dempsey. Singleton drew a walk, then Murray doubled to right, giving the Orioles a 6–5 lead that Stoddard protected. Suddenly, the Orioles were back. As Yankee owner George Steinbrenner fumed over the sweep, Baltimore's record stood at 64–44, just two-and-a-half games behind suddenly vulnerable New York.

The Orioles promptly lost two of three to the Royals before coming home for a crucial five-game marathon series against the Yankees, August 14–18. This turned out to be the most memorable home series of the season, not least because of the crowds, the likes of which Memorial Stadium had never seen during 20 years of August dog days. Stone paced a 6–1 win in the opener, before 49, 952. But the next night, John stopped the Orioles 4–3, outduelling Flanagan while 50, 434 screamed with every pitch. Cagey Gaylord Perry, a precious mid-season pickup, shot down the Orioles 4–1 in the third game, with 51, 649 frustrated by the lack of Orioles magic. Weaver burst onto the field during the game, laying into umpire Steve Palermo while pulling out several of his best routines: kicking dirt onto the plate, kicking and stomping on his cap, perching atop the keystone sack. "Earl figured that was the only way he could be as tall as we are," Palermo joked after the game, "But they don't make bags that tall." Star Yankee reliever Goose Gossage appreciated the performance: "That's a ten, no doubt about it. I'd pay to see that."[53] In the eyes of the American League, the routine was worth a three-game suspension. As with most of Weaver's histrionics, the outburst served as a pressure valve. While everyone buzzed about the hijinks, the team loosened up. McGregor's 1–0 gem against Luis Tiant, admired by 50, 073, set the stage for the finale, which Palmer won over Ron Guidry, 6–5, satisfying 51,528. Combined attendance shattered all previous home marks, but winning three of five games left the Orioles still two-and-a-half games back. The Orioles wound up 21–8 in August, and 76–52 overall, heading into September.

Over 11 days in August, they had faced the Yankees eight times, winning six. They consistently pitched around Jackson, loath to give the star any chance for heroics. They benefited from regular Oriole-killing third baseman Greg Nettles' absence due to hepatitis. Jackson hit only .120 for the 11 games, and the five-six-seven hitters who followed Reggie, a shifting array included Bob Watson, Joe Lefebvre, Rick Cerone, Eric Solderholm, Jim Spencer, and Aurelio Rodriguez, batted 91 times with 53 runners on base, yet somehow driving in not a single run. It was a standout pitching performance by the Birds' staff, while Jackson—who craved the game-winning chance—was so frustrated that one Oriole remarked, "He was swinging hard enough to hit it off the planet." "If I'd hit one, it would have gone nine miles," Jackson agreed. His struggles delighted the Orioles faithful who remembered his bittersweet Baltimore stint in 1976.[54] All in all, the Orioles handled the division leaders playing head-to-head. But they still trailed the Yankees, who continued to win when it counted. Led by tough veterans such as Nettles, Murcer, Bucky Dent, Lou Piniella, and Watson, enhanced by star Jackson, supplemented by role players including Fred Stanley and Bobby Brown, the Bronx Bombers were an old team. Besides Guidry, their rotation down the stretch depended on the 42-year-old Perry, 40-year-old Tiant, 37-year-old John, and 37-year-old Rudy May. The Yankee lineup averaged 35 years old.[55] But the Bombers were rugged mentally and too talented to wilt. No doubt the Orioles sometimes wished they could have back some of the games they booted away earlier in the season.

It is an old baseball bromide that September races reveal team character, and the burdens on the Yankees that month were enormous. When Jackson smashed into a fence to catch a ball during the series in Baltimore, Boswell wrote, "The wall should have been taken to the hospital for X-rays." Even Ray Miller was moved to grudging admiration. "When somebody on your team does that, you say, 'What guts! What a gamer!' When a guy on the other team does it, you say, 'What a dummy! There's no percentage in that!' But Baltimore's pitching coach was forced to admit that Jackson was built for such clutch performances. 'The only way Reggie could have made a better play on that ball was if he'd jumped over the fence and landed on Gossage.'"[56] Weaver, always a Jackson fan, agreed. "He's what you call a 'hard' player," Weaver explained. "He hustles, runs everything out, hates to embarrass himself. He'll take a guy out on the double play, or run into a wall, make a sliding catch.... He can reach a special level of concentration in the key situations that win games—just like Frank Robinson." Responding, Jackson was gracious. "I loved playing for Earl Weaver.... I could play for the little Weave. That man will chew you out, read you the riot act down to the ground, and then forget all about it."[57]

The hardened Yankees were not likely to collapse, although an exuberant Stone hoped otherwise. "If we don't win this thing going away, then call me a liar," he exulted.[58] It was left to Boswell to contextualize. "Stone wasn't a liar," the great scribe wrote. "He simply fell for that Scylla and Charybdis of every pennant race, a double lure that every hot team feels— natural pride in themselves and equally natural prejudice toward undervaluing an opponent."[59] The numbers gave Stone reason for confidence, since Baltimore played .692 baseball over the last 104 games of the year. But earlier missed chances—whether in April, or later pratfalls such as two late August losses to woeful Seattle—counted as much as their triumphs. That unavoidable fact reiterated itself every September night, as the Orioles kept winning and so did the Yanks.

On September 17, in the first inning of a home win against the Tigers, umpire Bill Haller called a balk on starter Flanagan. The game was just a few minutes old. No one suspected at the time that Weaver's subsequent tirade, captured on film, was destined to become his most famous. Haller was miked that night as part of a planned documentary on umpires. The filmmakers were in the stands with camera running. Later, the filmed version of the argument found its way to immortality via then-unimaginable YouTube. Haller and Weaver were longtime antagonists. On August 2, 1969, as the Orioles played against the Twins at Metropolitan Stadium, Haller noticed Weaver smoking in the dugout after the first pitch, a violation of the rules, and immediately tossed him out of the game. The next night, when Frank Robinson argued a called strike in the first inning, Weaver rushed in to join the rhubarb and wound up ejected during the top of the first for the second game in a row.[60] In 1972, as the Orioles tried desperately to overhaul the front-running Tigers, Weaver demanded that Haller be prohibited from calling Baltimore games, since the umpire's brother, Tom, pitched for Detroit. To the few horsehide cognoscenti familiar with this bad blood, the fact that Weaver stormed out to argue the balk in the first inning was unsurprising. To everyone else in attendance in Baltimore that hot 1980 night, it was a kind of unexpected bonus. At first the argument was conventional, if conducted in shouts. Murray led the opposition. But when Weaver offered his opinion that Haller and his crew were "here just to fuck us," the umpire's hook was prompt. Tiger first-base coach Dick Tracewski kept his composure, and no doubt struggled to keep a straight face, as the Oriole manager went off. "You can't wait to get me outta here," Weaver accused; "You run yourself, Earl," the umpire responded. "You're here for one Goddamn specific reason," Weaver continued, " to fuck us!" "Ah, you're full of shit, fuck you," answered Haller. Weaver wagged his finger in the ump's face, Haller poked the manager in the chest. Weaver swatted Haller's hand away. Then, the two men disputed who had touched the other first. Haller no doubt wanted Weaver suspended for making contact with an ump, while Weaver knew that if he insisted that Haller poked him first, he would gain cover. Each expostulated that the other was "no good." Murray and Flanagan drifted in and out of the scene as the extravaganza played out. Weaver and Haller accused each other of lying. "Your ass'll never have our games again," Weaver promised. "Well, what do I care? ... Why don't you go to the league office and ask them?" Haller inquired. "Don't think I won't!" Then Haller took the offensive. "The quicker you get outta here the better," he suggested. "You ain't goin' nowhere," Weaver pointed out. "You ain't, either," Haller answered back. At this juncture, Weaver told the umpire to "wait five or ten fucking years," when he promised to be in Cooperstown. "What for?" Haller demanded. "For fucking up World Series?" The proceedings went on and on. The best part, as far as the fans were concerned, was that each time the tidal force of the affair ebbed, Weaver stopped his retreat off the field and headed back to Haller. Each time he extended the fight, the Memorial Stadium crowd, already cheering, got more uproarious. "Earl! Earl! Earl!" they chanted. "Good job, Earl!" When Weaver finally departed, home ump Ken Kaiser was impressed despite himself: "Jesus Christ! We just started this goddarned thing!"

The spectacle of a short, florid man irked beyond reason was more funny than anything else, unless one wore blue and worked for the American League. It was not Weaver's most baroque performance, bereft of add-ons such as shredded rule books, tossed caps, buried plates, uprooted bases. But thanks to the umpire's hidden microphone and a future upload into the digital universe, this fracas would serve for generations as the template for those flare-ups that made summer nights in Baltimore so much fun for fans, if not umpires.[61]

Those who could see past the fireworks might have noticed two subtle aspects within this over-the-top comedy. The first was that the fuss started with a flustered Flanagan and a mad Murray. "He did not go behind the rubber!" the usually stoical first baseman pointed out several times, each time growing more impatient, as if Haller were a refractory child. The umpire and the Orioles' budding superstar were on the verge of their own ruckus. It was at that point, with Murray's choler mounting, that Weaver interposed himself, taking over the argument and letting his star cool down. The second aspect occurred when Weaver crossed the mound on the way off the field. "Did you balk?" he asked Flanagan. "Yes," admitted the pitcher. While Weaver railed against fate and umpires, the Yanks kept winning, all the way to a division crown. At the *Sun*, Maisel knew a tough outfit when he saw them. "Whenever they were backed up into a corner and had to come up with a key hit, pitch or play to hold the Orioles off, they did it," he wrote about the Yankees, adding that they did it while battling injuries to key players.[62] During the last three weeks of the season, the Birds battled to a 15–6 record, including winning streaks of five and six. On Thursday, October 2, they stood at 98–61, but needed the Yankees to lose to Detroit in order to remain alive. Jackson and Oscar Gamble homered in light rain, Gossage squelched a Tiger rally, and the Yankees' victory mathematically eliminated Baltimore. The Orioles won two of their final three, finishing 100–62. Their problem was that the Yankees went 103–59. Only two teams in the majors won 100 games that year, but the Orioles stayed home when the playoffs began. Perhaps tired by their dogged defense against persistent Baltimore, the Yankees fell promptly to Kansas City in the playoffs. The Royals, with their first pennant in the bag, took Philadelphia to six games before Tug McGraw's Phillies won their first World Series.

So, despite tantalizing chances and an excellent overall campaign, the Orioles' 1980 season mixed sweet and sour. The team had the second-best record in the majors, yet lost a divisional race they felt they should have won. Stone, en route to a 25–7 record, 3.23 ERA, and nine complete games, had a far, far better year than he ever did before. His Cy Young Award was his swan song; his reliance on the curveball did in his arm, and the next year would be his last. But as a Cy Young winner, Stone's star was fixed in baseball's firmament. The season sparked great memories and positive signs for the future. The Orioles' basic building blocks were intact, their lineup talent-rich and their pitching staff deep. The late–August five-game homestand against the Yankees emphatically showed that Baltimore was still in the throes of baseball passion.

Of course, Washington remained just down the parkway, ready for baseball of its own. Fans from the capital area joined in the Memorial Stadium enthusiasm and helped the Orioles set a new attendance record. Meanwhile, the far-seeing Boswell, who was making a career-defining

In 1980, the Orioles went 100–62. Only two major league teams won 100 games or more that season. Unfortunately for Baltimore, the other was the New York Yankees, who took the AL East with a record of 103–59.

study of Weaver that cemented the writer's reputation as baseball's best chronicler, wondered if Weaver, whom he called "definitely frayed" down the stretch, was nearing retirement. The manager told the reporter that two more years sounded right. "The older he gets," Boswell wrote of Weaver, late in the season, "the closer he comes to the end of his run, the more money gets stashed away in deferred payments so that he can spend his life in vegetable gardens, on golf courses, and at dog tracks, the harder it is not to find Earl Weaver appealing. "He's mellowing in the best sense."[63]

So Orioles fans could look forward to two more years with baseball's best manager. At the same time, owner Williams, consumed by the draining pennant chase, was making no ominous noises about relocation except to say that the matter was in Baltimore's hands. Record-setting attendance—1, 797, 243 in 1980, beating the 1979 record of 1, 681, 009, as well as broad cultural excitement across the Mid-Atlantic—made that formula reassuring. No matter where you went in and around Maryland—and in Washington, up to York, and out to lower Delaware—the Orioles were popular. *Sun* columnist Michael Olesker wrote at season's end of several episodes proving to him that interest in the team was at an all-time high. He recalled a mid-season visit to a comedy performance, not an ordinary venue for baseball fever. According to Olesker, when the comedian began his routine with a few baseball jokes, introducing himself as a New Yorker who liked going to Yankee Stadium, pandemonium ensued. "Those were the last words he would utter for a full five minutes. The crowd exploded in boos. The comedian stood there, stunned. Then somebody shouted, 'Gimme an O!' and everyone went through the Oriole cheer. And then somebody else took up the cry and everybody repeated the chant and then cheers for the Orioles were flung about the room like rice at a wedding."[64] Baltimore, which considered its baseball team magical in 1979, remained under the Oriole spell in 1980. There seemed no reason to be pessimistic about 1981.

3

SPLIT SEASON, DOUBLY FRUSTRATING (1981)

The backstory hanging over baseball's 1981 season was impossible to ignore: the labor dispute. The previous strike-averting settlement, which saved the 1980 season, was purely a stopgap, and unless players and owners came to agreement on the issues dividing them—including compensation for lost free agents, but also the general sense that the owners wanted to regain lost control of the sport—then 1981 would bring the showdown. That said, the Orioles made off-season moves which had fans and team feeling good that winter. First of all, a community relations effort led by Murray and Singleton not only enhanced Memorial Stadium diversity, it underscored the good feelings flowing between players and fans. Murray, moving into the mature phase of his career, on the cusp of true superstardom, was behind "Project 33" (his uniform number was 33), which set aside 50 upper box seats at every home game for disadvantaged Baltimore children. He was matched in the project by the Jaycees, who anted up for 4,000 tickets to be distributed across 33 city neighborhoods. At the same time, Singleton backed "Project 29" (his uniform number was 29), buying 64 lower reserved seats for every Sunday home game, earmarked for area senior citizen groups.[1] The two projects were added to an existing charitable portfolio benefiting Johns Hopkins Children's Center, fighting Sickle Cell Anemia, supporting the Kidney Foundation, and United Cerebral Palsy. Fans noticed, writing into newspapers and calling radio shows to compliment Murray, Singleton, and the franchise.[2] There were no such letters or calls about the Colts.

Such charitable endeavors enhanced the belief among fans that there was something inherently positive—a beating heart—at the core of their baseball team. It transferred and continued the cherished feeling of connection and specialness once associated with the old Colts, revered for their loyalty to the Baltimore community. It also pointed to a feeling among the team's leaders—and Singleton was the *de facto* leader, with Murray next to step into the role—that they were valued as leading citizens. There were ongoing efforts such as the continuation of the Orioles' charity basketball team. The off-season also brought Murray's new six-year contract, pushing his salary to nearly $1 million per season, a new level for the franchise. Negotiations with agent Ron Shapiro, himself a local attorney, had been swift and positive,[3] the atmosphere surrounding the Orioles upbeat and even virtuous. As usual in those days, the Colts provided a contrast. Despite a modest upturn to 7–9 under new coach Mike McCormack, owner Irsay still demonstrated disregard for local fans and politicians, who reciprocated. John Steadman of the *News-American*, and dean of Baltimore football writers, was a well-connected reporter at the national levels. Connections included a pipeline to Pete Rozelle, who, the writer insisted, "believes Baltimore is a solid base of NFL operations." Still, Steadman made it plain that Williams, of the Orioles, was easier for Maryland politicians to deal with than Irsay. The former continued to speak with Schaefer and Hughes about Memorial Stadium repairs and new stadium plans. Irsay preferred barnstorming "around the country on what amounted to a shopping spree."[4]

Another contrast was provided by other major league teams, especially the Yankees. Gammons noticed "some bad blood brewing" between the squads, so opposite in culture, so matched in talent. The Orioles were offended that spring when Gossage beaned Bumbry during an exhibition game[5]; the Yankees would be livid when the irrepressible Stewart pretended to deliver a pitch lefthanded during the regular season. Williams proved himself aware of his team's rare reputation when he commented on the Murray talks. "I've said all along that my number 1 priority is to keep this club intact. I think we've got a good, solid, young team with a great future.... I'm going to try to keep all the players and field a contending team next year, the year after that, and the year after that." In response, Shapiro contended that the a main factor in Murray's decision to re-sign with the Orioles was ""Eddie's abiding desire to remain in Baltimore."[6] Shapiro himself was a rare breed, an agent with good press. He was the focus of a major January article in the *Sporting News* about how players now used advisors not just for negotiations, but to plan long-term financial security. A photo of Shapiro talking with retired legend Brooks Robinson signified a Baltimore seal of approval if ever there was one.[7]

In Miami for the start of spring training, Boswell noticed and praised the good vibes, especially set against the murky conditions elsewhere. To the writer, the Orioles seemed the "lone keepers of the game's clean flame."[8] He admired the way they avoided spasmodic moves. Although frugal, they were able to re-sign and extend McGregor, would no doubt satisfy Flanagan, and still meet Murray's needs. They refused to entertain offers for Denny Martinez, believing that he was on the verge of ace status. No matter what turmoil the game experienced, or how hasty their rivals could be, Boswell wrote, the Orioles refused to lose faith "in their theories about the preeminence of starting pitching, flawless though not flashy defense, power over average, and (above all), boring fundamentals.[9] Among the principles they refused to traduce this spring training was their determination to stay patient with prospects. Thus, hard-hitting Rochester third baseman Cal Ripken, Jr. was not going to start the season on the Orioles, where his father was an admired coach and lifelong custodian of the Oriole Way. "While others are impatient for success," Boswell argued, "the Orioles are interminably patient, confident, at least in baseball, that is the only way to have long-term success."[10]

The accolades were not just regional. Boston-based baseball scribe Peter Gammons, national American League columnist at the *Sporting News*, waxed enthusiastic about franchise management in a winter article, "O's Prime Example of Good Management." Gammons, too, contrasted the Orioles to other teams, finding them refreshing as well as smart. "What has been going on in Baltimore hasn't created the headlines that the Great American Greed Machine has churned out in New York and Boston," he wrote. "But don't underestimate its relative significance."[11] He credited Williams' willingness to spend and Peters' sagacity in keeping top-tier talents like Singleton, Murray, McGregor, and Dauer on board. Next up would be Stoddard. He noted the difference from the mid-seventies, when Garland, Jackson, Grich, and Grimsley all left. Williams, he insisted, was the major difference. His devotion to fielding a winner extended to his willingness to pay to keep the roster intact, which in turn kept the players happy: "Winning means a lot," admitted Belanger. Flanagan gave Gammons a positive take on Weaver. "Because of Earl, we know where we stand, we're allowed the freedom to be ourselves in the clubhouse right up to game time. All in all, the fact is that the Oriole organization has created an atmosphere where we have fun playing. When you were a kid, you didn't play for money, but for fun."[12] Weaver was also having fun, filming a funny commercial for Jockey which made light of how much his physique differed from spokesmodel Palmer's.[13] Not for nothing did Gammons later credit the Orioles of this era as one of the major leagues' last fun teams.

But in 1981, money as well as fun was something the major leagues had to figure out.

That was much on Maisel's mind as he covered the team in Miami. Looking ahead to the likely outcome of the labor talks, he heard the owners talk about needing a victory, but also expected the players to hang on until management caved. "How can you blame them?" he asked. "They have gotten their way on everything since the reserve clause was ruled out, and history says labor does not give up gains already won, unless there is no way out."[14] Like many other writers, Maisel expressed bewilderment at rising ballplayer salaries. But what worried him most was the absolutist position he detected on both sides of the owner-player divide. Maisel's column warning of a work stoppage and resultant financial disaster stressed the Orioles' narrow margin for success or failure at the box office. It coincided with the delivery of a bombshell, in the form of a letter from Ray Grebey to Marvin Miller. The study committee, consisting of players Sal Bando and Bob Boone, and executives Frank Cashen and Harry Dalton, had met eight times to hash out a compromise on the free agency compensation issue, but come to no agreement. One member claimed that, whenever an agreement seemed close, the animus between Grebey and Miller reappeared, with one of the two antagonists preventing a deal.[15] Grebey's letter to Miller announced that the owners were set to unilaterally impose the free agency compensation scheme they favored, which the union vowed never to accept.[16] No matter how much goodwill suffused the Orioles, this would spill bitterness across the sport. The union's countermove was to declare a May 29 strike date. DeCinces, deeply involved in the game's labor issues, put it in baseball terms. "It was like a fastball up and in," he said of Grebey's unilateral declaration. "The players were going to respond to that."[17]

At the same time, there were the usual signs of normalcy when teams gather in the sunshine to work out the kinks of winter. There was organizational satisfaction at the spectacle of Frank Robinson being hired as San Francisco Giants manager, because he still enjoyed good relations with the front office, and because his selection validated the Orioles' quality coaching staff, as had previous hires of Jim Frey and George Bamberger, and ongoing interviews with Miller. More customary was the "certain indicator of spring" spotted by Nigro: Palmer's latest complaint about his arm. This time, it was torn muscle fibers in his shoulder, the pitcher explained, as he commenced camp under the tender touch of trainer Ralph Salvon. Nobody, including Palmer, seemed very worried. "I don't think this will have any effect on spring training," the pitcher predicted. "I hope not."[18]

Questioned about the team's prospects, Palmer was nearly giddy about the starting rotation. With 20-game winners Stone and McGregor returning, as well as Flanagan, Martinez, and himself, tall number 22 did not bother to hide his enthusiasm. The previous nicknames "Cy Young, Cy Old, Cy Present, Cy Future" were on many lips, while young Storm Davis, whose big-kicking delivery bore an uncanny resemblance to Palmer's, began to hear "Cy Clone." "This is our best pitching staff since I've been here," said Palmer, who was a rookie when the Orioles won their 1966 World Series championship.[19]

The biggest question that spring was what to do with Ripken, but the team had already assured all concerned that the prospect faced another year as a Red Wing. Ripken's hot performance in Puerto Rican winter ball whetted fan hopes for the best-looking rookie since Murray arrived four years before. Weaver fended off questions, while betraying manage's sky-high hopes for Ripken: "I have no idea what's going to happen with Ripken other than we'll take a close look at him in the spring. There's a possible chance he's another Eddie Murray, and if he is, the Baltimore Orioles have another Brooks Robinson and Frank Robinson on their hands."[20] It was 15 years since the Robinson combination not only won the World Series but entranced fans with their cross-racial friendship and dual commitment to winning. That the Orioles were willing to talk about Ripken and Murray in the same way, even contingently, showed a high degree of confidence in the pair, since management was customarily cautious about placing pressure on young players. Nor was Weaver alone in his optimism. Ripken was universally cited in every preseason annual as a top prospect, and out-of-town writers doubted the Orioles' promise to keep him in Class AAA for more seasoning.[21] Boswell was one of the few who trusted the team's commitment, having heard Weaver not only express concern for Ripken's development, but for DeCinces' feelings as the baseball world praised the rising young third baseman. "Let's not interfere with DeCinces getting off to a good start," the manager implored. What Boswell noticed about those remarks was that, out of all Oriole players, Weaver's relationship with DeCinces was perhaps the most strained. And yet the manager still tried to protect his current starter from insulting speculation.[22]

The manager, Boswell hinted, was no softie, but he did have a pragmatic instinct for insulating his players. DeCinces had avoided a back operation during the off-season and pronounced himself ready to produce. "Surgery is an athlete's worst enemy," he insisted, perhaps conflating cause and cure, but citing an admired peer on a nearby team playing a different sport. "Tell me about Phil Chenier."[23] Chenier, one-time star for the NBA

Bullets, had just gone through two operations and faced the end of his career. Clearly, DeCinces wanted to avoid such a fate himself.

While Weaver prepped for the season, Williams—who was still fighting cancer, busy with his law practice, widely involved in civic, charitable, and political causes, dealing with Annapolis on stadium issues, and running the team—took on even more responsibility as an increasingly influential member of the owners' lead negotiating cohort. Recently named to the owners executive council, Williams had two advantages not part of every businessman's portfolio. First, he understood that "macho posturing," as fellow negotiator Harry Dalton described some of the owners' pronouncements to Boswell, would do little good in the long run.[24] Dalton's uncensored moment cost him a $50,000 fine and the baleful enmity of Grebey, supposedly his negotiating team partner. Williams—whose financial resources came entirely from his law work—also understood that, with prime interest rates running as high as 18 percent, debt payments such as those needed to service his purchase of the Orioles would become particularly onerous in the event of a strike. Williams was as adept a negotiator as anyone in the United States, thanks to his courtroom experience. He could size up the strengths and weaknesses of each side. He recognized that, while Grebey leaned towards forcing an impasse en route to the "victory" owners so craved, Miller, having built the current system, was unwilling to see it disassembled. "There's no way he's going to give ground on it," Williams said to Barry Rona, a lawyer with the owners Players Relations Committee. "Marvin would commit suicide before he'd agree to that. In fact, the only way to achieve anything is to wait for him to die."[25] Those morbid words were both accurate and also psychologically noteworthy, since Williams, despite publicly losing not a step off his breakneck life's pace, knew he faced a potentially fatal disease himself. Perhaps this added to his sense of urgency, as well as his conviction that provoking a labor war was short-sighted. Williams used DeCinces and Belanger as back channels into the union ranks, simultaneously drawing closer to other owners more willing to compromise than endure a strike.[26] Each practice or exhibition in Miami brought not just Opening Day, but also the strike deadline, closer.

It was during this spring that press accounts first mentioned the possibility of building a downtown ballpark on the site of Baltimore's Camden Yards rail yard. Naturally, Williams was deeply involved in these talks, expressing disappointment in March that the City Council was skeptical. "I've found to my amazement that there could be opposition," he told reporters. "This has just happened in the last few weeks. I thought the city would be united on the stadium and I'd be glad to meet with the president of the City Council."[27] Baltimore politics being what they were, Mayor Schaefer supported Williams but the Council did not—yet. Having learned that other city politicians needed courting as well, Williams wooed them.

Back on the field, the brainy Singleton provided a long-term baseball perspective on Oriole preparations, along with his usual dose of explanations about fundamentals and details. "This is a serious drive toward April 10 [Opening Day]," the veteran pointed out after contributing to a March 12 win over the Rangers in Pompano Beach. "For instance, you'd think I'd be happy about today, since I had a home run and a single. But it's misleading. I'm a good breaking-ball hitter and I got both the hits off curve balls from Ed Figueroa. That doesn't prove anything to me. Figgy's getting older and he has to be letter-perfect with his control or he gets rocked. His control can't be sharp yet, so I can't get much satisfaction out of hitting him."[28] Boswell's delight at the scene always came through his columns, which gave readers not just an education, but a sense of the humor so much a part of the Oriole environment. For instance, after charting Singleton's reaction to the exhibition game's minutiae, Boswell recapitulated the car-dodging race of Stoddard, wearing shower-sandals, anxious not to miss the bus back to Miami. As his tall stopper raced through the parking lot, Weaver covered his eyes and thought of injuries: "God," said the manager, "Don't' do that." Boswell spoke for all baseball lovers in 1981 when, after the exhibition season opener, he concluded, "It's all started again. A good friend has returned."[29] But for how long? Fans, players, reporters—all wondered.

As the spring ripened, the blossoming of Murray into brightest stardom was the major storyline. Much of the coverage revolved around his low media profile as compared with other big-time big leaguers. "When Eddie Murray finally levels off at about 150 RBI a year, maybe he'll get noticed," Singleton drily intoned. "Already he's as good as they make ballplayers nowadays. He'll hit 500 home runs and be remembered as one of the all-time greats."[30] Boswell, like all who covered the first baseman, appreciated Murray's quiet excellence, and also accepted his reserved demeanor. "I'm not into publicity," Murray said. "Some need it. Some don't.... I'm not wild about the money either ... but if it's playing baseball you're talking about, I don't know how I could be having any more fun."[31]

He was, according to Boswell, "Baseball's best-kept million-dollar secret."[32] Such stories got to the essence of Murray. As his teammate suggested, the first baseman was destined for Cooperstown. As the writer understood, he was uninterested in more publicity. As his front office knew, he deserved a star's salary. But Murray loved the game, enjoyed his team, and had his best fun on the diamond.

A spring row surprised fans attending an exhibition against the Royals. In this game, Weaver broke new ground in his career-long onslaught against umpire slights and shortcomings. Weaver's ire was roused when Mark Johnson refused—despite the rules—to read aloud the list of Kansas City's substitutes so that the Oriole manager could jot them down on his ever-present lineup card. Johnson's omission was technically incorrect as AL president Lee MacPhail—at the game—explained later. But it was also in keeping with the more relaxed spring training code. "It is commonplace and accepted in spring training not to get so technical," MacPhail insisted. "Not accepted by me," Weaver riposted. So he pulled the Orioles off the field and forfeited the game.

That bothered the AL chief, who levied a three-game spring suspension for Weaver but acknowledged to reporters that any fine would be inconsequential. Showing "a look of benevolent despair," the long-suffering baseball executive only sighed. "I've fined Earl so may times..."[33] MacPhail's voice trailed off. His players certainly did not mind the early end to the exhibition, glad to get out of Ft. Myers and back to Miami. MacPhail, citing the fans, considered the forfeit inexcusable. Weaver remained puckishly unrepentant, citing another president as his inspiration. "If Lee told me, I didn't pay no attention. I'm using President Reagan's platform. I don't believe in a man—in this case, an umpire—taking a dollar's pay without a day's work. I'm protesting to increase productivity, to eliminate waste, to cut out the bureaucratic bungling."[34]

The performance earned Weaver's nomination to Clint Hurdle's all-hot dog team, unveiled that month, made up of players the Royals outfielder said he would pay to see. Weaver was manager, said Hurdle, because he scared the umps. Also from the Orioles was Palmer, because "He runs the whole show—players, umpires, sometimes even little Earl." The outfielder also included Dempsey, even then gaining renown for his vaudeville-caliber imitations of home-run swings and baserunning exploits between innings and during rain delays.[35] While there was some tut-tutting over Weaver's latest escapade, there were more than a few old-time observers, like sports columnist Mel Durslag, who found it refreshing. "Baseball will one day come to appreciate Earl Weaver," the writer predicted. "A manager who pulls his team off the field in an exhibition game can't be all bad."[36]

What made Weaver happier going into 1981 was the Orioles' evident depth. "It's conceivable we can win 110 games," he insisted.[37] What prompted this optimistic outburst were a few subtle yet savvy off-season moves, including the addition of Jim Dwyer—a left-handed hitter who could play any outfield spot and also first base—and Jose Morales, who was supposed to supplant Lee May as a DH/pinch hitter. "We're more versatile. I have a lot of guys I can put in there and still save a lot of guys."[38] This lapidary utterance came close to defining Weaver's idea of baseball paradise. It was what drew Dwyer to Baltimore in the first place. "I knew Weaver liked to use everybody on his bench," the new Oriole said, delighted to be out of Boston where the depth chart regularly went unplumbed.[39] The usually reserved Peters was not immune to the good feelings, either. He cracked a smile when asking reporters, "You have to like the way it's shaping up, don't you?"[40]

So ubiquitous was the positive coverage that, back in Baltimore at the *Sun*, Nigro noticed that some were already referring to the Orioles as the likely Team of the 80's. Young as the decade was, the seasoned reporter nonetheless saw logic in the label. "They are young, they play together, they're happy, they are all virtually signed for years to come, and they are very talented."[41] Economists have a term—irrational exuberance—for unexplained bullishness. But exuberance brimming all around the Orioles was not based on irrationality. It stemmed from recognition that they had extraordinary pitching and depth, a fetching blend of youth and experience, and palpably positive morale. But whether it was the manager tossing off figures like 110 wins, or the pitching leader crowning the staff the best in team history, or writers picking the team to go all the way, baseball experts always know that every season comes with its share of surprises. That was especially true of 1981, a season front-loaded with the troublesome, looming labor issue.

So overwrought was some of the rhetoric coming north from Florida to Maryland that it might have seemed that denial—especially of the danger that the season might end precipitously—was much in vogue. Certainly the Yankees, who had signed Dave Winfield as a free agent, and the Brewers, who had picked up Ted Simmons, Pete Vuckovich, and Rollie Fingers from the Cardinals via trade to accompany such stalwarts as Robin Yount, were not likely to be intimidated by the blue-sky Oriole talk.

When they got off to their customarily sluggish (3–6) start, it was unsurprising. In fact, the Orioles' April was, while mediocre, not bad for them, since they finished the month 7–8, good only for forth place, but also a mere three games off the lead. One notable performer was Dauer, who got off to a hot start at the plate, and generously gave departed Frank

Robinson, off to run the Giants, the credit. "Frank made me a completely different hitter. He moved me closer to the plate and told me to just spray the ball around. He finally got it through my thick head to do what I can do and not try to do more. He told me to forget about homers."⁴² At the same time, Dauer played peerlessly at second base, compiling long error-less streaks. The season's first month gave this quiet but vital player a rare turn in the spotlight.

Singleton, too, got off to a fast start. In mid–May, he was hitting .378 to lead the league, with eight home runs and 23 RBI's.⁴³ Discussing his promising early season at the plate, Singleton revealed one of those historical nuggets which so delight inveterate lovers of the game's connection to its past. The key to his batting success, said the Orioles' right fielder, was the instruction he received from Larry Doby during their time together in Montreal. Singleton came up as an Expo while Doby—the player who integrated the American League shortly after Jackie Robinson did the same in the National—was a batting coach there. "Doby worked with me every day and he convinced me that I could hit for a high average besides hitting for power," Singleton explained. "And he also taught me how to study the pitchers. I became a hitter instead of a swinger and started thinking about what I was going to do each time I went up to the plate."⁴⁴ Doby was never an Oriole, but his legacy for Singleton clearly showed that the Oriole Way had counterparts across the game, wherever serious baseball men took a smart and analytical approach to improving performance. At the same time, Frank Robinson's ongoing 1981 struggle to sharpen the Giants' less-than-organized approach, which drew attention from reporters around the big leagues, also provided a backhanded approval for the Oriole Way. "You can talk just so much about mental mistakes, but if they are not eliminated by the people who are playing, they won't play," the new San Francisco manager promised, in words which could have come from Weaver himself. "We have a lot of people who should know how to play."⁴⁵ Whether or not Giant fans knew it, Robinson was implementing a mindfulness upon their team that would pay dividends the following season, although it also contributed to his reputation of being tough on modern players.

A rare and unsettling occurrence transpired at Comiskey Field when the Orioles faced the White Sox on April 23. The two teams played a doubleheader, making up the previous night's rain-out. Just before game time in the opener, Dennis Martinez took a fan-hurled beer bottle full in the face, necessitating a hospital trip for stitches.⁴⁶ Frightening as that was, the pitcher and team were lucky it was not more serious. The attack was preceded by a standoff between Weaver and Chicago's young manager, Tony La Russa, who stationed himself between the mound and home plate to prevent the Orioles from taking batting practice and tearing up the sodden field. The Chisox skipped their own practice session but neglected to inform Weaver, who reacted with typical displeasure. Probably recalling his March argument with MacPhail, the manager rhetorically asked reporters, "What's the use of protesting when the league president tells you it's unimportant?"[47] An 18–5 drubbing in the opener was followed by a 5–3 loss that night as the White Sox swept the shaken Birds.

Roland Hemond put the Weaver–La Russa spat into perspective. "Earl missed his calling," said the White Sox GM. "He should have been Hamlet. Shakespeare would have loved him.... I remember one year in Baltimore, they called a game because of bad weather. Then, when we drove away on the team bus, they were taking batting practice in bright sunshine. I take his action today as a compliment to our field. He hasn't always been that nice to us."[48] Hemond had a good memory, which included a 1979 incident when Weaver railed against similarly wet conditions at Comiskey, likening the field to the Mekong Delta.

New York went 11–6 that April and continued strong into May, pacing the East and displaying few weaknesses. May was a far stronger month than April for the Orioles, as they went 21–8, more in line with the earlier optimism. Reporters enjoyed covering the ongoing Jockey underwear ad campaign featuring Palmer, who not only appeared in magazines, but who often made in-store appearances which drew appreciative crowds—many women wanted autographed ads—when the team went on the road.[49] Road fans in the stands found new ammunition for their gibes when Palmer pitched, but the unflappable star took it in stride. As May advanced, Weaver cancelled the traditional practice of having infielders and outfielders meet pre-game to plan their positioning for the opposing lineup. Belanger made light of the situation, because, he said, "The meetings were just shouting matches between Earl Weaver and Jim Palmer, anyway."[50] The manager also worried about home run totals, particularly since DeCinces' back was a persistent issue, threatening to rival Palmer's arm as the team's mainstay medical topic.

With impeccable although non-ironic parallelism, the third baseman engaged in a late May semi-public spat with Palmer. It was left to Weaver to defuse the quarrel before it blew up into a feud. He chose sarcasm. "I see no cause for concern," he said. "The third baseman wants the pitcher to do a little better, and the pitcher wants the third baseman to do a little better. So I hope we'll all do a little better and kiss and make up."[51] Weaver also identified Dan Graham's and Gary Roenicke's batting woes as areas of concern. Almost immediately, Roenicke's bat heated up. With his average on the rise and his power returned, the outfielder's mood improved and Weaver's words turned to praise. "The way Gary is hitting, it helps me keep his glove in there every day. And that guy can play the outfield."[52] Further detracting from clubhouse satisfaction were the new team uniforms, made in Japan, which several players complained did not fit well or feel comfortable. "The Japanese may know how to make stereos and cars," one player beefed, "But they don't know much about baseball uniforms."[53]

The Orioles managed to scrape into first place on May 9, then again on May 16. Each time, they dipped slightly, but on May 18, they grabbed a lead and held it for weeks. Their sartorial discomfort received no more attention. Weaver did, however. Durwood Merrill, working the plate in the May 18 game, a win over the A's, delivered the 79th ejection of the manager's 14-year career. Asked after the game why he ran the Oriole skipper, Merrill—whose physique was that of an offensive tackle—professed not to recall. "I don't remember," deadpanned the umpire. "It was probably the second time he buried home plate with dirt."[54] In fact, it was a short but intense disagreement over a pitch call by Murray, who himself was tossed, that riled Weaver up on this night. After the game, the manager continued his needling in his office, knowing full well that the reporters would pass along the particulars to Merrill. "I was so mad that it took me two innings to calm down," Weaver said.[55] Left unsaid was the fact that Murray rarely showed such emotion during a game, and that, by interjecting himself into the altercation, Weaver adroitly attracted the attention—and subsequent interrogations. Murray was left alone in the locker room. Weaver also recognized that Murray was on a hot streak, with four straight three-hit games.[56] He wanted no distractions for his first baseman.

Fellow ump Steve Palermo defended his crew mate. "Earl Weaver is a militant midget," Palermo insisted. "He just uses us umpires as props in his circus act. But baseball is not a circus and the game is not Earl's show."[57] The aggrieved umpires' feelings were understandable, but Palermo was wrong. If not a circus, baseball certainly was a performing act that placed a premium on entertainment. The canny Weaver knew this full well. So did Boswell, at the *Washington Post*, who chose that game to launch one of his very best columns, an all-time summary of vengeful quotes from umpires against the little manager with the big temper. Like so much of Boswell's work, the column would be a catalyst for future historians of the game, especially those in search of the accurate core of the Weaver legend. Boswell quoted Palermo to good effect. The umpire noticed that Weaver's rages usually served as pressure releases, loosening up or distracting his players. "With the years, I've noticed that Weaver usually gets thrown out exactly when he wants to. It's either to take the heat of defeat off his team or maybe to jack them up for the next day."[58] Still, Palermo was unforgiving, terming the Orioles' skipper a pest and clown.

A strike remained a persistent concern, especially when well-connected reporters like Dave Kindred dug for information and came up with the unshakable contention that the majority of owners looked forward to a strike, rather than fearing one. Several days prior to the late–May strike deadline, Kindred recalled the contretemps of March, when Harry Dalton's unguarded plea for compromise with the union fell flat before owners who wanted victory over Miller. Kindred saw the owner's recently announced $50,000 punishment of Dalton as both deeply troubling and monumentally unfair. "His words were harmless. He didn't say baseball is being greedy. He didn't say Bowie Kuhn is full of resin. He didn't say the owners are a gang of unreconstructed plantation massahs looking to bring back slavery.... He chose to be temperate in hopes a lowering of voices would cause sweet reason to settle upon the Lords."[59] Oddly, the five-member owners commission that sanctioned Dalton included Orioles' representation—Hoffberger, not Williams. The former owner was there due to his ongoing sinecure, and was clearly more of a hard-liner than his new boss. Soon, as the talks spiraled down into depths of mutual recrimination, it was the new owner, not the old one, who made his presence felt. In the process of being nudged aside from Redskins control by Cooke, Williams hardly needed to cede control of the team he did own to Hoffberger.

Part of what disturbed the far-seeing Ken Denlinger was the owners' evident determination to keep their positions and negotiations strictly hush-hush. There were few baseball writers with more connections and respect than Murray Chass, who described the five-man punitive commission as secret, chiding the owners for refusing to admit its existence even as its composition leaked. Along with Hoffberger, it included Peter O'Malley of the Dodgers, John Fetzer of the Tigers, August Busch, Jr., of the Cardinals, and William Wrigley of the Cubs. After canvassing owners, Chass came away convinced that they were unimpressed with recent offers by the union, as well as unconvinced that the players truly meant to strike and stick with it. A move to put the entire situation before the National Labor Relations Board struck Chass as reasonable, but unlikely to avert a stoppage, given that governmental agency's penchant for slow delibera-tions.[60]

The Orioles had moved into first place on May 18, and were there at 28–14, up by three games, when the May 29 strike deadline finally arrived. Had the season stopped at that point, their ultimate 1981 fate might have been very different. But a last-ditch agreement to postpone the strike deadline for at least a week meant more baseball. The players proclaimed themselves glad, in words that came back to bite them. "Anything that postpones this strike is good because neither the players nor the owners want one," opined Stone—whose arm hurt and who might have been expected to relish some rest. "We've fought a long time to get baseball interest to the level it is now and we don't want to lose that. And if post-poning the negotiations is the way to do it, I'm for it," the sore-armed pitcher added. Meanwhile, Murray said, "It's got to be good for us because we're going good right now." Bumbry was more hesitant, since the under-lying issues seemed unresolved. "Unless the basic issues are addressed, it's only a matter of time," the outfielder predicted.[61]

Those reactions bore parsing. Stone's gave lie to the notion that players were unconcerned about the game's overall health. Murray showed strong awareness that the Orioles were on a hot streak. But it was the speedy outfielder nicknamed "Bumble Bee" who got it right. The strike was a matter of timing. The Orioles were in first place when the first strike deadline passed. The interlude kept the game going until June 11, but did nothing to advance a settlement. It gave Baltimore time to fall into second place, two scant games behind the Yankees. That seemed inconsequential in the scheme of a normal season, but 1981 was nothing like normal.

During the extension period, the NLRB suggested an injunction designed to postpone implementing the owners' negotiations for a year, to allow more time for settlement moves. Since there was no movement at all that June, the question was whether or not a federal judge would approve or deny the injunction bid. If he approved it, the season would continue with the owners unable to act unilaterally. If he denied it, the players would strike. So explained Miller, who added that he was prepared to let the player representatives handle negotiations themselves, lest the owners argue that it was his personality which constituted an impediment. The judge was Henry F. Werker, whose United States District Court included New York, where MLB had its headquarters. Grebey's policy of keeping ownership proposals cloaked continued, while Miller made public the union's latest offer, which would see each team designating one player for a pool from which franchises could select compensation upon losing a free agent. That idea was rejected by the owners, so everyone waited for Werker's ruling.[62] The players, with the NLRB's agreement, also insisted that the owners must "open their books," revealing the true state of their finances to back up their claims of great losses. This, of course, was a non-starter in major league boardrooms.

At the same time, the nation's attention was split by another labor dispute involving the national air traffic controllers' union. That gave baseball negotiators the chance to cite flight disruptions as another impediment to solving their problem through talks. Press accounts identified Williams and Rangers boss Eddie Chiles, two of the newer owners in the game, as forces urging Kuhn to step in and broker a season-saving deal. But those same articles described the two compromise-minded owners as stymied by a harder and larger cabal which wanted a strike, in hopes that the union would eventually back down and lose power. Some writers speculated that Williams might publicly disassociate himself from the rest of ownership, which would have been an unprecedented break in solidarity.[63] Grebey seemed almost to dare Williams to make such a move. "We've got 25 solid votes from the owners and only one loose cannon running around," ownership's lead voice publicly claimed. Williams' response was just as cutting. "I can't believe—no, I find it hard to believe—that our principal negotiator would show such bad judgment," intoned the lawyer, who always said precisely what he wanted to.[64]

The bad news hit on June 11, with the Orioles in second. The strike was on. Players across the majors packed up their gear, their reactions ranging from lugubrious to defiant. Owners were tight-lipped, as per Grebey's desire. Photographs of major leaguers in mufti carrying suitcases struck fans as pictures of players arriving in Spring Training usually did, but in the opposite way. It seemed a repudiation of all the hopefulness that makes the coming of the game each spring such a blessed relief. In Baltimore, brilliant *Post* writer John Feinstein surveyed player reactions. "It's a sad thing for a lot of people who love baseball," Singleton said. "But I think that most of us are glad it's finally come to a head. This thing's been dragged out and postponed for a long time.... The only way this thing is going to end is for the owners to be a little less stubborn and stop thinking we're going to take the compensation that they want us to."[65] Peters, who of course spoke from management's side, was noticeably conciliatory. "Someday we're going to have this unfortunate situation behind us and we're going to be operating again as a baseball team," he said, adding that the team would handle travel logistics for the players' trips home, regardless of the stoppage.[66] Traveling Secretary Phil Itzoe booked all the tickets and distributed them by hand.

Peters' perspective and willingness to help with travel plans no doubt reflected Williams' own position. Equally satisfying to Oriole players and ownership was the local fan reaction. While across the country there was significant reaction against well-paid athletes striking for any reason, in Baltimore, Wild Bill Hagy led a rally in front of an otherwise empty Memorial Stadium, replete with O-R-I-O-L-E-S. Hagy, a cab driver, spoke pointedly. "I don't think the owners deserve compensation," he argued, directing reporters' attention to the 200 or so fans who showed up. "I'm happy with our turnout." After some cheering, he asked fans to pause a moment to contemplate "what may be the death of baseball," before leading his disciples to a bar on 33rd Street, where they could at least quench their thirst for baseball with their other great love.[67] Peters surveyed the empty stadium with his eye on the bottom line. The team would have made about $1.2 million over the course of a coming 10-game home stand, now cancelled. "This came at a bad time. It's the middle of June, the pennant race is starting to heat up, school is out, and a lot of groups start coming to the games."[68] It was not hard to hear, in the words of the GM and the wishes of the owner, a determination to keep the Orioles players as happy as possible, and the fans as loyal as possible, under trying circumstances. But accounts that the team laid off 17 scouts as a money-saving measure showed that some would feel the costs.[69]

WFBR-AM, bereft of programming, started carrying Rochester Red Wings games across the radio network, so fans hungry for news kept up with Ripken. Farther down the system, promising new signee Mike Young tore up class-A ball in Miami. The most compelling development from the minors was the amazing 33-inning marathon between the Red Wings and Pawtucket, finally won by the Pawsox.[70] Networks tried broadcasting Japanese games. But the biggest story in Mid-Atlantic baseball circles during the strike was Williams. Rumors of his tireless maneuvering to get past irreconcilable difference and prevent a killed season took on sufficient detail to give them credence. In New York, Chass wrote of the stalemate with no obvious end in sight.[71] From Baltimore, Nigro added that in all Williams' years as an attorney, he probably never suffered so many setbacks as he had recently among his fellow owners. Chass pronounced Williams shaken by the opposition, especially when his last-ditch effort to insert Kuhn into the process failed, thanks partly to Steinbrenner's opposition. Only three clubs—the Orioles, Rangers, and Astros—were alienated from the PRC, Chass contended, before quoting a resigned-sounding Williams. "There's nothing I can do at this point," said the attorney. "Sometimes you have to go back and ponder and mediate. I will say that Baltimore will stand tall.... Eddie [Chiles] and I are in Lower Slobovia."[72]

Williams made his rounds and made it clear that he was actively working to end baseball's absence. With Chiles as his wingman, he repeatedly approached owners with his settlement-oriented message. Despite frequent rebuffs, every day that the players maintained their solidarity lent additional credence to the Oriole owner's argument that there was more money to be made by returning to action than by waiting on a union-busting pipedream. Chiles, a Texas oilman, made light of his reputation as part of baseball's odd couple, terming himself "bloody but unbowed" while wearing a fake bandage around his head. Williams and his ally insisted that theirs was the long-term vision. "There are major changes that are going to come in baseball," he predicted. "Maybe they are not quite so imminent, but they are as inevitable as tomorrow."[73]

Several Orioles filled their time with guest appearances as weathermen on local TV. Dennis Martinez appeared in a Chicago court when the fan who hit him with the beer bottle was charged. Stone tried to rehabilitate his aching elbow, while Palmer, a quiet voice on the labor issue, filmed *Love Boat* and *Dynasty* episodes. The tall righthander did sound off eventually, wishing aloud that baseball had a more proactive commissioner, bemoaning lost salary, and echoing Williams' earlier description that Grebey had negotiated the owners into a corner.[74] Players conducted their own workouts at Towson State, while Peters counted lost dollars as the team's voided home dates piled up. Weaver and Santarone had their picture taken next to their famous tomato plants, as the manager explained the reason his were in the lead: "A special mixture of cow flops and water."[75] There were fan protests around the nation. Predictably, in Washington, D.C., there were calls for Congress to intervene. But the nation's capital, which was used to silent springs and summers at RFK, also noticed Kuhn's contention that, while the labor problem went on, the problem of baseball's absence from the nation's capital was now "solved. The solution for Washington at the present is the Baltimore Orioles," insisted the commissioner.[76] Meanwhile, from June 12 until August 10, Baltimore fans appreciated the fact that Williams was a voice for baseball's return, which was of course the public's major desire.

The end to the strike, when it came, supported Williams' position. Ownership had never been entirely unified, although Grebey's cloaking device covered up the fissures. Rumors of a settlement midwifed by a federal mediator floated in late July, but failed to materialize. Then, according to subsequent reportage, a dissident eight-owner group led by Williams—who utilized his persuasive skills to round up this cadre—called an American League meeting. This occurred soon after players, gathered in Chicago, vowed to end the season themselves, which shook hard-line owners waiting for a union climb-down and gave credence to the dissidents, who insisted that any more dead time meant no more baseball at all in 1981. In the end, Miller and MacPhail spoke substantively, the eight owners and AL President joined forces, and the settlement finally emerged. It was like watching someone bleeding to death," Williams described the process. "You had to stop the bleeding."[77]

There were some exhibitions scheduled against the Phillies in early August before the season recommenced, but these were inconsequential. There would be a whipped-up All Star Game, too. What mattered was the split-season format agreed upon for the rest of the season. Some fans expected the season to continue where it left off, but instead, major league owners chose to go with a format lifted from the bush leagues. The Yankees, A's, Phillies, and Dodgers, all in first place when the season was suspended, now found themselves assured of a spot in the "mini-playoffs," which would pit them against whoever won the season's second half. Owners liked the idea of an instant pennant race involving every other team. Skeptics figured out right away that having the better overall record, always the major league standard for post-season qualification, was no guarantee in 1981. Weaver was among the gimmick's doubters. "Are you kidding?" he asked reporters wondering about his position. "Who in the hell would vote for it? The Yankees and Oakland'll vote for it, because they've already won it, but none of the other 12 teams would."[78]

As it turned out, Weaver was not off the mark. The Yankees, their playoff fortunes assured, tailed off considerably down the stretch. But the Brewers found August and September conducive, surging ahead of the Orioles, who yet again found themselves in pursuit of a division leader. They finished 11–9 in August, as their starters had to regain their mid-season form, finishing the month two games off Milwaukee's pace. September brought them a 14–13 record, including 6–4 against New York and Detroit to close out the season. As to the Yankees' incentive, it was sufficient to let them split eight games against the Orioles during the last two weeks, contributing to another "almost" AL East season in Baltimore. The Reds finished with baseball's best overall record, but with neither a first-half nor second-half title, they stayed home. The Cardinals suffered similarly, as did the Orioles. Baltimore had a better overall record than their rivals, but they watched the playoffs on television, while the Yankees advanced to the World Series, where they lost to the Dodgers.

There were some bright spots: Stewart won the AL ERA race, and Murray led the league in home runs. Cal Ripken, Jr., arrived after a late-season call-up. With Belanger flailing at bat, the muscular Sakata came up from Rochester, too, impressing all with his bat as well as his biceps. There were late-season pennant race thrills, including Lowenstein's 12th-inning single for a victory over the Royals. "These are the kind of games that produce gray hairs coming out of your nose," Brother Lo said.[79] But there were also disappointments as the Orioles failed to catch the Brewers. For once, instead of attracting plaudits, Weaver's moves raised eyebrows. Against the Yankees, for example, he was stuck with a sore-shouldered Stoddard on the mound, who gave up a three-run shot to Murcer. The manager was uncharacteristically defensive in post-game interviews. An August 31 arrest for DWI not only cost Weaver his driver's license for 60 days, it added to rumors that he was failing to cope with the stressful season.[80] Baltimore bats, including Singleton's, cooled noticeably. Graham and Dempsey were unproductive at the plate, while Morales failed to provide the big punch off the bench Weaver had dreamed of in the Spring. Dauer pressed, resorting to his ill-advised quest for power, winding up in a slump. Peters saw the hardships as temporary but unfortunately timed. "Part of the problem is some of our people are very hard-headed about what they need to do to be successful," the GM said, addressing the collective slump. "You wonder how low the averages have to go before the players wake up."[81] Williams, who now enjoyed discussing on-field issues as well as back-room dealings, was no less cranky about the team's woes. "I don't know whether it is the split season or what but this kind of play has been a big disappointment," he said as the second half slipped away.[82] At season's end, he resorted to humor, announcing that he was rooting for Steinbrenner's team. "If the Yankees, win, it will keep George out of the free agent market," Williams kidded. "I want him lying fat and content. I don't want him out there hungry."[83]

But for Williams, topsy-turvy 1981 was, he said, "In a lot of ways ... the worst year of my life." He felt like throwing a party, the owner claimed, because the trying season was finally over. But when Maisel interviewed Williams to end the season, there was some newsworthy information buried amidst all the backward-looking wistfulness. The lawyer, wrote the *Sun* veteran, had recently visited the new downtown Inner Harbor, gem of redevelopment planned by James Rouse and shepherded to completion by Schaefer. He admired the crowds lined up to shop at Harborplace and visit the National Aquarium. "The only piece missing to the picture down there is a stadium," the owner asserted. "And there is one piece of land left in the area to build one."[84]

Baltimore's 1981 concluded with the Colts' atrocious season. Late in December, however, reports circulated that Williams and Schaefer were talking seriously and often about that particular piece of downtown land.[85] Where the Colts fit in was unclear. It was not hard for Baltimore fans to decide whether the football or baseball situation was most promising. One owner presented an unstable public stance, lurching from one public relations fiasco to the next. The other was closeted with Baltimore's mayor, talking about a new stadium at Camden Yards.

4.

THANKS, EARL (1982)

Any account of sports in Baltimore in 1982 needs to first consider the Colts. The previous year was the most humiliating to date for the 29-year-old NFL franchise, once the pride of Maryland. A 2–14 season featured the Colts beating the Patriots in the first and last games of the season, losing 14 straight in between. The crash plunged the suffering fan base deeper into gloom. The defense was historically inept, the offense overmatched, the team's ineptitude epitomized by one of the largest negative point differentials ever. But what rankled most was the notorious episode on Sunday, November 15, with the Colts en route to a heavy loss against the Eagles. In one of the weirdest scenes ever at Memorial Stadium, a visibly agitated, intoxicated Irsay lost patience, exploded at the coaching staff, and started phoning in plays from his booth. The coaches on the sidelines were confused, the players shocked. "Irsay couldn't have told you how many players there were on the field," quarterback Bert Jones later recalled, "Never mind what plays we had. All he was trying to do was embarrass the coaches and players. When he told me to run, I threw. When he told me to throw left, I ran right."[1] The episode unfolded in full view of reporters.

It was a nightmare for the image-conscious Rozelle. Press coverage ensured that fans knew about it, and the few remaining faithful became yet more alienated. The season also saw coach McCormack benching Curtis Dickey for lack of effort, which the running back—key cog in what little there was of the offense—blamed on Jones. Former Colt star Bill Pellington commented to John Steadman that he felt sorry for the current team, which he called "whipped." "Baltimore is a good football city," Pellington insisted. "When we were winners, we would pack them in. But this is a blue-collar town. There aren't many people willing to pay $50 to see losers.... The pendulum has swung to baseball."[2] The Colts' ugliness was rendered harder to ignore by the nearness of the improving Redskins. At RFK, the Skins went 8–8 under the bright and young coach-GM combination of Joe Gibbs and Bobby Beathard. Washington fans sensed the rise to greatness. Never had football in Baltimore seemed so down-and-out. "Help!" was the message of *News-American* writer Steadman in a plaintive editorial written for the *Sporting News 1982 Football Yearbook*, but there was no succor forthcoming. On Valentine's Day, 1982, the *Sun* printed a letter from a fan, Frank J. Ruzek, who suggested, "It would be best for the Baltimore Colts if Mr. Robert Irsay kept Bert Jones and traded himself."[3] Another fan spoke to Steadman about the disparity between Baltimore's two franchises. "Football is at its lowest point now since the franchise came to Baltimore," contended Bill Michael, of Catonsville. "There's too much dissension.... After 25 years, I'm one of those idiots that still sits out here. But the Orioles are the number one team here now because of the difference in management. These Colts people just don't get involved."[4] The Colts ended the McCormack era by hiring tough-guy coach Frank Kush, from Arizona State by way of the Canadian Football League's Hamilton Tiger-Cats. The ever-hopeful Steadman, for whom Baltimore football was a sacred trust and who had seen every game the Colts ever played, hoped in print that the no-nonsense coach would fix what ailed the dysfunctional roster.[5] But those with more cynicism than hope mulled over the fact that Kush remained a hero in Phoenix, one of Irsay's potential relocation destinations.

Compared to a Memorial Stadium partner like that, the Orioles could have done nothing during the off-season and still looked pretty. But the baseball team did not stand pat. Instead, the Hot Stove League featured a big trade: the increasingly disgruntled DeCinces went to the Angels, along with pitcher Jeff Schneider, for hard-hitting outfielder Dan Ford. DeCinces was a Californian whose Baltimore years included many great performances. But he suffered from being sandwiched between Brooks Robinson and Cal Ripken, Jr. "Disco Dan" Ford was not, at first glance, an Oriole type of player. The charismatic outfielder hesitated before agreeing to the trade. Ford was best-known to casual fans for posing nude in the June 1981 *Playgirl*, which hardly endeared him to buttoned-down Angel manager Gene Mauch.[6] Ford worried that Weaver would not like him, either, but his new manager was more concerned with performance in uniform. "I've always been successful doing things my own way," the outfielder maintained. "If I play tight, I can't be Dan Ford."[7]

It was precisely Dan Ford whom Peters and Weaver had coveted for years. Ford's bat was especially appealing, and he had a strong arm. In the strike-shortened 1981 season, Ford hit .277 with 15 home runs and 48 RBI. In 1979, when Baltimore played against him during the playoffs, Ford stood out on a star-studded Angels team. Peters and Weaver looked at Ford and saw a starting outfielder and hitter who would protect Murray in the batting order. At the same time, they knew that 1982 would be the younger Cal Ripken's first full season. It seemed assured that Junior would play third, rendering DeCinces expendable. Sakata, whose season-ending recall the year before left the team optimistic, was penciled in as the regular shortstop despite some question about his arm. The Orioles also swung a trade with the Reds, offloading prospects for catcher Joe Nolan, who took over for Graham as Dempsey's backup.

The Orioles also made a push to reacquire free agent Reggie Jackson, but Mr. October, after five years with the Yankees, opted instead to sign with the Angels. Peters also worked on a long-rumored deal for Cardinals shortstop Gary Templeton. San Diego wanted some combination involving Bumbry, Stewart, Roenicke, shortstop Bob Bonner, or outfield prospect John "T-Bone" Shelby in exchange for Templeton; the Orioles caviled at the price. So the Orioles missed on some front-page moves, but still managed to work over their lineup. They resigned old acquaintances Ross Grimsley and Don Stanhouse to deepen the bullpen when Stewart's elbow began to hurt and Stoddard's shoulder to ache. Heading to camp, the Oriole bench boasted Crowley, Lowenstein, Ayala, Morales, Bonner, Shelby, Dwyer, and Nolan.[8] They soon traded Morales for Leo Hernandez. Once again, Weaver had his precious "deep depth." And once again, Weaver would be the top story, since 1982 was slated to be his final year. Writers, well-aware that the Brewers and Yankees were coming off postseason berths, nevertheless predicted that Baltimore would contend. "We are definitely a contender, definitely," Weaver told Nigro, of the *Sun*.[9] "Who has better starting pitching?" he demanded rhetorically of Gammons.[10]

In Miami, one of the first stories revolved around the shoulder and contract status of Flanagan. For once, there were few young pitchers moving onto the staff, so the Orioles hoped for a bounceback season from their lefthanded former Cy Young winner. Nobody was more excited at that prospect than Flanagan himself, who spent the winter undergoing rehabilitation with Dr. Arthur Pappas, renowned Massachusetts orthopedist. "I've been feeling great, super," the pitcher said. "I've been throwing regularly and the ball is getting to the plate much quicker."[11] The momentum for the pitcher's comeback gained speed when his coincident salary-arbitration hearing was called off. The reason was unusual: for only the second time in arbitration history, the team set a higher figure than the player. The salary figure of $485,000 submitted by the pitcher and his agent, Jerry Kapstein, was below what the team offered, $500,000. Nor did Flanagan seem upset. Instead, he called himself satisfied, looking forward to the season and a contract extension.[12]

One major item from the off-season pertained more to team history than the future. That was the Hall of Fame election of Frank Robinson, voted in alongside Hank Aaron. Coverage of the former Oriole right fielder's honor prompted national reminiscing over the famous-in-Baltimore/notorious-in-Cincinnati trade, and the subsequent glory that followed. Fans still related to him, as the "HERE" flag still fluttered over Memorial Stadium's left field wall. Cooperstown meant that the Orioles' best seasons, with one of their best players, would be rehashed later that August at the induction ceremony. Robinson's plaque featured him in an Oriole hat, signaling that the Oriole Way, for which number 20 was such a fierce avatar, remained viable as a formula for success. This was not to be taken for granted. Despite the arrival of Ripken, it seemed that the vaunted farm system was producing fewer front-line options. Gammons noticed, and speculated about what he called the season of "De-Weaverization" would mean for the team's operations.[13]

There were some rookies who excited onlookers. Possibility is one of baseball's best pleasures, and during spring training, the speedy John Shelby was the rookie most fans were talking about—besides Ripken. "I really think we've got some talent down below again," Peters assured reporters. "You know you've got good prospects when you look at your 40-man roster and see it's starting to get a little tight."[14] Peters' words were reassuring. But the "again" reminded reporters that the GM aimed to rebuild the farm system; maintaining the Oriole Way was an ongoing process.

That off-season, Singleton won the Roberto Clemente Award for his charitable works. The banquet, held in the Florida governor's mansion, was as much a testimonial to the deceased Pirate great as to the current winner, and Singleton knew it. His acceptance speech paid homage to Clemente. "I played for him when he managed in San Juan," the Oriole remembered, "and I always followed his advice to set my goals high."[15]

A theme in camp was whether or not it really would be Weaver's last year. Poor Disco Dan Ford even confessed to a nightmare scenario. "The worst thing that can happen to me is to have Weaver quit and Mauch replace him next year," the former Angel fretted, adding that he hoped his relationship with Weaver would be good.[16] Here, Ford unintentionally put focus on the difference between the Orioles, customarily thought of as a conservative franchise, and the "my way or the highway" style of managers such as Mauch and Vern Rapp. Weaver and the front office were obsessed with performance, but cared little about tangential issues. Players needed to dress for travel, but there was little pressure off the field. Nor was management bothered by labor activism, so long as the players did well on the field and did not disrupt chemistry in any way that led to losing. Ford learned that, despite his earlier worries, he did not have to play tight to be an Oriole. In Miami, he visibly enjoyed himself.

Also in Florida, *Sun* reporter Nigro speculated that Williams would probably try to talk the manager out of retiring. The owner plainly loved the manager. Peters wondered aloud if the manager was really destined for the golf course. "We respect his decision and we're taking him at his word, but whether it will really be his last year remains to be seen," the GM explained. "I think maybe he needs a sabbatical, not retirement. Sometimes you need a year or two to recharge the batteries. Earl's too young to talk about early retirement."[17] There was plenty of room for maneuver in that artful utterance, although it probably upset the umpires who read it.

The previous year, Palmer had supplemented sniping with Weaver by arguing with DeCinces. In Miami this season, he and Stone attracted attention as they battled injuries and age. Stone had rehabbed hard for over a year, but never recovered his 1980 Cy Young form. "I don't want to go out as a fifth starter swing man," Stone insisted, although Sammy Stewart had that role nailed down tightly. "Thirteen years of experience tells me that I have almost no value in that role.... Give me a set time before Opening Day and decide by then whether or not I'm in the rotation. If I'm not, then let me go or release me."[18] Stone, coming off a 4–7, 4.57 season, was one of the few players as well-spoken and palpably intelligent as Palmer, and (it turned out) on the brink of becoming one of the game's best color analysts, on cable network WGN. Palmer, at 36 a year older than Stone, went 7–8, 3.76 in 1981's split season. He and Stone were competing for the last rotation spot, behind Flanagan, Dennis Martinez, and McGregor. The betting was on Palmer, partly because he looked young again during camp; partly because Stone's injury seemed unresolved; and partly because, as Thomas Boswell noted, Weaver had a strong loyalty to his all-time best starter. "The last man to lose faith in Palmer will be Weaver," the *Post* writer predicted. The manger was non-committal. "This is what we come to Florida for.... To look at all our options."[19]

There turned out to be no spot for Stone. The Orioles opened the season on Monday, April 5, with a 13–5 win over Kansas City. Starting pitcher Dennis Martinez went only four innings, giving up six runs, but

Stewart came in for five innings of strong relief to nab the win. The Orioles prospered thanks to four home runs, by Ripken in the second inning, Murray in the third, Roenicke in the third, and Ford in the seventh. Fans buzzed about the rookie, also about Ford's arrival. Disco Dan supplemented his homer with strong throws from right field. The Orioles batting order that day looked like this:

CF	Bumbry	3B	Ripken
C	Dempsey	LF	Roenicke
RF	Ford	SS	Sakata
DH	Singleton	2B	Dauer
1B	Murray		

For the most part, that was the shape the team kept. There would be usual Weaver moves, such as the leftfield platoon of Lowenstein and Ayala. Dempsey would fall down the order, while Ripken rose to third. The biggest shift occurred in the field, with the rookie shifting from third base to shortstop. That turned out to be the last, and one of the biggest, successes in Weaver's long career of tinkering.

Opening Day was a feel-good event, and the sellout crowd in Memorial Stadium went home happy. Plenty of those were fans who drove south on I-95 or the B-W Parkway after the game. They were residents of the D.C. metro area, many from the Maryland suburbs of Montgomery and Prince George's County. Baltimore offered Washington fans twin benefits: reasonable convenience—that "40 mile" figure so often tossed out—and winning baseball, as the Orioles were good and played attractively. But there were many in the nation's capital who, while they enjoyed Orioles Magic, never stopped believing that their own hometown deserved a team. The Washington issue, contrary to commissioner Kuhn's vaguely phrased formula, may have been solved *for the present* by the Baltimore Orioles. But that did not mean the Orioles were Washington's best long-term answer.

Shirley Povich, keeper of the baseball flame at the *Washington Post*, was at his paper in 1924 when Walter Johnson pitched the Senators to a World Series title. Povich marked 1982's Opening Day with a column of protest in the Outlook editorial section rather than the sports pages. "Dammit, we've been banished from the mainstream," he complained. "They tell us now not to weep, and to go root for the Orioles." This, he admitted, was a reasonable thing to do. But the Orioles had one big problem. "They don't have 'W-A-S-H-I-N-G-T-O-N' written across their chests. They are Baltimore's team. They live in Baltimore. They eat and sleep in Baltimore and play ball in Baltimore, and are loved in Baltimore. They are Baltimore's darlings.... At best the Orioles offer an escape valve, a sneaked joint, a temporary high for Washington's most addicted baseball fans. These are said to account for 10 percent of the Orioles' attendance."[20] There was plenty to dwell on for thoughtful readers of this column besides a 77-year-old's startling use of a marijuana metaphor. First, even Povich accepted the fact that a significant fraction of Oriole attendance came from the DC area. Second, as he explained, the proximity of Memorial Stadium sounded much better when one did not have to make a 40-mile shlep each way. Povich did not charge fans who adopted the Orioles with being traitors to D.C. Instead, he classified them as the sort of devotees for whom baseball is a need rather than an option. Sports junkies are always the core, but never the majority, of any fan base. By implication, his message showed that attention paid to Baltimore supported, rather than undercut Washington's future big league prospects, since it verified that there was real horsehide passion in the capital region. Of course Povich knew enough to read Kuhn's signals that there was no swift answer to his wishes for a DC team. In his mild but deeply informed way, the dean of Washington sports gave a pragmatic sanction to his home's embrace of the nearest team, while pointing out that the Orioles should not be viewed as the permanent answer.

Elsewhere at the *Post*, this balancing act between covering the Orioles out of practicality and maintaining the rightfulness of the Senators-replacement position, was epitomized by Boswell. The younger man was every bit the native Washingtonian as the *eminence grise;* Boswell also adored baseball and, as a writer, needed a subject to cover. Once aboard the Orioles beat, he described the prodigious upside of what he saw, but he never turned away from his desire to see the Nats return.

Since it was Weaver's last year, the tradition of a slow start had to be kept. The team fell below .500 in game five, eventually digging a 2–10 hole that took the whole season to escape. They went 6–12 in April, 17–12 for May. There was little panic at the outset, but the baseball world did wonder if the team felt the pressure of Weaver's farewell tour, and when they would straighten out. Not until June 8 did the Orioles surmount .500 for good, sitting then at 27–26. Weaver had implemented his big idea, switching Ripken to shortstop from his supposedly "natural" position at third base. Far more than an intuitive hunch to spark the club or flex the lineup, the shift looked like sacrilege or stupidity to many. Junior was simply too big for many to see him as a shortstop, particularly when the slender "Blade" Belanger, or short-quick Luis Aparicio, formed the recognized mental template of what that position called for. Third base was convenient, too, since it put Ripken into the slot vacated by DeCinces. But Weaver stuck with the switch. While the organization looked nervous, the manager's decision was validated by none other than trusted coach Cal Ripken, Sr. "That's where he's supposed to play," the crusty, Orioles Way-saturated father said of his son.[21]

Ripken, Jr., of course, turned out to have superb mobility, a strong arm, and fine instincts. He rearranged the vision of what a shortstop could be. The move did not hinder him at the plate. After going 3-for-5 with his first homer on Opening Day, the youngster's output plummeted. Over the next 10 days, Ripken managed just one hit in 21 at-bats, with an 0-for-17 stretch that dropped his average at .154. When the team finally crested .500, he was batting .233. Again, Cal Sr. provided calm perspective whenever the subject of his son's slow start at the plate came up. "Almost all young hitters go through this same thing," the baseball lifer insisted. "They go into a little slump and they go to the plate trying to get a hit instead of trying to hit the ball." Senior cited Dauer and Singleton as examples. "It isn't a mechanical thing with Cal, but 90 percent of slumps are caused by your mental approach. That's what Cal's fighting now. I asked him if he could hit and he said, 'Yes.' I said, 'Well, dammit, go up there and hit the ball.'"[22] By July 4, his average was up to .262 and he was obviously figuring out major league pitching. Given the team's slow start, Ripken never became the focus of negative attention. Instead, the entire team's doldrums were analyzed, while Weaver took the brunt of inquiries over the position shift. The whole Cal, Jr. story took on a new dimension that summer when the Orioles drafted brother Billy and sent their newest Ripken to Bluefield in the Appalachian League.[23]

Ripken stuck at shortstop. Sakata did have trouble making the throws from third base, and reverted to a utility role in which his skills served him well. He spelled Dauer at second, filled in elsewhere as needed, and pinch-hit. Weaver's decision to make the switch would leave its mark on the Orioles lineup for 21 years. Another move he made, far less consequential, shored up his reputation as a manager solicitous of his players. When Singleton, Ford, and Morales all complained about a new rule requiring ear flaps on the batting helmets, claiming that they could not find decent fits, Weaver pounced on the chance for a showdown with the league and promised that he would not make his veterans wear them. The issue faded, but once again Weaver had placed himself between players and officialdom.

One pitcher whose spring was calm and who started the season well

was Palmer, whose record stood at 6–3 by the end of June. More impor-
tantly, the tall righthander was pitching late into games, showing excellent
command, and demonstrating no arm woes. Having reasserted himself as
the team's stopper, he discussed his relationship with Weaver: "A lot of
things Earl says are not meant to be negative, it just doesn't come out in
a positive way." What number 22 had in mind was a late–April outburst
in which Earl read the riot act to his starting rotation. "Every time he gives
us a dissertation on pitching I remember the Dave McNally line, 'The only
thing Earl knows about pitching is that it's difficult to hit.'" Palmer added
that he thought Weaver's anger was premature, and that the rotation would
settle in.[24] All Weaver had to say was that Palmer, who that night tossed
a complete game to beat the Angels 9–4, "pitched a good, intelligent ballgame."[25] The rotation did indeed improve, with Palmer himself finding his
season-long groove from that point on.

The pitcher whose health would not cooperate was Stone. His return
kept being postponed. "It's not good," he admitted after feeling elbow pain
in April. "Essentially, I have to start all over. It's so disheartening. I spent
three weeks in camp and I threw the ball as well as anyone. Then, my arm
lets me down."[26] Such news made swingman Stewart all the more valuable
to the team. He was working on an improbable addition to his repertoire,
a sweeping overhand curve, which prompted his manager to say, "That's
why I still enjoy coming to the ballpark. You never know what the hell you
might see."[27] But the jocular Stewart offered other forms of comic relief
besides new pitches. Pure country in his small-town North Carolina way,
he often serenaded teammates in the clubhouse with renditions of blue-
grass and rock favorites. He thrived on the uncertainty of his swing role,
never knowing in advance if he was slated for a short or long stint, or perhaps might be plugged in for a start. "I have to be ready right away, so I
do stretching exercises. But if I see one-two-three in the first inning, I just
sit down and start telling stories," he explained.[28] His happy-go-lucky
approach to life made him comfortable with the ambiguity of his situational role and he never expressed resentment or demanded a move from
the bullpen. On May 15, with the team mired in fifth place, 14–19 and
eight games back, he expressed sanguinity. "On most teams, it might be
Panic City right now, and I'd be saying 'Hey, I want to start!' But not here."
Pressed, Stewart expressed trust in the system. "Why not give Earl the
benefit of the doubt?" he asked. "Stick with what we've got. My time will
come."[29] He was simply expressing his own assurance, but the cheerful,
long-haired, 6'3" righty might have been speaking for the entire franchise.

The Orioles sat in third at 44–38, 3½ games back, on July 11, the start of the All-Star break. Their lineup that afternoon differed slightly, but significantly, from Opening Day's.

Bumbry, CF	Ripken, SS
Dauer, 3B	Ford, RF
Singleton, DH	Sakata 2B
Murray, 1B	Dempsey, C
Lowenstein, LF	

This was hardly gimcrack, but the idea that Dauer—one of the game's best-fielding second basemen—belonged at third was hard to swallow. This fueled critics of the Ripken-to-short move. Clearly, naysayers pointed out, Weaver had made the big change without a solid answer to the team's third-base situation. Just as clearly, Weaver thought that Dauer, Sakata, and others could handle the position, while Ripken brought something special to shortstop. The rookie displayed less angst over the position change than anybody. Meanwhile Singleton, trying to adjust to his DH role after years in right field, struggled. "Just being the DH makes the game seem awfully long," he noticed.[30]

Weaver did not go to Montreal for the All-Star Game, turning down an invitation to be honored there. But his first baseman made the AL team, the only Oriole to do so. As Murray headed to Olympic Stadium, his batting average was a comfy .306. He was earning the attention which eluded him in previous seasons, when he was often referred to as the quiet, or overshadowed star. With free agency not upon him until 1986, Murray was securely in the Oriole fold. "O's Murray a 'Regular' Superstar," headlined a full-spread, two-age *Sporting News* feature. The theme was his self-description, "Just regular." In the piece, Nigro charted the Los Angeles native's childhood "just outside of Watts," described as stable and positive, marked by endless baseball playing with his brothers and sisters. The Murray kids invented a game of hitting Crisco lids, tossed like flying disks, which he credited for sharpening his eye. "I don't know how it started, but I think it helped us a lot hitting curveballs later on," he said with a smile. The article charted his swift rise through the minors, noted his at-plate consistency since his 1977 rookie year—27, 27, 25, 32 were his HR totals; 88, 95, 99, 116 his RBIs; .283, .285, .295, .300 his batting averages. Nigro also alluded to the pain Murray felt at his 1979 World Series performance, when he slumped in the final five games, going 0-for-21, after reacting negatively to, and denying emphatically, a written account about his family and its allegedly low opinion of Oriole scouting. The bitterness still lingered, intensifying the private Murray's suspicion of outsiders.

"There are very few people I trust," he said. "But I don't like to talk about myself anyway."[31] His agent, Shapiro, did not mind talking about him, though, suggesting that Eddie might wind up as baseball's first $3 million-per-year man. But that was years away. For now, the laconic first baseman was the central weapon in the franchise arsenal as they trained their attentions on catching up with Milwaukee. Weaver liked comparing his young star to his old one, returning to the Murray-Frank Robinson similarities in a June account. "I'm not gonna put a weight like that on the kid's shoulders," he said, doing precisely what he said he wouldn't. "But he is like Frank Robinson in a lot of ways. If you need a stolen base in the sixth inning, he'll get it. If you need a home run in the ninth, he'll get that, too."[32]

All season long, the Orioles put up with speculation about who would succeed Weaver. John McNamara, of the Reds, was one rumored candidate. Frank Robinson and Jim Frey were two with organizational ties, and the fact that the Orioles' 1982media guide was dedicated to Frank Robinson—in honor of his Hall of Fame election—only fueled speculation about him. Pitching coach Miller, the elder Ripken, and Joe Altobelli were also reportedly in the mix. Altobelli was third-base coach for the Yankees, but his Oriole Way pedigree was solid; he'd served as longtime manager of Rochester before heading off to San Francisco in 1977, where he managed for three seasons.[33]

When the majors took their mid-season break, Williams returned to the news. This time, he was written about as part of Bowie Kuhn's preferred inner circle. The commissioner now ran a "unified" major league set-up, without the separate American and National leagues setup of old. Kuhn's power base was intact, enemy owners resentful at the way the 1981 strike played out, yet evidently not able to push him off his perch. As part of Kuhn's rearrangement, he named Williams to the prestigious Executive Committee. Having seen the attorney's backroom abilities and negotiating strength during the stoppage, Kuhn wanted the Oriole owner on his side. Williams was having no problem rising to a position of prominence among a group of very prominent men.[34]

It was after the All-Star Game that the intensity of the farewell-Earl stories picked up. His memoir, *It's What You Learn After You Know It All That Counts*, co-authored with Barry Stainback, came out that summer. It received A-list treatment in the *Post*, where lead critic and Oriole fan Jonathan Yardley, whose unabashed devotion to the manager was well-known, wrote a loving review. But Yardley's review stressed that the book's most surprising and appealing aspect was that the tempestuousness of

Weaver's character was not the dominant theme. Rather, the text showed the manager's deep baseball knowledge. Straight-up strategy and tactics trumped irreverence in this book, making it a suitable read for all serious fans of the sport. Yardley did not miss a pregnant phrase. He drew readers' attentions to Weaver's contention in the book that he would retire to Florida, "perhaps after the 1982 season." "To any Oriole fan," Yardley wrote—and he was one himself—"That 'perhaps' is as momentous—and as welcome—as a Murray home run in the bottom of the ninth."[35]

Less partisan, the *Sporting News* followed its major spread on Murray with an even larger one on Weaver. This was a pastiche, covering his famous umpire run-ins, his tomato competition with Santarone, his relationship with Palmer, and his place in the all-timer pantheon alongside McGraw, Mack, Miller Huggins, Casey Stengel, Walter Alston, and Joe McCarthy. It also speculated—not idly, as things turned out—that Weaver might find himself back in a big league dugout before too long.[36] Other speculation came from the world of television. Weaver, it was widely reported, was in line to replace Tony Kubek as the number one color analyst on NBC's *Game of the Week*, where he would work alongside Vin Scully. He was also talking to ABC.[37]

But Weaver had his mind on overtaking Milwaukee and Boston, who sat ahead of the Orioles in the standings. "Naturally, the first goal is to win every game," he said before an August road swing. "After that, it's to win every series. If we do that, it will mean we're in good shape, because we've taken three out of four from Boston, one of the teams ahead of us."[38] August turned out to be a decent month, 18–14, but as it ended, the Orioles were still in third place, five games behind the Brewers and a half-game behind the Red Sox. August closed with Palmer going the distance for a 1–0 road shutout against the Blue Jays, making the veteran's record a gaudy 12–3. Further good news from the mound came when McGregor, who had battled tendinitis, stopped New York a week later, pitching 5⅔ innings of shutout ball, pushing his record to 13–12, and pronouncing his arm fine. Stewart was sharp in closing things out. "Vintage Scotty," was Dempsey's verdict; "Looked great," said Weaver. "Big day," the pitcher enthused, delighted with his renewed mastery of the change-up, his go-to pitch. "If something hadn't gone right with [the shoulder] pretty soon, we might have had to forget the rest of this season."[39] Instead of being on the shelf, McGregor would be on the mound as the Orioles focused on the pursuit ahead. His win marked the team's ninth in a row, pushing them to just two games behind Milwaukee in the loss column, and three games back overall. The winning streak would stretch to 10, followed shortly by a stretch with 10 wins in 12 games. The Brewers were hardly fading, but they could certainly hear footsteps approaching from below.

On September 20, the Orioles hosted Detroit for the first of a three-game set, to be followed by three in Milwaukee's County Stadium, home of the Brewers. But just before the Detroit series began, there was a formal "Earl Weaver Day" in Baltimore. A crowd of 41,194 showed up to see their sawed-off hero presented with a new van, a Caribbean cruise, a customized golf cart, and a song written in his honor by Terry Cashman called "The Earl of Baltimore." The game, an extra-inning affair against the Indians, turned into pure Orioles Magic when Dauer smashed a 10th-inning, two-out, two-run home run. As Dempsey scored from second ahead of Dauer, he tore off his helmet and threw it into the second deck.

But according to Weaver, the best gift of all was a controversial call from umpire Steve Palermo. The ump, never shy about his dislike of the manager, made what Boswell termed "a rare and dicey call" by calling Ripken safe at second when the rookie made a hard slide and Tribe second baseman Mike Fischer tried the "neighborhood play," his foot coming near the sack before he threw to first. "Yes, it's ironic that I'd make a call that might have kept his team from losing, especially on Earl Weaver Day," Palermo confessed. "We've had a bad history in the short time I've been in the league. Maybe now Earl'll admit that we call 'em the way we see 'em; that we're not out to get him."[40] Such an admission by the manager might have been miraculous, but this was a night for Orioles Magic, and after Dauer's obligatory curtain call, the crowd called, "Earl! Earl! Earl!" When Weaver came out of the dugout and blew kisses, it might have seemed like his career's emotional capstone.

Perhaps the magic, or excitement, wore the team out, or perhaps they were due to come to earth against the Sparky Anderson–led Tigers. The Tigers were learning to win under their own legendary manager, and their future was promising. After a 3–1 series-opening triumph, the Orioles dropped two straight. In the second game of the trip, young Storm Davis, who so resembled Palmer in his delivery, lasted but two innings before giving way to recently-promoted rookie Mike Boddicker, then John Flinn, then Stanhouse. The Orioles were shelled 11–1 that night as Milt Wilcox kept O's batters in check. Next, Detroit gutted out a 10–5 win as McGregor went just four innings, giving way to Davis, Stewart, Tippy Martinez, and Flinn. Baltimore arrived in Milwaukee frustrated, feeling more so after losing the Brewers series opener 15–6. Don Sutton took that win, running his record to 16–9, while Flanagan's loss put him at 15–11. Now, instead of seizing the chance to cut a two-game lead to nothing, the Orioles had let the Brewers rebuild their cushion to four. The second game in Milwaukee loomed large. Fortunately for Baltimore, Palmer was slated to start against ace Pete Vuckovich. The two were rival contenders for that season's Cy Young, and this showdown went to the Oriole. In pitching a complete game four-hitter for the 7–2 victory, Palmer improved to 15–4, while Vuckovich stood at 18–5.

Maisel led off his September 27 column with a question for fans: "Tell the truth now, how many of you gave up on the Orioles after they were blown out by Milwaukee 15–6?" The writer did not blame loyalists for "losing a smidgen of heart," given that the team had given up 36 runs over their badly timed three-game collapse. Watching them reminded him of following an NBA team that falls 20 points behind and spends the balance of a game trying to cut the margin to zero. But, Maisel said, there was still hope, and that was because the Orioles possessed sufficient character to keep battling, and perhaps enough talent to win. Palmer's shut-out woke up the echoes of past glories and gave everyone reason enough to hang in there, through what little remained of the season-long chase. Like everyone else, Maisel hoped against hope that the season-ending four-game series against the Brewers, slated for October 1–3, would be meaningful. But, he allowed, a glance at the schedule showed another matchup with Detroit preceding that finale, and "It won't mean much unless they can play the Tigers better in Detroit than they did in the recent series here."[41]

They could not. Baltimore arrived in Detroit for another three-game set at 90–66, a pair of games behind Milwaukee, playing in Boston. The Brewers took care of road business, taking two of three from the Red Sox. In a repeat of the previous week, however, the Orioles could not find their way past Anderson's Tigers, who took the first two games 9–6 and 3–2. The second game was especially demoralizing, as journeyman John Wockenfuss put the Tigers ahead with a ninth-inning, game-winning home run. This time, late-inning magic favored Detroit, not Baltimore. The shock prompted Boswell to issue the death certificate for the Orioles 1982 season. "Nothing in baseball is quite so depressing as losing a long, hard pennant race," he intoned. "A club bleeds to death collectively, one tiny nick of fallibility after another, watching its chances drain away, until, finally, the last cut feels more like a decapitation than a scratch."[42]

Only a wild 6–5 nail-biter in the third game kept the Orioles alive. Down 5–1 in the top of the seventh, they showed either desperation or a faint flash of magic, rallying behind clutch hits from Bumbry and Singleton in the seventh and a game-winning RBI single by Roenicke in the ninth.

Fans tuned in back home could be forgiven for appreciating a nostalgic note: old friend Dave Tobik, who gave up the fateful DeCinces homer in 1979 to kick off the Orioles Magic era, was on the mound during most of the rally. So the Birds were still alive, if barely: three games back with four to play when the Brewers came to town.

The Brewers team of 1982 was one of the colorful squads of the era; also one of the best. At the start of the season, predictions noted that, if their pitching held up—which it certainly did—their overall solidity could make them the best bet for a divisional title.[43] With their grizzled, admired manager, their wild hairstyles and moustaches, their superb starting trio of Mike Caldwell, Vuckovich and Sutton, and their mammoth power, the Brew Crew not only won big and often, they did so with flair. Their batting order had no holes:

Paul Molitor, 3B	Gorman Thomas, CF
Robin Yount, SS	Roy Howell, DH
Cecil Cooper, 1B	Charlie Moore, RF
Ted Simmons, C	Jim Gantner, 2B
Ben Oglivie, LF	

Yount and Molitor were future Hall-of-Famers, while rugged veterans such as Cooper, Simmons, Oglivie, and Thomas wouldn't shy away from anything. Stormin' Gorman led the league in home runs that season, with 39. The Brewers were good and they knew it. So did their fans, who made County Stadium resemble itself during the late 1950s.

Milwaukee fans, hungry for a true winner since the Brave glory days of 1957–1958, responded emotionally to this Brewer team, and the rest of the baseball world—except in Maryland—looked on appreciatively as Kuenn's squad staved off the frantic Oriole charge, week after laborious week. Milwaukee had kicked off the franchise movement craze of the 1950s, opening up the west to the majors, emphasizing to a nation that the same old cities that had dominated baseball since the 19th century needed an infusion of fresh markets. But Wisconsin also experienced the shattering decline of Brave fever, suffering through the team's move to Atlanta after the 1965 season. Only the fast action of car magnate Bud Selig, who purchased the Seattle Pilots in 1969 bankruptcy proceedings after the American League botched its expansion into the Great Northwest, put Milwaukee back into the bigs. Their mini-division title of 1981 was a positive sign, but in 1982, the Brewers faithful sensed bigger triumphs ahead. At the same time, the Green Bay Packers wandered through a post–Vince Lombardi wilderness. Milwaukee had its own sports anxieties, and Harvey's Wallbangers were the best bet to lay those to rest. Beating Baltimore to win the AL East would do just that.

The Brewer-Oriole rivalry of that season would be immortalized in an unusual way that few knew about at the time. On June 10, 1982, writer Daniel Okrent covered the game between the two teams at County Stadium. He used the 9–7 Milwaukee win as material for an enormously successful literary experiment: a thick description of what he and his publisher referred to as "The Anatomy of Baseball as Seen Through the Playing of a Single Game."[44] A long piece appeared in *Inside Sports*, before Okrent expanded his insights into a classic of baseball literature. *Nine Innings* appeared in 1985, giving scholars and fans a lasting and revealing look into the Orioles, and especially the Brewers, circa 1982. Okrent could not have known that the two would battle down to the season's final day, but the fact that they did lent his book additional resonance.

There was a sense of playing for pride as the Orioles took the field for the first game of a doubleheader on Friday, October 1. Fans were glad the team would finish at home, hoping at least that they would not go quietly, sending off the Earl of Baltimore with a display of grit if not magic. On the other hand, anyone who remembered 1979 knew that no lead was safe until a series was complete. The second-largest crowd ever to see a baseball game in Memorial Stadium, 51,833 in all, understood what Boswell wrote that night: "The Orioles needed only to think of themselves in the final three disastrous games of the 1979 World Series to understand," he pointed out.[45] Fans and players alike understood this even better after the first game, an 8–3 Oriole win. Pitching by Martinez was one key: Dennis went 6⅓ to notch the win and Tippy closed things out, while Vuckovich took the loss. Singleton homered, Nolan tripled, four Orioles doubled, and there were several great fielding plays, leading to a sense that the breaks that night were in Baltimore's direction. That sense only intensified when the Orioles prevailed again, 7–1, in the nightcap. Murray started things with a home run in the first, joined later by Sakata, Shelby, and Ripken. The Wallbangers were silenced, the Orioles' power bats unstoppable. As the throng exited the brick ballyard and flowed down 33rd Street, they dwelt upon the fact that six hours earlier, their favorite team faced a seemingly insurmountable lead. Now, Baltimore was one game behind with two to play.

The next game, Saturday night, was another Oriole rout. Once again, Stewart came in early after an ineffective start, this one by McGregor. As the Throwin' Swannanoan went 5⅔ to capture the win, Baltimore batters teed off on Doc Medich and the Orioles bullpen. The two teams were now tied, facing what amounted to a winner-take-all, one-game playoff the next time out. "Now, it's a toss-up," was Dwyer's apt summary of the situation.[46] "I'm throwing up every four minutes," owner Williams jested. "You couldn't ask for a greater confluence of circumstances. We're playing the team with which we're tied. For the East championship. In beautiful weather. A packed stadium. And no pro football."[47]

Sunday dawned bright and crisp, an apple of a fall day in Baltimore. Another sellout crowd admired what they had waited all season to see: the Oriole flag fluttering in the first-place spot atop Memorial Stadium. Two Cooperstown-bound aces were ready: Palmer and Sutton. What could have been more appropriate than for Weaver's last scheduled regular-season game to feature the starter with whom he had such an enmeshed relationship? "After all the tough games we've had, who knows how you're going to do?" Palmer answered when reporters queried him about the upcoming duel. "My arm doesn't feel well now. With the back injury, it puts pressure on the arm. I really hope the club plays well and I can just keep them in the game. That's really all you can hope to do with a club like Milwaukee."[48]

Palmer was right to forecast a tough game. Sutton turned out to be the winner, while Palmer gave up four runs and the Brewers later shelled the bullpen for a five-run ninth. Yount homered twice to lead the Milwaukee attack and bring Harvey's Wallbangers their thoroughly deserved win. Not only did they cop the divisional crown, the Brewers' triumph likely assured Yount of the MVP award, and Vuckovich of the Cy Young, since Palmer, his top competition for the award, took the loss.[49] As the Sunday brightness gave way to fall's chill, Orioles Magic had nothing left to offer. Or so it seemed.

It was after the game that the Baltimore highlights came. First, the still-full stadium did the O-R-I-O-L-E-S chant, hardly needing Hagy's prompting. They applauded another season of excitement, albeit one that again fell short of total satisfaction. Then, as Weaver waved and headed into the dugout while "Auld Lang Syne" played on the sound system, events went off-script. The impromptu took over from the predictable. "W-E-A-V-E-R" became the new spelling exercise, supplanted by the well-loved chants of "Earl! Earl! Earl!" It went on and on; it grew louder and louder; it would not stop. The ABC crew, covering the game for a national television audience, cut back from the victorious Brewers' party to cover the raucous post-loss celebration on the field and in the seats. Howard Cosell was even more verbose than usual, yet this time his narration was full of admiration for Baltimore. Over and over he praised the fans, the owner, the team, and the manager. He talked up the downtown renaissance, especially Harborplace, sounding like an Oriole Advocate himself. Prior to the game, Cosell had friendly talks with fans and predicted an Oriole win. Now, he lauded those same fans to a national audience, and praised Schaefer, too.

There was no narration inside the stadium, where banners read "Weaver 4 Prez," and "Thanks, Earl." Fans tucked away the brooms they waved high before the first pitch, and instead shouted their love for the retiring number 4. Williams came down to the field, saluting and embracing his skipper, as Weaver himself cried unashamedly. He bent into the O-R-I-O-L-E-S shape, leading the cheer. The players, while stung from their loss and the sudden end to a whole season of pennant-chasing, applauded the scene. And the fans would not go home. It was unlike anything in the ballpark's memory, and it provided one of the best-loved moments of the Orioles Magic years: that time the fans ignored a devastating loss and instead celebrated the career of their franchise's best manager. "An act of love," the lead editorial in the *Sun* called it the next day. "The Orioles lost, but Baltimore fans never looked better."[50]

Later, after the unexpected and unplanned hour-long ceremony wound down, Weaver spoke to the gaggle of reporters anxious to collect his post-game thoughts one last time. He steered the conversation to the Brewers. "The Brewers are an awfully good team, and it's a great organization," he said, mindful that old boss Harry Dalton sat in Milwaukee's GM chair. "Our division will be well-represented in the playoffs." Palmer concurred, saying, "The Brewers are not the kind of club you can get by without good stuff, and that was shown in the last game." Complimented for his glittering 15–5 season record, Palmer waved it off; "It wasn't quite good enough." Weaver was asked whether he thought Murray or Yount would win the MVP. "I'm very partial to my player. I wouldn't be here and you'd be in another city if it weren't for Eddie Murray. But it would be hard to top Yount's performance today. He was outstanding."[51]

As the Brewers went on to nip the Angels three games to two in the playoffs, clinching their first (and still only, as of 2016) American League pennant before losing a hard-fought seven-game World Series to St. Louis, the Orioles had some unfinished 1982 business. Cal Ripken, Jr. won the league's Rookie of the Year honors, which helped counterbalance the end of an incredible streak dating back to 1967, which was the last time before 1982 that no Oriole starter won 20 games over a full season. The big matter at hand, of course, was the continued search for a new manger. Threaded throughout every reporter's coverage was whether the team would insist

Left: Before the 1982 campaign got under way, Earl Weaver announced his intention to retire at season's end. The Orioles chased the Brewers all summer, battling the Brewers down to the final game. The post-game farewell scene that day at Memorial Stadium drew national attention when fans stayed to cheer despite a loss. *Right:* In August 1981, then-minor leaguer Cal Ripken, Jr., was promoted to Baltimore, where he joined his father, the Orioles coach and former minor league manager. He would win the Rookie of the Year Award in 1982, then enjoy MVP seasons in 1983 and 1991. Ripken may be best remembered for the evening in 1995 that saw him break Lou Gehrig's consecutive-games-played mark, a record long thought to be untouchable.

on an Oriole Way heir, hiring someone with organizational connections, or start afresh. Peters tipped his hand, but only slightly, in October. "Some background with the organization would obviously be a factor," he said. "But not the deciding one. There are other things I might consider more important."[52] Speculation at the time swirled around three possibilities: McNamara, Robinson, and Altobelli. The first two would make different kinds of splashes; McNamara, because he would not be a former Oriole; Robinson, because he was a franchise icon but still tied to the Giants. Miller and Ripken, Sr. also rated mention in the guessing game. But when the decision came in November, the choice was Altobelli. "I'm qualified," the new manager said by way of low-key introductions.[53] Right away, the new man announced that he would retain all five coaches: Ripken, Sr., Miller, Hendricks, Williams, and Ralph Rowe. What he promised was not a new direction, but continuity. "As a rule, whenever a new manager is introduced, his first words are something like, 'We're going to turn things around here.' With the success this organization has had, we just have to keep it moving smoothly." His first interview ranged over his recollections of handling seven current Orioles—Flanagan, Dennis Martinez, McGregor, Murray, Bumbry, Crowley, and Dauer—when they passed through AAA under his tutelage. He likened Miller to former pitching coach George Bamberger. Altobelli praised the elder Ripken, by way of easing any dissatisfaction Senior might have felt on not earning the skipper's nod himself. All in all, he made it clear that the Oriole Way was still intact, although of course he could not vouch for Orioles Magic. On the matter of replacing a famous predecessor, the former Yankee coach and Red Wing manager was forthright, and sensible, a style that quickly became his signature. "Succeeding someone like Earl naturally is difficult," the new Oriole manager said. "But if you win, it doesn't make any difference, and if you lose, you're going to be in trouble anyway."[54]

5

CHAMPIONS (1983)

Baseball is famously the game in which success is measured by minimizing unavoidable failure. The best batters fail to get a hit about 70 percent of the time; the best teams lose 60 games or more. The Orioles knew this like the hedgehog who knows one big thing. They were, as usual, a team noted for quiet self-possession; a conviction that their organization controlled what could be controlled, and that being in contention year after year would give them the chance to win championships. "We try to judge every decision in the organization by the same standard," Hank Peters would put it. "We ask, 'Is this change a plus for us, or a minus?' If you want to stay on top, then over the years, you better make a lot more plus moves than minuses."[1] Over 26 years, the Orioles had baseball's best record, proving that they had made many more plus moves than minuses.

But there were pressures—silent, inevitable—stalking the 1983 team. It was three years since this talented squad had won a division title, 13 since they'd won a World Series. Their core was showing its age: Singleton and Bumbry would turn 36 during the season; Palmer, 38. While their two young stars, Murray and Ripken, had many years ahead of them, it was clear that the Orioles were staring at the later stage of this phase of team history. Retooling was already underway. Going into 1983, one question was, would this version of the team, the Orioles Magic iteration, ever win it all? If they did not, might they go down in history lamenting 1979's near-miss, having never baseball's summit? A 1983 team publication listing Oriole accomplishments and fan attractions was relentlessly positive, stressing: "Orioles Baseball is far more than just winning a pennant or a World Series, as anyone who attended the final game of the '82 season will attest."[2] True enough—that impromptu celebration of Weaver and 1982 was indeed special, although impossible to quantify. However, baseball is a quantifying pastime, as the rise of new statistics-minded analysts attested. The standings never lie: the Orioles had come close again in 1982, but that was it.

　　Another question heading into camp was how Altobelli would do as Weaver's heir. Certainly, the new manager was no splashy hire, but the Orioles were no splashy team. Like his predecessor, Altobelli was a baseball lifer: 17 years as a minor league player, 12 additional years as a minor league manager, two of those at Bluefield and six at Rochester. He knew many current Orioles. As Red Wings boss, he finished first four times and won two International League championships. His Red Wing alumni abounded on the Oriole roster. His three years with the Giants, 1977–1979, represented that team's attempt to import some of the Oriole success into their own system, while two subsequent seasons in the Yankee organization put him in position to understand Baltimore's main rivals.[3] Temperamentally, Altobelli was milder than Weaver. A powerfully built 6-feet, 180 pounds, he exuded more quiet strength than fiery passion. But fans with a penchant for Baltimore baseball history might have recalled the old Orioles, who replaced the peppery McGraw with the genial Wilbert Robinson.

　　It was conceivable that the absence of Weaver would remove a consistent stress element, with all its inherent drama. Perhaps the veteran team would react with relief to a more relaxed environment. Certainly Altobelli was the choice for those who wanted continuity, and, given the team's success, who did not? Fans got to know Altobelli's style through a marketing campaign aimed at driving attendance past the never-achieved 2 million mark. The campaign, "Two Million Time," featured television spots and billboards. The commercial showed Oriole players thanking their fans and urging them to come out in 1983. "Thanks a million," said the players. "No," interrupted Altobelli. "Thanks, *TWO Million!*" That filmed advertisement was far more auspicious than the near-disaster which befell the new skipper at his first formal event in Baltimore. At a January banquet, as he moved back to make room for Weaver, rising to give a speech, Altobelli fell off the back of the dais. He plunged five feet and headed to the hospital. Fortunately, his injuries were slight. In fact, he betrayed *sang froid* when asked about the accident. "Instead of getting up and saying I was okay, I should have laid on my back and moaned and sued 'em."[4] Whether his lawyer boss, Williams, found this funny went unrecorded.

　　Before spring training started, other items drew fan attention. One was the abysmal Colt situation. That troubled team reached its on-field nadir in 1982, as the NFL suffered labor turmoil resulting in a 57-day player strike. In the truncated season, the Colts went 0–8–1, winless for the first time in their history, playing before increasingly small and hopeless crowds, setting up even more unflattering comparisons with the baseball club. For every feel-good development surrounding the Orioles, the Colts seemed to suffer a morale-sapping embarrassment. Another one came when the Colts selected Stanford's star quarterback John Elway with the first NFL draft pick. Elway refused to sign, wishing to avoid playing for Irsay. The football star expressed willingness to play baseball as a Yankee minor leaguer instead. Executive Ernie Accorsi was certain that the Colts could call Elway's' bluff, winding up with the franchise-saving star they needed. But Irsay worked out a trade himself, and peddled the young QB to Denver. Fans, angry at Elway, were equally scornful of the owner. Colt haplessness was also underscored when the Redskins won Super Bowl XVII. *Sun* columnist Michael Olesker, who, like many Colt fans, had deep ambivalence towards Washington's football team, was moved to grudging admiration. He remembered when it was the Skins who struggled while the Colts were an NFL power. "We rejoice with Washingtonians in the moment of vicarious athletic thrill," before adding that the neighboring city's fans rarely showed any respect for the Colts during those glory seasons.[5] Clearly, at least in Olesker's case, the presence of a Super Bowl champion one hour south, added to the ongoing issue of a D.C.-based Oriole owner, continued to accentuate Baltimore-Washington differences rather than paper them over. Meanwhile, Williams, who had formerly run the Redskins, was now on the outside.

The other winter occurrence was pleasing to Baltimore fans. Just as Frank Robinson's 1982 election to Cooperstown provided that season with an emotionally rewarding historical element, so did the January 1983 vote putting Brooks Robinson into the Hall. Upon hearing the news that he would be inducted along with Juan Marichal, the former third baseman was typically gracious. "This is the utmost thing that can happen to you as a player," he explained, "So many players in the Hall of Fame were idols of mine growing up in Little Rock." He interpreted his election as a vote for defense: "Most of the players in the Hall of Fame have offensive statistics that are awesome and that worried me a little."[6] He also made sure to thank his early managers and coaches: Paul Richards, George Staller, and Joe Schultz. Richards, of course, helped to sign Robinson as a rookie and managed him in the majors. Staller, who later would be an Oriole coach, and Schultz, who later managed the expansion Seattle Pilots, "cared about me," he remembered, "And you can't imagine how important that is, especially when you're 18 and 19 years old." He laughed, recalling

Schultz's salty advice: "You'll never get to the big leagues eating ice cream and drinking pop, Arky. You got to pound that Budweiser."[7] That very phrase received less-than-flattering recollection in Jim Bouton's book about playing for the Pilots, *Ball Four*. According to the kindly Robinson, there was more to his mentor than Bouton perceived. In any case, it required no prescience to guess that thousands of Baltimore fans would make the August trek to Cooperstown. How the present team would be doing at that time had yet to be seen.

Another story made little news in Baltimore, but it did reflect upon the character of team owner Williams. In 1980, his undergraduate alma mater, Holy Cross, found itself in a hard financial spot and there were rumors that axing the school's football team was on the table as a cost-saving measure. Crusader athletic director Ron Perry wanted to save the team and tried to hire promising coach Rick Carter, who had a record of reviving frail programs. By 1983, Holy Cross was back on solid gridiron footing. The story emerged that, during the crisis, Williams was deeply involved in convincing Carter that the team could be successful and the university would back it.[8] The account of Williams' work on behalf of his old school showed those aspects of his personality—a loyalty and a willingness to work hard behind the scenes—that were not always reflected by his "superlawyer" reputation, but which were very much in evidence as he worked alongside Baltimore's Mayor Schaefer to come up with proactive stadium solutions to keep the Orioles in town. Just as he did not publicize the draining nature of his long battle against cancer, Williams did not advertise the stubborn loyalties which he developed during his unglamorous Hartford childhood.

That winter, Ellie Hendricks returned to the Oriole fold as a coach; *Sun* beat writer Ken Nigro left to work for the Yankees and was replaced by Jim Henneman; WFBR-AM took a chance on hiring a young Bay Area–raised announcer, Jon Miller, whose experience included calling A's and Red Sox games. The radio opening came as longtime announcer Chuck Thompson moved exclusively into television, pairing with Brooks Robinson. Miller's rich vocabulary, baseball knowledge, and intellectualism mingled with a subversive sense of humor. This helped him to form a contrapuntal duo with holdover partner Tom Marr, who was not averse to rakish humor. Once, he recorded a parody session of "Manager's Corner," in which he let Weaver run loose with intentionally profane responses to fake questions. That episode, meant as a private joke, found its way into the public sphere and helped to cement Marr's own reputation as a cut-up. The Orioles radio booth promised to be spicy in 1983.

Avoiding a bad April—those season-starting slumps that dogged so many Weaver teams, necessitating the late-season rushes—was clearly a priority in Miami. But first, the new roster had to be determined. There were some rising prospects who had crested without making enough contributions to the big club. These included pitcher Dave Ford and catcher Dan Graham, both once highly prized, now expendable. They were let go. Speedy outfielder John Shelby deserved to play, and would share centerfield duties with Bumbry. There were other youngsters scrutinized for their ability to offer immediate help, especially on the mound. Allan Ramirez, John Flinn, Don Welchel, and Cliff Speck all had decent results at Rochester and got plenty of looks in Miami. So did promising righty Mike Boddicker, whose 10–5 Red Wing mark earned him a September call-up in 1982. Boddicker hardly looked intimidating on the mound, at 5'11" and 172 pounds. He had a good fastball, but especially effective off-speed pitches, such as a forkball, which some called his "fosh." If the 26-year-old from Norway, Iowa—a small town with a famous baseball tradition—showed sufficient command, he would be a potentially effective new staff member. Just how confusing his array of off-speed stuff was for major league hitters was the key question, but with instruction from pitching coach Miller and Hendricks, not to mention mentoring from Palmer, Martinez, Flanagan, and McGregor, Boddicker would get every chance.[9]

Role players John Lowenstein and Joe Nolan, both having been through the reentry draft, were Orioles again. Injury concerns revolved primarily around relief pitcher Stoddard's recovery from knee surgery. Trainer Ralph Salvon also kept an eye on McGregor and the aging Palmer during pre-camp training sessions in Miami.[10] Other Orioles—Boswell at the *Post* called them "Memorial Stadium Moles" because they frequented the old ballpark's hidden tunnels, full of batting cages and pitching spaces; a crypt-like space excavated for player workouts at Weaver's suggestion—preferred to winter in Baltimore. Despite their claims that they were working to stay in condition, the scribe, who by now knew this team as well as anyone, discerned different motivations. "They're here for the same reason that fans walk through the snow to buy the *Sporting News* on Christmas Day. The Orioles can't wait to get back to the game, get back to each other, back to feeling the tools of their trade in their hands. 'Welcome to the catacombs,' says Flanagan."[11]

This was the kind of all-in attitude that made the Orioles appealing to observers, including writers and purists from beyond Maryland. In fact, as 1983 approached, the team received plaudits from many sources. They received credit for their advanced use of metrics. None may have been more meaningful than that from Kansas-based baseball analyst, Bill James. Author of the annual *Baseball Abstract*, he was the John the Baptist for what practitioners were already calling "sabermetrics." The term credited the Society for American Baseball Research, and stood for, explained James, "The mathematical and statistical analysis of baseball records."[12] This movement marked a paradigm shift in the way devotees would approach the game and its lush statistical yield. As the lead pioneer in the use of advanced statistics to assess baseball performance and decision-making, James used his pre-season write-up on the Orioles to explain Weaver's use of strategic tools. Adept at number-crunching, James was also a talented writer whose explanations were as elegant as his equations. He was quick to credit Boswell for explaining to the public over several years the pith of Weaver's approach, a preference for big innings over one-run-at-a-time ball. In his forecast for the 1983 season, James covered a large number of factors, credited Weaver with making the team better than its talent over many years, and came to a conclusion sobering for Oriole supporters: "The only question in my mind concerning the Baltimore Orioles in the post–Weaver era is whether they will fall apart this year or next."[13] According to James, the window was still mostly open for a strong season, and he gave them a 60 percent chance of winning more than 88 games. But he saw this version of the Orioles as needing to win the big prize immediately before their opportunity vanished.

One statistic that emphasized the team's effective use of match-up statistics was the 1982 Orioles' American League record of 11 pinch-hit home runs. The new mark broke the previous record set by the 1961 New York Yankees, falling just one shot shy of the major-league standard set by Cincinnati in 1957. The left-field platooners figured large in this effort, as Roenicke and Ayala boasted two each. Dwyer also hit two, as did Crowley. Ford, Lowenstein, and Nolan also went long as pinch hitters. This naturally drew attention to Weaver's ability to make in-game decisions based upon his awareness of match-up trends. It was this kind of calculation that writers wondered whether Altobelli could replicate.[14] Recognizing the inherent pressure as well as the team's talented roster, *Street & Smith's* was pithy in their summation. "Pity poor Joe Altobelli," they suggested. "Or envy him."[15]

Peters defended the hiring. "Joe was just a natural," he insisted. "So often, some teams make changes just for the manager. But we believe in that consistency throughout the organization. We don't know everything, and we consider recommendations, but we think the way we do it has paid off."[16] In other words, the team would continue to enjoy the benefits of the Oriole Way with Altobelli at the tiller. As if to reassure the fretful, the team brought back Mark Belanger and Lee May—two fan favorites whose departures rankled—as spring-training aides. May and Belanger were welcomed to Miami by Altobelli himself.[17] With such a small gesture, the former Red Wing boss made it clear that he still appreciated the contributions of the old Orioles. Belanger's departure in particular had been marked by bitterness, so this homecoming did much to reintroduce cross-generational comity to an organization that prized same.

The new manager scoffed at the notion that Spring Training would represent some kind of massive switch. He had, he explained, "been to spring training for the club many times before. When I was the manager in Rochester, I always went to spring training with the major league club. Everyone was familiar to me, even the writers.... I used to go to Baltimore for about six games a year to watch. So it was like a homecoming for me. I knew the surroundings, the organization, and the people in it."[18] In Miami, Altobelli's equanimity was favorably noted, as was his cheerier demeanor. According to Palmer, "The first time Joe said hello to some guys, he broke Earl's record.... That was the old school approach. Chain of command. Never speak to a player if you could avoid it. That's basically how Earl was."[19] But Altobelli? Closer Tippy Martinez was direct: "Joe breaks the ice and takes the first step toward you. It's a little more comfortable situation."[20]

Boswell was, as James pointed out, an apostle of sorts for Weaver's genius. But he wasted no time recognizing the new leader's positive attributes. Among these, the writer noted, was an admirable refusal to ape his predecessor. Friendly and familiar though he was, Altobelli was his own man. Altobelli resolutely parried questions implying that he represented some break with the past, asserting time and again how well he knew the club and understood its situation. His demeanor was invariably calm and quietly confident. Indeed, Boswell was among those who first hinted at the fact that the absence of Weaver's dominant personality might prove a relief of sorts. From spring training, he wrote, "Weaver is still spoken of here with universal respect; it's always acknowledged that he will be missed. His status as living legend, quick-witted celebrity, future Hall of Famer and Runyanesque character is unchallenged. Officially, Weaver is welcome to put his feet up on anybody's desk any time he wants.... In the parking lot, there's still a space reserved with the one word 'Earl' painted in script." But when the writer asked Palmer if Weaver had visited practice that Spring, the veteran answered: "Who?"[21]

It was not surprising that the managerial shift dominated attentions throughout the Spring, because the kinds of personnel moves the team had to make were not headline-grabbers. They resigned Nolan, Sakata, and Stoddard, lending depth at catcher, infield, and in the bullpen. They also inked Boddicker, Rayford, rookie infielder Glenn Gulliver, and a host of others destined to shuttle between Rochester and Baltimore.[22] Anticipating a positional weakness, they acquired veteran third baseman Aurelio Rodriguez. This former Senator, Tiger, Angel, Padre, and Yankee was one of the great fielders at the hot corner during his era, although he played in the shadow of more famous third basemen such as Brooks Robinson, Clete Boyer, and Graig Nettles. Altobelli knew full well that Rodriguez was still a defensive asset. "Joe was very impressed with Aurelio," Peters explained to reporters, showing that, like Weaver, the new manager had a say in personnel moves.[23] Altobelli would have all the options Weaver ever did.

The Orioles lineup was largely set. Murray remained the dominant player on the team, "always a legitimate MVP candidate" in the words of one preseason annual.[24] 1982 Rookie of the Year Ripken was of course a bright spot at shortstop, "gradually developing a reputation as a clutch hitter and someone who has the ability and the discipline to hit behind runners and move them up a base ... a definite asset in the field, with an outstanding arm ... and better than average range."[25] Such write-ups validated Weaver's decision to move the rookie from third. The outfield featured the usual cast: Bumbry, Ford, Shelby, and, in left, the three-headed Roenicke-Lowenstein-Ayala platoon. Singleton was the presumptive DH. On the mound, McGregor, Flanagan, Dennis Martinez, and Palmer represented four proven aces; Storm Davis, coming off an 8–4, 3.49 season, represented a promising talent, while rookie Boddicker was unproven. Stewart would continue to play his swing-man role. Altobelli announced that the Orioles would turn to a five-man rotation that season. "I've averaged four or five [extra] losses since 1979 because by July and August, I couldn't reach back and make the big pitch in the seventh or eighth inning," observed Flanagan. "I expect that to change now."[26]

The team that broke camp and headed to Baltimore for Opening Day was mostly devoid of suspense and controversy. The biggest change in the season's first game was the absence of Bumbry from the starting lineup for the first time in eight seasons. Shelby started instead, but "The Bee" returned to the lineup for game two, scoring four runs and making it clear that his playing days were far from done. In fact, the most discordant note to emerge that Spring had nothing to do with baseball as such, but with fan culture. The switch from Weaver to Altobelli prompted the front office to make a switch in Memorial Stadium's soundtrack. "Thank God I'm a Country Boy" had, went the thinking, run its course, as had "Orioles Magic." They were to be replaced by "That Magic Feeling," a commissioned song unveiled on April 4. The song, played in the seventh-inning stretch, prompted more boos than the season-opening 7–2 loss to Kansas City. Afterward, business affairs executive Bob Aylward admitted, "We could have played 'White Christmas' or any of the most popular songs of all time, and they would have booed. I think it was a reaction to the change and not the song itself."[27] To their credit, the team was not slow to react, returning the old songs to the playlist in the eighth. The new number would be worked into a rotation, but "Orioles Magic" simply had the reference to Weaver dubbed out. As for "Country Boy," fans would not tolerate any pinch hitter for John Denver. The other highlight in the Opening Day loss was a brief snow squall, which gave the irrepressible Miller a chance to recite Christmas carols over the air, to Marr's laughter and the amusement of listeners.

April was notable for what it was not: a bad month. There was no typically slow Oriole start in 1983. The team was not hot, but given prior seasons, a mediocre beginning was nothing to scoff at. 3–2 after five games, 6–4 after 10, the Birds were 11–9 at the end of the month. The last time the team started reasonably well was 1979. To some on the roster, the balanced start was exciting. "I think it's going to be a fun year," McGregor enthused after beating Cleveland 4–1 in a nippy night game, April 17. "For a few years, we expected to win, but this year we want to win and it's a nice feeling."[28] Testifying to the truth of the lefthander's remarks, Boswell, wrote, "After only 10 games, the Baltimore pitching staff is already showing the signs of life that usually don't arrive until late May. The clubhouse rings with laughter. Altobelli waltzes through the clubhouse in his goofy head-to-toe union suit while the whole clubhouse is in muzzled hysterics."[29] What had them laughing that night was not their skipper's long johns, but Rick Dempsey's allegedly accidental beaning of Mike "The Human Rain Delay" Hargrove on an errant toss back to the mound. Ironically, Hargrove would one day manage the Orioles, but on this night, Dempsey's throw served as a reminder that the Orioles were willing to play tough.

It was vintage Dempsey. The catcher, never a slugger, was known not just for sterling defense and able handling of the staff, but for a hard-nosed approach that belied his zany reputation. By then a favorite around the American League for his pantomime routines trotted out during rain delays, Dempsey was already proclaiming his intention to extend his career into the 1990s. Having first reached the majors in 1969, he spied the chance to be an active major leaguer across four decades. Queried about the feasibility of his ambition (which would be realized), the catcher dead-panned, "Why not? I haven't lost a step since I've been here."[30] Later, he feuded with Royals outfielder and base-stealer extraordinaire Willie Wilson. When Wilson refused a call-out with disdain, saying, "I don't fight .190 hitters," the catcher asked reporters to convey a message. "Ask Willie how high I have to get my average before he'll fight me," Dempsey said. Weeks later, he returned to the topic. "I notice Willie's down to .280 and I'm up to .240."[31] His switch-hitting experiment generated more laughter than hits, but the catcher's blend of pugnacity, tough play, and humor entrenched him as a favorite among fans and reporters alike.

The Orioles continued winning in May, going 15–13, spending 10 games in second place and four in third, but otherwise leading the AL East most of the month. The main problem was Dennis Martinez, whose record in May stood at 1–4. Altobelli displayed patience with the Nica-raguan-born ace, who was—unknown at the time—facing alcohol prob-lems. Martinez's eventual triumph over this addictive phase became one of the proudest aspects of his long career, but during 1983, the situation remained mysterious and reporters speculated about the reasons for his mound woes. Pitching coach Miller was frustrated, yet loyal to his charge. "I wish everybody could watch Dennis throw between starts," he said. "Great heat on the corners, yackers off the table.... Looks like the best pitcher in the league until he gets in the game. It's gotta be driving him crazy, because it's driving me crazy."[32] Bullpen coach Hendricks was sim-ilarly puzzled. After warming up Martinez, he said, "I'd bet my house Den-nis will pitch a shutout." When that failed to transpire, Altobelli was dry: "Well, it's a good thing Elrod doesn't bet or he wouldn't have a house."[33]

Another note in a minor key was struck by Stoddard, still struggling with his post-operative knee as well as a diminished role since Tippy Mar-tinez was firmly ensconced as the closer. The two factors pushed him into a rare display of discontent, which he aimed at his new manager. "If he doesn't want to pitch me, then I want to get out of here," the tall reliever complained to Hendricks. "I don't want to pitch here no more."[34] The com-plaints were picked up in the press. In other hands, either case might have boiled over into a full-fledged controversy, but Altobelli's low-keyed, matter-of-fact responses avoided a publicity mess. He expressed continued confidence in Stoddard, but allowed that there was no place on the team for someone who wanted out. The tall pitcher quieted down and adjusted to his new situation.

The outfield platoon system worked extremely well in both left and center. Altobelli had no difficulty emulating Weaver's switches. Blithe spirit Lowenstein led the club in RBIs by mid–May, with 13, despite being a role player. Shelby hit safely in eight of his first ten games, hitting well from both sides of the plate. Ripken's average stood comfortably over .300 while Murray was off to a steady start. Heading into Memorial Day, Ford was hitting .345 with 15 multiple-hit games, and the entire team racked up 10 or more hits in 16 of their first 30 games. Adding to the positive vibe was the kind of trip that would have been impossible when the Senators served as baseball's outpost in the nation's capital. Since May was National Amateur Baseball Month, the White House invited several Orioles to a ceremony with President Ronald Reagan. With the President and owner Williams serving as co-masters of ceremony, GM Peters beamed alongside Altobelli, Palmer, McGregor, Dempsey, and Singleton.[35] Just days later, however, in keeping with the bifurcated nature of Washington's baseball awareness—the Orioles were a popular antidote to the absence of a home team, but the city's fans still wanted the Senators replaced—Redskins owner Cooke termed the return of a DC franchise "As inevitable as tomorrow, though not so imminent." In fact, he said, "I'm going to get one."[36] Exactly how he would evade the NFL rule against cross-sports ownership that helped to kibosh Williams' control of the Redskins, Cooke left unsaid. But since his team won the Super Bowl, few questioned that, if Cooke set his mind to something, he might well achieve it. This came on top of the ongoing negotiations in Annapolis to fix up Memorial Stadium, which increasingly took on the look of an Oriole-specific endeavor since the Colts' Irsay was more or less off his chain. By this time, the local media was in full-bore discovery mode, and not from a friendly direction. Details of Irsay's life that varied from his official biography started to emerge, including discrepancies regarding his claims of education and football experience at the University of Illinois, as well as the details of his military career.[37] While the Orioles were rolling along to the delight of fans on both ends of the B-W Parkway, long-term answers to regional questions about stadiums, franchises, relocations, and the like were very much in play. Some already assumed that the Orioles and Redskins would wind up being shared by both Washington and Baltimore when the Colts headed out.

The Orioles cruised into June in a three-way tie for second with the Yankees and Red Sox. The tightly-bunched trio trailed the surprising Blue Jays by a half-game, while the defending pennant winners, the Brewers, were a mere two-and-a-half games back. Baltimore promptly went on a run, winning nine of ten, 12 of 15. Night after night, the starters went deep and earned wins. Among them was Boddicker, the rookie surprise. Pitching the Orioles past Toronto on June 4, the slightly built Iowan pushed his record to 3–2, with a 3.34 ERA. Because of the Stewart factor—the long reliever came in during the sixth, pitching the last four innings for a save—Boddicker and other starters knew that, even if they suffered a bad outing, the rotation would not be disrupted. To a large extent, Stewart's versatility helped to minimize Dennis Martinez's erratic performance, which in turn allowed Altobelli to continue handling the starting rotation with a gentle hand. This was also the case when Flanagan took a lengthy turn on the disabled list thanks to a knee injury, while Palmer was plagued by back trouble. June was a good month for the Orioles, who went 14–11. Despite four three-game losing streaks in mid–June and early July, Baltimore's record at the All-Star break stood at a healthy 42–34, good enough for second place, one game behind plucky Toronto.

Played in Chicago's Comiskey Park, where the White Sox were enjoying a banner season, the 1983 All-Star tilt was a 13–3 laugher for the American League. No Oriole graced the starting lineup, but Murray and Ripken appeared, the former subbing for Rod Carew, the latter for Robin Yount. Tippy Martinez was also named to the team, although the relief ace did not pitch. For the rest of the Orioles, the break represented a welcome chance to rest and to gauge their chances over the rest of the season. While their start had not left them far behind, it remained to be seen if they would finish the season in their customary strong fashion. It was in July that the already-winning Orioles really asserted themselves, going 19–7 on the strength of three winning streaks that ran to six, five, and four games apiece. They entered August 59–41, tied for first with the Tigers, renascent under Sparky Anderson, while the rest of the division began to sink.

The winning was inspiring, of course, although without the frequent Weaver-umpire dramatics, some of the old excitement was absent. But the ingredients of Orioles Magic remained firmly in place. Nightly, Memorial Stadium was a happy place to be, with Hagy leading the cheers, either from the upper deck or the dugout roof, Miller and Marr describing the action. Perhaps the most reassuring aspect of the season as sultry August proceeded was that every potential derailment—Dennis Martinez's problems, Flanagan's knee, Tippy Martinez missing four weeks with appendicitis, Ford missing two weeks after having his own knee cleaned out arthroscopically, Nolan winding up on the 15-day DL—failed to check the team's momentum. "We've never had this many key injuries," longtime

Summer night games at Memorial Stadium could be hazy and humid, but during the Orioles Magic years, the fans turned out nevertheless. By the end of the 1983 season, attendance had topped 2 million for the first time in franchise history.

second baseman Dauer said, bewildered.[38] Third base remained a chronic problem, since the aged Rodriguez no longer resembled his earlier golden-gloved self. But a host of short-term players provided effective stopgap solutions. At catcher, John Stefero briefly replaced Nolan, garnering some clutch hits, while highly touted prospect Mike Young made a visit from Rochester to plug an outfield hole. Fans grew as familiar with the Rochester roster as with Baltimore's.

On June 30, the Orioles made a roster move which barely registered around the league, but which proved to be a crucial step in solidifying the lineup. Weaver's much-debated decision to move Ripken to shortstop the previous season had been more than justified by the young star's performance. But it did leave a hole at the hot corner. Age had robbed 35-year-old Aurelio Rodriguez of his form in the field. Leo Hernandez filled in, but was a bit too slow throwing the ball to second for the whiparound 5–4–3 double plays that stymied opposing rallies. So the Orioles ventured farther afield to solve their third-base problem, purchasing the contract of Todd Cruz from the Mariners. Cruz had been a shortstop, so his range was unquestioned. His glove was dependable, and just as important, he was a loose and positive clubhouse influence, fond of jokes but glad to be aboard a contender. A light hitter, he headed to the bottom of the batting order. Cruz, Dempsey, and Dauer occupied the 7–8–9 spots, and were promptly nicknamed "The Three Stooges" by good-humored teammates such as Flanagan. Cruz was Curly, Dempsey was Moe, and Dauer was Larry. The three liked the appellations, especially as they showed a penchant for clutch hits that made their lowly nicknames amusing, not insulting.

The successful new arrivals added to the folkloric belief that Orioles Magic was still operative. Equally convincing was the team's ongoing habit of winning in clutch or unusual fashion. If one series could be said to have clicked on the magic button in 1983, it was a wild and wooly three-game home set against Toronto, August 23–25.

Heading into the trio of games, the Orioles were in second place, a mere half-game behind Milwaukee, with Toronto one behind the O's. Clearly, the Blue Jays, enjoying their first season of real contention, hoped to overtake the teams ahead of them. *Sun* columnist Alan Goldstein learned as much when he spoke with their DH, Cliff Johnson. "You see any chumps in this clubhouse?" the powerful veteran asked. "No, not a one," the writer responded. "Well, then why does everybody turn thumbs down on us? These guys have more character than any team I've been with.... They just don't want to lose."[39] They did not lose the Tuesday opener, clubbing Baltimore 9–3. Flanagan, newly returned from the DL, struggled. It was an auspicious start for the confident team from Ontario. But the next night saw one of the most unusual games in Memorial Stadium history, distilling Orioles magic and method, adding madness to the mix.

The atmosphere in Baltimore had already heated up. Two games earlier, the normally sanguine Altobelli was ejected from a loss against the Royals. After the game, he grumbled about home plate umpire Dave Phillips. "He said a few things to me," the manager complained. "I'm not really pleased with what I've heard from umpires the last couple of times I've gone out to argue. It's not fair. They know you can't punch 'em in the nose."[40]

The August 24 game attracted 25,882, the kind of mid-week attendance that kept the team's pursuit of the two million mark on track. McGregor started for the Orioles, going nine innings while scattering eight hits and giving up three runs. Blue Jay starter Jim Clancy matched him, allowing three over eight and ⅔. The Orioles began the game with a customary lineup:

Bumbry, CF	Singleton, DH
Ford, RF	Dauer, 2B
Ripken, SS	Cruz, 3B
Murray, 1B	Dempsey, C
Lowenstein, LF	

Thanks to Altobelli's substitutions and platoons, the lineup morphed as the game progressed. By the bottom of the ninth, down 3–1, the manager accelerated his wheels-within-wheels approach. Lowenstein struck out, but Shelby, inserted earlier as a pinch runner for Singleton, reached first on a bunt single. But Clancy struck out pinch hitter Roenicke, and the O's were down to their last out. Clancy walked Sakata, in for Dauer, and was pulled by manager Bobby Cox. In from the bullpen came lefty reliever Dave Geisel. Altobelli sent Ayala up to the plate to bat for Nolan, who had pinch hit earlier for Dempsey. The manager later claimed, "I wasn't thinking of a base hit by Ayala, I was thinking of a three-run homer."[41]

Instead, Ayala's single to center scored Shelby. Bumbry then hit a grounder to third that glanced off Garth Iorg's glove and skittered into right field. Sakata scored on the play to tie the game, which headed into extra innings when Joey McLaughlin replaced Geisel and struck out Dan Ford to end the ninth. But now, Altobelli's bench options were beyond exhausted, and he had to figure out a defensive alignment. It was novel, to say the least:

1B	Murray		LF	Ayala
2B	Lowenstein		CF	Bumbry
SS	Ripken		RF	Ford
3B	Roenicke		C	Sakata

Roenicke, Lowenstein, and especially Sakata were now out of position. Sakata had not played behind the plate since age nine. Lowenstein had the briefest stint as a second baseman to his credit—for the Indians, way back in 1975. Roenicke had never played third. Ayala, despite plenty of experience in left field, was the weakest glove man of the platoon at that position. This was catch-as-catch-can baseball, but Altobelli had no better options. The embarrassingly makeshift setup looked like it would blow up in the manager's face. Blue Jay batters took one look and imagined running rampant on the utility infielder-turned-catcher's arm. Stoddard, on the mound to spell McGregor, promptly gave up a solo home run to DH Johnson, putting the Jays up 4–3. He followed this by giving up a single to Barry Bonnell. Tippy Martinez came in.

Bonnell took a suitably large lead at first, since everyone on the field and in the stands knew he would run at the first opportunity. Martinez noticed and, with a sneaky quick move, picked the erstwhile baserunner off first. The reliever then walked speedy pinch hitter Dave Collins. The entire Blue Jays bench howled, because Collins was a good base-stealer. Martinez looked in at the batter, then threw to first, catching the overeager Collins leaning the wrong way for a second pickoff. Next up was Willie Upshaw. Upshaw chopped a blooper to second, where Lowenstein awkwardly turned a routine play into a base hit. Next, Martinez threw to first, picking off Upshaw. The Orioles' closer had not retired a single batter at the plate, but had picked off three runners at first. The crowd was hysterical, but the Orioles were still down a run in the bottom of the 10th. Ripken promptly solved that with a lead-off home run. Murray and Shelby reached base, and, with two outs, "catcher" Sakata came to the plate. His motivation was powerful, he admitted after the game. "I didn't want to throw," he said to reporters. "I didn't want to give away my secret weapon, the one-hop throw to second."[42] Thanks to a game-winning three-run homer that barely cleared the left-field wall, Sakata did not don the catcher's tools again. Tippy Martinez put the craziness in perspective in front of a celebrating clubhouse. "I knew they were anxious to get going, so thank God for Lenny," he said. "I was really just thinking of making as many throws over to first as possible. Eddie's really good at deeking guys."[43]

The next night saw more magic. Storm Davis and Dave Stieb dueled through eight innings of shutout ball. Tippy Martinez relieved Davis in the ninth, while Stieb finished his ninth before giving way in the 10th to Roy Lee Jackson. In the top of the 10th, Martinez gave up a go-ahead homer to Bonnell, and the Jays took a 1–0 lead into the bottom of the extra inning, against an Oriole lineup that had managed only four hits. Dwyer popped to short before Nolan, pinch hitting for Dempsey, singled to right. Bumbry moved Nolan to second with a scratch single of his own: men on first and second, one out. Up came Ford, whose double to right scored both runners with the tying and winning runs. Again, the players flooded out of the dugout and carried the party into the clubhouse. Again, the fans headed home convinced that the Orioles played under a protective cloak of fate.

Magic or not, the Orioles never looked back after this series, gaining first the next game behind a Boddicker shutout of Minnesota and never relinquishing their lead. The two wins over Toronto kicked off an eight-game winning streak, followed by winning five of the next six. They also made some roster tweaks. One was acquiring Cardinals outfielder Tito Landrum, just before the September deadline for postseason eligibility, as the player to be named later in the deal that sent Floyd Rayford to St. Louis back in June. Few noticed this small move. On Friday, September 9, the Orioles hit New York up by five over the second-place Brewers, with the Yankees a half-game behind Milwaukee. A sweep would put New York back in the title mix. But after losing the opener, the Orioles took three in a row, then another three straight in Boston to maintain their lead over the Brewers. By mid–September, fans were beginning to count down the magic number.

In his owner's box, Williams remained as nervous as ever, unsettled by Commissioner Bowie Kuhn's unexpected loss of ownership support earlier in the season, leading to lame-duck status and an uncertain replacement search. On September 20, the Orioles were six-and-a-half ahead of the second-place Tigers. But that Tuesday night, Detroit thrashed Baltimore 14–1. Talking to reporters, Williams reminded all that, when he ran the Redskins, his in-game nerves won him the nickname, "Panic Button." Until the magic number was zero, he said, he would remain on edge. "The most excited I will get is the night we clinch the Eastern Division—If we clinch the Eastern Division."[44] Holding forth, he opined that Tippy Martinez's appendix attack was a hidden blessing, giving the reliever a month-long rest and leaving him fresh and effective for the stretch and—perhaps—the postseason. Williams also reviewed his own performance since purchasing the team in 1979. The formula was, he explained KISS: Keep it Stable, Stupid. He described his respect for the way Miller shepherded the team's traditionally strong stable of pitchers, and pronounced himself proud of fending off free agency losses, as well as making cagy trades like the one bringing catcher Nolan to the Orioles. Looking at the season, he could not help pointing to the three-pickoff game on August 24, zinging Toronto's Cox. "Hate to say this, but that was a case of a manager losing the game. I mean, Tippy Martinez cannot throw a curve ball because Lenn Sakata cannot catch a curve ball. In fact, he can't even see through the catcher's mask bars. Now, when Tippy throws a fast ball, the odds are at least 8–1 they're gonna hit it into the infield. And if they do, who in the hell knows whether it'll get stopped." Recollecting Roenicke at third and Lowenstein at second, the owner turned his attention back to the unfortunate Cox. "Instead, he lets the three runners on first base get Saint Vitus' dance. They are so hot to go, like three horses trying to break out of the starting gate."[45]

There were no guarantees, of course, especially with the ache of the 1979 World Series collapse still throbbing. But Williams' thoughts, and those of the fans, were turning to the playoffs, where the revived Chicago White Sox, with a rugged pitching staff, a homer-happy batting order, and bright young manager Tony La Russa were waiting. The Birds clinched the division on Sunday, September 25, beating the Brewers 5–1. Back in Baltimore, fans sat in the stands watching the Colts upset the Bears, listening to the baseball game on their radios. Memorial Stadium cheered in unison when Milwaukee made its last out. In the regular-season finale, a 2–0 whitewashing of the Yankees, the stadium loudspeaker played a favorite, "You Can Do Magic," by America.[46]

Playoffs: "Orioles Magic" versus "Winning Ugly"

The 1983 White Sox were as ready for the playoffs as the Orioles were. Their young manager, Tony La Russa, already had a dual reputation for being brash and a master tactician. Unafraid to argue his points, once, when ejected from a game, he refused to leave the dugout, much to the umpires' consternation and the fans' amusement. In a move that Weaver could have applauded, La Russa once yanked up third base and hurled it into the dugout in protest against a call. But he also complained about the Orioles' penchant for riding the men in blue, which he saw unabated after Weaver's departure: "They moan and groan at the umpires so much, maybe it's part of the spring training program."[47] To this, Altobelli replied, "What am I, an American Legion manager and he's a major league manager? Why can't I be a major league manager, too?"[48] Since both clubs had been in control of their division for much of the season, they had eyeballed each other for months, and a sense of incipient rivalry developed. The Chisox had their own motto, "Wining Ugly," describing their delight at playing hard, rallying when necessary, doing things their own way. Everything worked for them that season. They even had a theme song, "Na Na, Hey Hey, Kiss Him Goodbye," by Steam, which fans chanted when opposing pitchers headed off to an early shower. Their record was 99–63, better by one game than the Orioles' 98–64. The White Sox scored 800 runs, giving up 650. The Orioles? 799 and 652. Chicago won the AL East by a whopping 20 games over the Royals, meaning that La Russa had weeks to prepare his team for their postseason.

The White Sox had star power, with Ron Kittle (.254, 35, 100) in left field, Carlton Fisk (.289, 26, 86) at catcher, Greg Luzinski (.255, 32, 95) at DH, and Harold Baines (.280, 20, 99) in right. They rounded out their positional lineup with talents like first baseman Tom Paciorek (.307, 9, 63), center fielder Rudy Law (.283, 3, 34) and gritty role players like third baseman Vance Law (.243, 4, 32), second baseman Julio Cruz (.251, 1, 40) and shortstop Jerry Dybzinski (.230, 1, 32). Players like Tony Bernazard and Scott Fletcher gave La Russa the depth for the moves he loved to make. Their starting rotation was fearsome. 28-year old LaMarr Hoyt was the stopper, with a glittering 24–10, 3.66 record. He was followed by Richard Dotson (22–7, 3.23), Floyd Bannister (16–10, 3.35), Britt Burns (10–11, 3.58), and old Oriole tormentor from the 1969 Mets, Jerry Koosman (11–7, 4.77). Dennis Lamp, their closer, had 15 saves, while pen mate Salome Barjoas had 12. Their season series with the Orioles was close: 7–5 Baltimore. The Orioles' playoff rotation had long been set: McGregor (18–7, 3.18), Boddicker (16–8, 2.77), Flanagan (12–4, 3.30), and Davis (13–7, 3.59). Palmer (5–4, 4.23) and Stewart (9–4, 3.62) waited in the wings for long duty, while Tippy Martinez (9–3, 2.35, 21 saves) remained atop the bullpen. The intimidating Hoyt and Dotson gave the White Sox a slight edge, according to some reporters. At the *Post*, Boswell made a prediction that could scare the Baltimore faithful: "The White Sox have such suffocating starting pitching that, like the Orioles of '79, they may be in the Series before they ever have to face a truly frightening game. If Chicago wins the first game of this playoff, they could certainly sweep."[49]

On the Orioles' side of the ledger, what Boswell and others identified as an advantage was the team's recent record of coming close. Three times, he figured, "they came up short by narrow margins. Now again, the Orioles face a team that is their match but not their superior. If they don't get over the hump this year, they probably never will."[50] Citing the near-misses of 1979, 1980, and 1982 as an advantage might have seemed counterintuitive, but the sagacious Boswell was on to something. The rest of the press corps also picked up the whiff of intensity from an outwardly relaxed Baltimore squad. In fact, the Orioles were a desperate team. Because of their experience, they were in a state of equipoise rather than panic. But up and down the roster, players clearly understood that this might be the last, and perhaps best, chance for the Orioles Magic team to go all the way. Trades, free agency moves, and inevitable overhaul promised to alter a roster that was no longer young. If veterans like Singleton and Bumbry were ever to win the World Series rings they coveted, it might have to be now.

Baltimore fans, however, perhaps less cognizant of such deep currents, remained upbeat. They betrayed little concern about the mighty bats and strong arms propelling the White Sox into Baltimore. It was that franchise's first post-season in 24 years, since the long-ago Go-Go Sox of 1959, and South Side fans were delighted. Reporters from across the land canvassed Baltimore and Chicago in search of good fan copy. One such Baltimore venue was Attman's, the fabled delicatessen which was the sole remaining linchpin of the former downtown Jewish neighborhood adjacent to Little Italy. "I got my tickets for all the playoff games and the Series," owner Stuart Attman explained to *Washington Post* Style reporter Michael Kernan. "I've been to 25 games this year. I don't think it's registered yet.... I have a friend in Philadelphia, and we're gonna go together in both cities."[51] Baltimore's reigning Corned Beef King was clearly confident. The Phillies were favored to top the Dodgers in the National League Playoffs.

The Sox showed no signs of stage fright as the teams opened the series with a Wednesday, October 5, afternoon game. Hoyt went the distance, giving up only one run. McGregor was nearly as good but not quite, and the White Sox' 2–1 win put them in position to test Boswell's proposition. Oriole highlights were few. Singleton had a double but was stranded on second. The Birds rallied in the ninth, when Landrum—pinch running for Ford after his double—scored on a Ripken single. With Junior on first and Murray at the plate, the 51,289 sent up their usual, imploring, "Eddie! Ed-die! Ed-die!" chant. But Hoyt coaxed a grounder to short and the Orioles were down a game in the best-of-five series.

The next game was at night; the 8:40 start was more than an hour later than usual, so the coolness of the evening combined with nervous anticipation, rendering the sellout crowd loud and fidgety. In the bottom of the second, Roenicke doubled off Bannister, then scored on a fielder's choice by Singleton. The Orioles led 1–0. In the fourth, these two did it again. This time, Roenicke walked and Singleton doubled: 2–0. Bannister was otherwise effective, but it was rookie Boddicker who dazzled this night. Again and again, he either struck out Chicago batters or put the ball in play where his fielders handled things. His off-speed pitches—especially the fosh—were practically unhittable. Roenicke homered in the sixth with Ripken on base, extending the margin to 4–0, while Boddicker shut down every incipient White Sox threat, going the distance, striking out 14 batters, equaling the playoff record set by Joe Coleman in 1972 and matched by John Candelaria in 1975. Down at 33rd Street and St. Paul, along the main route to the stadium, the Johns Hopkins fraternity boys at Alpha Delta Pi expressed their appreciation with a homemade bedsheet banner:"*GOD*IKKKKKKKKKKKKKKKER!"

The Orioles broke serve in Chicago in Game 3, battering Dotson en route to an 11–1 rout. The game revealed bad blood between the two teams, with brushback pitches and an irate La Russa protesting a Murray steal of second in the top of the eighth with the Orioles up 6–1. "We hear about how Murray had a bad foot and that he can hardly walk," complained the manager, "And then he does something like that. I guess you can't believe everything you read."[52] Ron Kittle, still angry after being hit by a fan's spilled beer while manning left field in Game 2, was equally frustrated after being beaned in the knee by Flanagan on a 3–2 pitch in the fourth. He called out to the mound in anger, explaining later, "They hit two of our guys [Paciorek and Luzinski] ... So when Flanagan hit me, I said, 'Hey, this has to stop.'"[53] It is doubtful that Flanagan wanted to put the leadoff batter on, and the Orioles were known for not throwing at the opposing team (not necessarily out of virtue, but because of a belief that the free base was too much of a risk) but Kittle's reaction reflected the tautness of emotions. Ripken took the retaliatory pitch next inning with a broad smile. Murray snarled at Dotson's next brushback, and La Russa ran out to join the back-and-forth. Benches and bullpens emptied, umps issued warnings, but the dramatics dwindled without any punches thrown. Four runs in the top of the ninth capped the Oriole romp, leaving both teams uncertain what Game 4 had in store.

What it had in store was more outstanding pitching, and precious little run production. The Orioles knew that, if the series went the full five, Hoyt awaited. Facing the huge righthander in shady, chilly Comiskey with the pennant on the line sounded like a formula for more post-season heartbreak, so Baltimore definitely wanted to put the series away. But inning after inning, Britt Burns set them down. Storm Davis went six shutout innings himself before giving way to Tippy Martinez, who entered during the seventh after Greg Walker's leadoff single signaled a nascent Chisox threat. Martinez got out of that inning and pitched three more shutout frames. Meanwhile, Burns' shutout continued through the regulation nine, and the gutsy lefty took his gem into the top of the tenth. He started off the extra frame well, catching leadoff hitter Shelby looking for a strikeout. Up came right fielder Landrum, the late-season acquisition from St. Louis, inserted into the starting lineup for this game by Altobelli in a bid to find an advantageous matchup. Landrum's Oriole career thus far had been quiet, and he was certainly the least-known player on the team. Burns had thrown a whopping 149 pitches, but his mastery kept him on the mound. Burns delivered a fastball, which Landrum—chasing a hit, hoping to become a baserunner, wanting to spark a rally—met squarely. The ball shot up, carried, flying into the left-field upper deck. The disbelieving White Sox watched the seldom-seen substitute trot around the bases. The Orioles were up 1–0. A disgusted Burns wiped his brow, suddenly and plainly exhausted. Barojas came in to quell the rest of the order. But Ripken singled, then scored on a Murray single. Murray then scored on an Ayala sacrifice fly, and the Orioles went into the bottom of the tenth with a 3–0 lead. Martinez, pitching his fourth inning, got Fisk to pop up to Roenicke in left field. Baines reached on a single, but Martinez struck out Luzinski and Paciorek. The pennant was Baltimore's again. The World Series was next.

Retrospect provided plenty of numbers to analyze. One of the most notable statistics was that the White Sox stranded 35 baserunners during the series, including 18 in the seventh, eighth and ninth innings. The 19–3 cumulative Oriole scoring margin was misleading, given the lopsided Game 4. The Series was otherwise tight. Roenicke hit .750 with a home run in three games and might have been a suitable MVP selection. Murray helped to overcome the image of his 1979 World Series struggles with a .267 average, a homer, and three RBI. But the MVP of the playoffs was Boddicker, since writers realized that his stunning Game 2 performance was a series-saver, putting Baltimore in position to avoid Hoyt in a Game 5 at Comiskey.[54]

For the first time in five seasons, the Fall Classic beckoned Baltimore. But first came celebration. Naturally, attention focused on the newest Orioles Magic performer, Landrum. "Pinch me a couple of times when I leave here to see if I'm still alive," he laughed as the champagne sprayed.[55] He credited hitting coach Ralph Rowe with correcting an undercut before the pivotal at-bat. Having sent his new team to the World Series, ensuring himself a permanent spot in team lore and reigniting the talk of magic, Landrum recounted a season in which he expected to reach postseason play with Louisville, the Cardinals' AAA affiliate, for whom he played 111 games before the trade. Had he expected to be dealt? "You hear rumors," he admitted, "But nothing was taking place." When it did, he decided, the swap to Baltimore was a blessing. And now, he enthused, "I feel like Muhammad Ali."[56] As Landrum spoke, Murray and other Orioles sang their own version of the Chisox theme song, "Na na na na/Na na na na/Hey hey hey/Good bye!" "We were all rooting for Tito in the bullpen," recounted Hendricks. "Jim Palmer was talking about him doing something big to help the team. I guess we've just become used to somebody different doing something to help us win all the time, regardless of who they are."[57] Landrum was just the latest hero. But with a World Series to come, would he be the last?

World Series: The I-95 Contest

The Philadelphia Phillies locked up their National League East championship thanks to a 10-game winning streak down the stretch. This clutch drive subdued the Expos and Pirates, giving GM-Manager Paul Owens' squad a playoff berth. Along the way, the team enjoyed the 300th career win by the great Steve Carlton, which softened his losing (15–16) season.[58] The Phillies were at the tail end of the best era in team history, having won their first World Series championship in 1980, following three division titles from 1976 through 1978. Their 1980 glory was epitomized by reliever Tug McGraw's standout performance and vocal optimism, which put the Phillies atop the baseball world for the first time in 97 seasons. Since the City of Brotherly Love's five other World Series triumphs were earned by Connie Mack's A's, who left town in 1954, the Phillies' win was an occasion for jubilation from South Jersey to Lancaster, from upper Delaware to the Poconos. By 1983, Phillie fans no longer thought of their team as a sad-sack squad, but rather as a composed collection of veterans.

Their rotation was especially strong at the front end, where Carlton was complemented by John Denny (19–6, 2.37 ERA). The unimpressive back of the rotation was balanced by a deep bullpen, with closer Al Holland leading the way. He had help from durable Ron Reed and Willie Hernandez, ably backed by others (including once-and-future star Tug McGraw). An undeniable aspect of the 1983 Phillies was the way they perpetuated the influence of Cincinnati's old Big Red Machine. Pete Rose (.245, 0, 45) and Tony Perez (.241, 6, 43) shared duties at first base, while Joe Morgan (.230, 16, 59) started at second. The team's leader was mighty third baseman Mike Schmidt (.255, 40, 109), while shortstop Ivan DeJesus (.254, 4, 45) rounded out the infield. Bo Diaz (.236, 15, 64) caught. The outfield saw Garry Matthews (.258, 10, 50) in left, Gary Maddox (.275, 4, 32) in center, and Von Hayes (.265, 6, 32) in right.

Bench depth was good, with outfielders Joe Lefebvre, Greg Gross, and Bob Dernier joining other effective substitutes, including catcher Ozzie Virgil, outfielder Sixto Lezcano (long coveted by the Orioles) and former Oriole infielder Kiko Garcia. They were an old team, with four players 40 or older (Rose, Morgan, Perez, and reliever Reed), two 39-year-olds (Carlton and McGraw), and but one positional starter, 24-year-old Hayes, under 30. No wonder the writers referred to these Phillies as "The Wheeze Kids" (a play on "Wiz Kids," the nickname of the 1950 Phillies, the franchise's 1950 World Series entry).Their age prompted writers to dub them "The Old and the Relentless," as the Phils beat the Dodgers in four games to win the NL pennant.[59] They charged to the flag behind the hot bat of "Sarge" Matthews, who hit .429 against the Dodgers. Torrid coming into the series, having won 25 of their last 32, the Phillies shut down Los Angeles in Game 1 behind eight innings of Carlton's shutout ball. The Dodgers got to Denny in Game 2, taking a 4–1 decision behind Fernando Valenzuela. But Philadelphia slugged their way to a 7–2 win in Game 3 before clinching the National League crown with another 7–2 triumph in Game 4.

The 80th World Series opened in Baltimore, but Philadelphia prevailed 2–1. The first highlights made Oriole fans happy. Before the game, John Denver performed the national anthem wearing an Orioles jacket (he also sang "Country Boy" atop the dugout during the seventh-inning stretch). In the top of the first inning, Joe Morgan headed for second on a hit-and-run. Rose's swing missed and Dempsey gunned down the veteran at second by three yards.[60] A Jim Dwyer solo shot in the bottom of the first Denny gave the Orioles a quick lead, but Morgan knotted the score with a sixth-inning home run off McGregor which reminded many viewers of the pitch he threw to Stargell in 1979's Game 7. Then, in the eighth, Matthews continued his hot streak with a clout that cleared the wall in left. Only an over-the-fence catch by Lowenstein prevented Diaz from making it back-to-back homers. Denny and Holland, who relieved for the save, scattered five hits. The game—not to mention the team's overall position—justified Owens' penchant for platooning. But Matthews' post-game comments showed a difference in clubhouse atmospheres between the two teams. "I don't want to get into anything controversial," he said, "But I have not accepted being a 'role' player.... A lot of us have had to do things this year that we didn't want to do. We had to reach down and be professional. I haven't been given a fair chance to show what I could do this year."[61] It seemed a strangely dissatisfied remark coming from the playoff MVP and Game 1 star.

So, just as in the playoffs, Boddicker started Game 2 looking to prevent his team from falling down an 0–2 hole. And, just as he did in the playoffs, the rookie went the distance, pitching a three-hitter, striking out six, and allowing just one run as the Orioles evened things by winning 4–1. The fifth inning was their big chance, and they took advantage of it by scoring three off Hudson. Lowenstein started things off with a homer, Dauer singled, and Cruz dropped a bunt that saw Morgan slow to cover first, leaving Schmidt handcuffed. Dempsey's double drove in Dauer, and Boddicker, in his second career at-bat, pushed Cruz across with a sacrifice fly. Willie Hernandez replaced Hudson on the mound and escaped the inning, but three runs were plenty for Boddicker. Had Murray not mis-played an easy toss in the fourth, the Iowan would have had his second straight post-season shutout. The first baseman also went 0-for-4 at the plate, prompting press and fan mutters that perhaps his 1979 World Series funk had not been a fluke. Boswell, at the *Post*, said Boddicker managed to turn the World Series stage into "merely some mown and tended corn-field turned into a diamond."[62] It was the third rookie-hurled three-hitter in Fall Classic history, and the first since 1919. "I had a better curveball against Chicago, but I had a better fastball tonight," explained the plain-spoken Oriole starter.[63] He also threw more of his patented "foshballs" due to Philadelphia's heavily left-handed lineup. As if in response to Matthews' prior complaints, the irrepressible Lowenstein joked about his own part-time status. "I have no desire whatsoever to play every day. It's too tiring.... Hell, I don't even want to play the third game. Carlton's pitch-ing."[64]

Having split the Baltimore games, the two teams traveled by bus for the short trip to Philadelphia's Veterans Stadium. Before Game 3, the Ori-oles received a big dose of the kind of positive PR that their relationship to Washington's leading journalistic echelons made possible. The praise came from George Will, who wrote a national column entitled, "The Ori-oles and Civic Virtue." The Orioles, insisted the 42-year-old Pulitzer-winning writer, "with the best record in baseball in nearly 27 years, are one of two American institutions of consistent excellence." The other, he said, was the phone company. Worrisomely, "The government is fiddling with that, so the Orioles may soon have cornered the market on quality."[65] The baseball-loving political pundit went on to express joy that the World Series occurred four times more often than presidential elections, which he saw as a sign of healthy national priorities.

Will also inserted a dig at the Vet's artificial turf. Oriole-watchers knew that the team had struggled on fast surfaces in the past. *Sun* jour-nalist Steve Parks noted that in 1982, the team went only 9–10 on turf, including a disastrous 0–6 in Kansas City, which could be said to have cost the team a division title. But 1983 saw a turnabout, as the Orioles played their way to a 16–8 mark on artificial surfaces. The key, argued Parks, was an Altobelli innovation. Whereas Weaver had played his fielders up in a bid to stymie opposing speed on turf, Altobelli backed up his infielders and bunched them towards the middle to cut off hits up the middle.[66]

The big news going into Game 3 was Pete Rose's absence from the

Cal Ripken, Jr., and Phillies catcher Bo Diaz wait for a pitch during the 1983 World Series. The Orioles would win the showdown in a romp, four games to one.

lineup, with his longtime Cincinnati teammate Tony Perez earning the start at first base. Meanwhile, Steve Carlton would become the first 300-game winner to pitch in a World Series since Grover Cleveland Alexander took the mound for the 1928 Cardinals. Matthews staked the Phils to a quick 1–0 lead when he belted a Flanagan pitch into the stands to start the second. Morgan extended the lead to 2–0 with his own solo shot in the third. The Orioles' Ford halved the margin with a homer in the sixth. With two outs in the seventh, Dempsey doubled, Carlton uncorked a wild pitch, and pinch-hitter Benny Ayala had a crucial RBI single that tied the game, chased Carlton and brought in Holland. At this point the glare of the spotlight discombobulated customarily smooth-fielding Ivan DeJesus, who booted a hard grounder from Ford which scored Ayala, putting Baltimore up 3–2. Jim Palmer, on in relief for the fifth and sixth, earned a World Series win with Stewart and Tippy Martinez shutting the door over the last three innings. The symbolism of the Orioles' veteran hurler gaining the positive decision, with Carlton suffering the loss, was lost on nobody. Nor was Rose's displeasure at being benched. Owens warned reporters not to "make a big deal out of it," adding, "Everyone thinks Pete's done something wrong, but this isn't his fault. He's done nothing wrong."[67] But Rose said he still felt embarrassed. Palmer was asked by the press if he felt embarrassed, being relegated to relief. "I'm just hurt, I'm not embarrassed," he insisted. "The guys in front of me deserve to pitch. They got us here. How can you fault the pitching selections by either manager in this World Series? We got a strong game from Scott McGregor in the first game, and Mike Boddicker pitched great the other night. I got my chance and I'm thrilled the way things turned out."[68]

Game 4 kept the Oriole Magic talk going, since it represented Baltimore's third straight come-from-behind win. They staked themselves to a fourth-inning lead when Rich Dauer tagged Denny for a bases-loaded single to right, scoring two. But the Phillies responded in their half, rallying behind singles from Rose and Schmidt, followed by Lefebvre's double. Matthews drew a walk to load the bases, but Storm Davis coaxed a double-play grounder from Gross, the Orioles still ahead 2–1. But the Phillies went ahead in the fifth on the strength of three doubles, taking a 3–2 lead. In the sixth, Altobelli sent up a record four pinch hitters. Lowenstein singled with one down, followed by a Dauer double. The manager then sent in Nolan to bat for Cruz. Setting up a potential double play, Denny gave Nolan a free pass, followed by an unintentional walk to pinch hitter Singleton, which forced home a run and tied the game at three apiece. Shelby batted for pitcher Davis, facing Willie Hernandez, and drove in Dauer with a sacrifice fly, putting Baltimore up 4–3. Ford came in for Bumbry but failed to keep the rally going when he fanned against Ron Reed.

In the seventh, a Dwyer double and Dauer single gave the Orioles an insurance run, which they wound up needing since the Phillies scored once in the ninth. But Tippy Martinez escaped. The final batter was Joe Morgan, known for his clutch performances over a Cooperstown-caliber career and already boasting two homers in this series. A calm Martinez threw a curve, inducing a soft liner to Sakata, who clutched it tight for the final out. The score was 5–4 and the Orioles were up three games to one. Asked about pitching under late-game pressure against a future Hall-of-Famer, the Orioles' stopper was up front. "To be honest, I wasn't too worried about Morgan," he said. "I've never pitched to him before so he has never seen my curve ball. Our reports said Morgan has a certain power zone and as long as I kept it away from there, I knew I could get him."[69]

All Oriole players, fans, and reporters remembered 1979, so there was no sense of inevitability. In fact, as everyone combed over the numbers for hints, they noticed Murray's 2-for-16 slump. The question of whether or not the star first baseman was overwhelmed by Series-level pressure was much discussed. Baltimore's new booster, Howard Cosell, defended Murray and predicted a breakout Game 5. Phillie fans sarcastically mounted an "Ed-die! Ed-die!" cheer of their own each time he failed at the plate in Games 3 and 4. But Murray remained unfazed. In the top of the second inning, he clubbed a home run off starter Hudson to lead off the inning and give the Orioles a 1–0 lead. Dempsey hit his own home run in the third. Then Murray did it again, with a fourth-inning, two-run shot off the scoreboard that netted the Birds a 4–0 lead. They scored their fifth and final run in the top of the fifth on a double by Dempsey, a Diaz error, Bystrom's wild pitch, and a Bumbry sac fly. On the mound, McGregor shut down the Philadelphia batters all afternoon, going the distance, striking out six, scattering six hits. The lefthander had the satisfaction of gaining the Series-clinching win after losing two previous games, including the last game of the 1979 World Series. When the last batter, Maddox, lined softly to short, Ripken grabbed the ball, held it aloft in two hands, and the on-field celebration began as Jon Miller told the home fans, "The Orioles are the champions of the world!"

Was Murray conscious of the ragging by Phillies fans or nervous because of his slump? Reporters wanted to know. With his father visiting in the clubhouse, the soft-spoken first baseman was mild in his answers. "All I thought was one to nothing," he said of his first homer. "I also thought I took the crowd out of the game."[70] As he spoke, 240 bottles of champagne were uncorked; Murray and Ripken drank from their bottles with their arms draped around each other's shoulders. The Series MVP was the unquenchable Dempsey. When President Reagan phoned in congratulations, Dempsey advised him, "Mr. President, you go tell the Russians we're having an awful good time over here playing baseball!"[71] He was a fitting MVP choice, thanks to his .385 series batting average, which included four doubles and a home run. Asked about his run-ins with Weaver, the catcher was gracious. "He never wanted me to say anything to the pitchers, But I'd feel they needed a push now and them," Dempsey said. "We fought every step of the way. But we had the same game plan—winning."[72] As to the freer atmosphere under the more laid-back Altobelli, Dempsey stressed that he tried to be more than a funny player. "Maybe I'll do something a little crazy from time to time," he admitted. "But I'm no flake. I don't swallow goldfish or anything. I just like to have a little fun."[73] Altobelli was generous in response. "Rick is a team spark plug, a great handler of pitchers," the manager insisted. "But frankly, anything he does with his bat is a bonus." Dempsey, coming off his best-ever hitting performance on the sports highest stage, agreed, "When I hit a home run, it's something of an event," he laughed.[74] Williams moved through the clubhouse, hugging every player, laughing, reveling in his team's triumph and appearing as happy as a man could be.

The Orioles celebrated well into the Philadelphia evening, and the party continued when they got back to Baltimore, where thousands of chanting fans awaited their bus. Patrick McGuire, covering the merriment for the *Sun*, discerned as much relief as release. "Permanently retired with that last out was the choking memory of 1979's Paradise Lost," he reported from a packed saloon. "Replacing it was the sweet ring of the words 'World Champions.'"[75] Dauer was in a community-minded mood. "I'm proud to be a part of the Baltimore organization and proud to be a resident of Baltimore," the second baseman enthused. "I've said all along I'm fortunate God gave me this talent to play baseball. I've said all along, 'Why abuse it?' It's been a great season for us."[76] Williams, visibly moved, complimented the fans: "The way I feel right now, there has been no greater feeling in my life than this world championship. We held the team together and kept it together with the magnificent support of the fans."[77] In Norway, Iowa, there was a celebration as well. Dolly Boddicker, the pitcher's mother, expressed satisfaction that Mike had done his share for the world champions.[78] Murray made a point of stressing that the team's strength went beyond Ripken and himself. "We have a ball club that isn't made up of just two ballplayers," he reminded reporters. McGregor echoed that sentiment: "We proved that you have to have 25 guys to win a world championship."[79]

There were 40,000 fans outside Memorial Stadium when the team bus pulled in to the parking lot at 11:30 p.m. Murray waded into the adoring crowd and shouted, "We are the best of '83!" The fans' reaction was 100 percent predictable: a chorus of "Ed-die! Ed-die-Ed-die" rent the night sky. GM Peters, showing more emotion that usual, addressed the fans directly. "We brought you the only thing we could to pay you back for what you've done for us," he said, alluding to the "Thanks Two Million" campaign that cemented Baltimore's ability to hold on to its team.[80]

Seventeen hours after Ripken caught Maddox's liner, Baltimore had the parade fans had waited for since 1970. The crowds began showing up at 9, and the parade kicked off at noon at Mount Vernon's Washington Monument, wending its way down Charles Street, east on Baltimore, north on Holliday, to City Hall. "Aww, now we gotta ride through that stupid parade,"[81]Dauer had joked earlier. Now, he and his delighted teammates were stuffed into open convertibles and soaking in the warmth of the fall sunshine along with the cheers. Part of the procession was a flatbed carrying all the members of the Section 34 club, led by Wild Bill Hagy, doing his spelling cheer over and over again. Everyone joined in. Clutching his trademark Budweiser, Hagy said that he had taken a 28-minute break between the previous night's imbibing and the current day's. At City Hall, Brooks Robinson was official Master of Ceremonies. Mayor Schaefer wore an Oriole cap and gazed out at the crowd of more than 200,000. He was no doubt enjoying the event more than his interactions with Colt owner Irsay, as he chatted with the ebullient Williams. The owner and mayor were already looking ahead to putting a new stadium at Camden Yards, not far from where they were celebrating. With the thousands of adoring fans cheering O-R-I-O-L-E-S, such fantastic dreams seemed possible. Williams, channeling Shakespeare's Henry V, called the team a band of brothers, while fans and players mingled, calling affectionately and loudly to each other. It was the culmination of years of hope, and seemed to justify all the belief in all the magic that marked Orioles baseball.

There was still more fun in store. One week after the Series win, a biography of Williams appeared on bookshelves around the country. *A Lawyer Who Plays Hardball: Edward Bennett Williams for the Defense*, written by Robert Pack and published by Harper & Row, covered the attorney's amazing career, right at the moment of his greatest achievement as a sportsman. At the same time as they celebrated the Orioles' success, Washington fans noticed that press coverage of D.C.'s efforts to replace the Senators were now revolving around Jack Kent Cooke, rather than speculating on the Orioles moving into RFK. Williams was busily talking up his own team's prospects for 1984. "You're always moving in this business—either forward or backward," he said. "We've got to continue to look for ways to improve ourselves."[82] Mike Boddicker received the *Sporting News* nod as Rookie Pitcher of the Year, and Ripken won the BBWAA's American League MVP award. Typically, the young star credited Murray, his mentor. "The absolute perfect ending to this year," he said before the award was announced, "would be to finish tied in the voting with Eddie. That would be the most appropriate finish to an unbelievable season." After he won the prize, Ripken continued in the same vein. "If Eddie had won and I finished second, I'd feel just as excited. There's no way I would have had the success I had if I wasn't hitting in front of Eddie all year." Murray sounded just as satisfied. "I've been asked often how I would feel if Cal won the MVP award," the first baseman reflected. "I feel he deserves it and I hope he does it again next year and the Orioles win the world championship again. The Orioles' success comes from the team approach and I know no better teammate or friend than Cal."[83]

The baseball press lauded the team again and again, stressing the consistency and depth; the roster-wide approval of role-play duties; the combination of thrift with selective splurges on star players; the blend of player types which somehow resulted in team harmony; and now, a World Series title. "Oh, Those Orioles!" sang out the front page of the *Sporting News*. *Street & Smith's* featured a shot of McGregor and Dempsey hugging after the last series out, and praised the whole organization in an article titled, "The Orioles' Winning Style." *Sports Illustrated* featured a smiling Dempsey on its cover. A *Sun* piece celebrated the Oriole Way on the day of the triumphal parade, quoting Peters: "I believe in consistency, patience, and fairness. We just don't bring people in and out. We tinker with the machine, but we don't overhaul it. Every time the season opens, we have a chance to win something. It sounds like a lot of corn, but you win because of the people in your organization, top to bottom. It's hard to define. I really don't know why players come here from a multitude of backgrounds and succeed."[84] During that off-season, there was broad agreement that the Oriole Way had led naturally to 1983's outcome. What few foresaw was that the 1983 World Series also marked an end point for the team's quarter-of-a-century model for success.

6

THE MAGIC RUNS OUT
(1984 AND AFTER)

It was a strange part of the Maryland sports scene in those days that the baseball team reached the sport's ultimate height while the football team's fortunes spun beyond Baltimore's control. The Colts' 7–9 1983 record was encouraging to fans. The better record sparked a tentative upswing in attendance. But this dawn was false. After the season, even as the Orioles continued their stadium talks, Irsay shuttled between Phoenix and other cities before finally deciding on Indianapolis. While Maryland legislators debated whether or not they could prevent a move through eminent domain, Irsay ordered the movers to pack up the team's belongings and head west on I-70. The Colts' notorious nighttime departure took place in the wee hours of March 28–29, 1984. Thus, when baseball's opening day came just days later, the world champion Orioles were the only big league team in town. Baltimore would wait 13 years for another NFL team (the relocated Browns, renamed the Ravens). During the hiatus, fans adopted a USFL team in 1985, then a CFL team in 1994 and '95. They also followed every relocation and expansion development with obsessive interest. Particularly galling was losing out to Charlotte and Jacksonville in the NFL's expansion derby. Baltimore's old sports-induced fear—that it was not up to major league standards—was intensified by the NFL debacle. Fury lasted until Art Modell announced his team's arrival, in 1995. That move, ironically, kicked off a national conversation about franchise relocation, but Baltimore fans felt they already knew that story. Schaefer calculated that the agony Baltimore fans and politicians felt at the loss of an NFL team could be put to effective use in building support for a new stadium complex. Whereas Annapolis had long nickle-and-dimed the Mayor's proposals to refurbish Memorial, the new mood saw many legislators willing to take hitherto unimaginable steps to keep the Orioles from following the Colts out of town. Schaefer became governor in 1987, meaning he could fend off any attempts to derail the Camden Yards plans he had supported as mayor.

The Orioles set out to defend their championship in 1984 only to be left in the dust by a record-setting Detroit Tiger team which won its first nine games, then went 35–5 over its first forty. The Orioles finished a respectable 85–77, hardly a reason for panic. Their theme that summer was "Catch the Tigers by the Tail," but the year belonged to Sparky Anderson's "Bless You, Boys" team, which ultimately swept the World Series from San Diego. More worrisome than not winning the title was finishing fifth, behind not only the incredible Tigers, but also Toronto, New York, and Boston. The year marked the end of Palmer's productivity, as well as Bumbry's and Singleton's.

Just as Bill James had predicted a year earlier, the Orioles were suddenly old, and needed an infusion from Rochester. All in all, the season was hardly abnormal, given Peters' formula of patience. But Williams—who was still battling his illness, and who was increasingly frustrated with Altobelli's low-key style—appeared frustrated. He promised a shake-up. Where the GM saw patience, the owner saw complacency. They were plainly at odds when they met late in 1984 to plot an overhaul that included the outright releases of Ayala, Singleton, Bumbry, and pitcher Tom Underwood. Williams plunged into the free-agent pool into which Peters had dipped only carefully, coming away with Fred Lynn, Lee Lacy, and Don Aase. Watching the sudden shift in direction, Boswell recognized the end of an era: "The Orioles as we have known them for the last quarter-century—placid, excellent, hermetic, slow to change, tasteful, and conservative—are gone."[1]

The new roster was expensive, and the pressure was on to win in 1985. The team finished fourth, 16 games behind first-place Toronto. These O's were a hard-hitting club, but the pitching showed signs of decay. Boddicker slumped to 12–17, 4.07; McGregor went 14–14, 4.81, Dennis Martinez 13–11, 5.15; Davis 10–8, 4.53. They were never really in the race, which drove the free-spending Williams to distraction. Increasingly frustrated with Altobelli, he called his recent world championship-winning manager "cement head" and yearned publicly for Weaver's intensity. Williams fired Altobelli halfway through the season, bringing Weaver back from retirement, hoping to reignite the old fires. Altobelli felt ill-used and said so. Weaver's record over the second half was .500, the team's final mark just 83–78.

1986 marked the last attempt to fire up the old system in conjunction with new free agents. Peters sought to shore up the bullpen via free agency, which highlighted the fact that there was nothing worthwhile coming through the Rochester pipeline. The season had its high-water mark in August, when the club got hot and seemed set to overtake the division-leading Red Sox. But the Orioles collapsed down the stretch, finishing 18–43, including 8–24 in September and October. Instead of charging into contention like Weaver's teams of old, this Oriole squad disintegrated, falling all the way to 73–89, good enough for dead last. Weaver retired again, this time without the sentimental outburst of his previous departure, but certainly without any second thoughts.

Cal Ripken, Sr., finally got his chance to manage the big league club. But the 1987 Orioles were atrocious, playing a brand of ball fans—and manager—barely recognized. They lacked quality pitching and defense, featuring only power at the plate. The front office looked uncertain whether to patch the roster or blow it up. Their record sagged to a once-unfathomable 67–95. At season's end, Williams fired Peters but retained Ripken as manager. Prospects for 1987 were grim, lightened only by the arrival in Baltimore of Billy Ripken, giving fans the pleasure of seeing the manager handle his two sons. Discouragingly, the senior Ripken found himself teaching young pitchers and players skills and routines they would once have learned in the low minors. Obviously, the systematic vertical integration of training and method that long marked the organization's best practices was disappearing. Word began to filter up in the press that, down at Rochester and Charlotte, the emphasis was on winning rather than training players to play Oriole baseball. "That's a big change," said one *Washington Post* source. "It used to be that the goal was to get them ready for Earl. Period. Nothing else mattered. You could throw a no-hitter at AAA and get chewed out. These guys come up now and their mechanics are terrible and they have no idea how to pitch."[2]

At this time, Williams' cancer was recurring, interfering with some of the best career options he ever faced. All of Washington was abuzz in 1987 with the story that the Orioles owner was President Reagan's choice to take over as director of the CIA. He longed to accept the post, but demurred due to his uncertain medical status.[3] One of the more discouraging aspects of the Orioles' fall was the way Williams' impatience focused on Murray. The owner, desperate to regain a winning edge, wanted his superstar to assume an assertive leadership role. But the quiet and reserved Murray was no firebrand, and ill-suited to the kind of clubhouse role Williams imagined for him. The owner complained about his star to reporters, which Murray could never forgive. It set up Murray as the fall guy for the team's intrinsic woes, paving the way for his trade to the Dodgers after the 1988 season. As for Ripken, Sr., he was set up to fail. With the minor league teams in chaos—their ownership groups feuding and management distracted at best—his new talent was as poor as his veterans were undistinguished. With former White Sox head Roland Hemond at the GM spot, the Orioles started 1988 0–6 before Williams pulled the trigger, firing his manager, running the grave risk of alienating the younger Ripkens, and reaching out to Frank Robinson to rekindle the old spark. It did not work, at least not right away, as the 1988 team went into the record books with a 21-game losing streak to start the season. Now the Orioles were as notorious as they were once admired, the butt of late-night comedians and opposing fans before they became, simply, too pathetic to mock. As they staggered to a 54–107 record, the Orioles came full circle back to 1954's inaugural season, when the relocated St. Louis Browns won 54 games against 100 losses. But there was one highlight that season. When the Orioles returned to Baltimore after winning their first game on the road, 50,402 fans showed up to cheer. The mood in Memorial was upbeat, the 1–21 start notwithstanding. A 9–4 win over the Rangers made the evening feel like a celebration of Baltimore's baseball tradition.[4] So did the announcement that the team was prepared to sign an agreement to remain in Baltimore, building a new ballpark at the Camden Yards site long coveted by Williams and Schaefer.

Governor Schaefer devoted much of his political clout to pushing a stadium bill through the legislature, ensuring the Orioles' future in Baltimore and—it was devoutly hoped—attracting another NFL team. The season ended not just with losses, then, but with hope for the future. It was fortunate that Williams was there for the announcement. Mere weeks later, he passed away, finally the victim of the cancer he had battled for so long. But despite the fallen state of his team, the high-flying celebrity lawyer did leave his Baltimore legacy intact. Widely viewed as likely, if not bound, to move the Orioles to Washington when he bought them in 1979, Williams was as good as his word when he said that Baltimore fans would have the chance to show their mettle and keep the team. "For so long as the city will support this team, it will stay here," he vowed in 1979.[5] The 1,660,738 who came through the turnstiles to see 1988's worst team showed that Williams was correct. He paid them back by inking the Camden Yards deal.

Williams had brought in a junior lawyer, Larry Lucchino, to help with team operations. Lucchino's first foray into sports was helping his boss with the Redskins. By the late 1980s, Lucchino was deeply involved with the Orioles, especially on the stadium front. The two attorneys bonded deeply because both the senior and junior partners battled cancer, and Williams became a personal, not just a legal, mentor to Lucchino.[6] Over the next few seasons, it was Lucchino who would make many of the decisions affecting Baltimore's baseball future. He assisted with the estate sale of the Orioles in December 1988. The new purchasing group included Lucchino, majority partner Eli Jacobs, who was a New York investor, and the Maryland-based Shriver family. Both Lucchino and Jacobs wanted the new Camden Yards stadium to be something memorable and different, and it was they who negotiated with the HOK Architectural firm to come up with the model for a ballpark that included old-fashioned intimacies and historically accurate touches along with modern amenities. Their success in arriving at a balance between the old and new, and at designing and constructing a stadium which fit into its neighborhood rather than looming over it, resulted in Oriole Park at Camden Yards becoming the gem of the majors, and the forerunner of a whole generation of emulative parks across the country.

The woes of 1988 made 1989 all the more pleasurable, as a young Oriole team shocked baseball by going 87–75 and challenging the division-winning Blue Jays until the last weekend of the season. Frank Robinson's managing job that year was astounding. In 1990, the Orioles slipped back to fifth, going 76–85. They skidded further in 1991, going 67–95. Robinson was fired, replaced by onetime Oriole catcher Johnny Oates. But by then, attentions were moving to the imminent move downtown. The final game at Memorial Stadium was a celebration of its baseball past. Rick Dempsey read a poem of his own, "The Lady in Red," while as many former Orioles as the team could track down came to the ballpark. They surprised fans, greeting them at the gates before the game, and assembling on the field afterward for a farewell scene fit for the ages. Home plate and the distinctive outfield foul poles were to be carted downtown to the new ballpark, and for one last time, the fans filled Memorial Stadium with their O-R-I-O-L-E-S. But some things had changed. Wild Bill was on a semi-strike, having been kicked out years prior for protesting the new ban on bringing beer into the ballpark by ceremoniously tossing his cooler from the upper deck. In Section 13, the infamous red line had appeared in 1984. Seats below that line, which were the equivalent of higher-priced seats nearby, went up in price, much to the dismay of that section's loyalists. So moving from Memorial seemed appropriate, since changes were already underway. In 1992, the Orioles opened their new digs to incredible, unprecedented levels of acclaim. The ballpark was the star, the most celebrated new stadium since Dodger Stadium. The team responded positively, climbing to 89–73.

Like the 1982 farewell to Weaver, the farewell to Memorial Stadium was one of the most moving sports ceremonies anyone ever beheld. But this time, too, there was a second act; more life for the well-worn, well-loved park. The AA-level Bowie Baysox, who moved from Hagerstown after 1992, needed a place to play while their Prince George's County stadium was being built. So, in 1993, while the Orioles played downtown, the sounds of ballgames once again could be heard on 33rd Street. Attendance was minuscule, but nostalgic fans found their way back for a last baseball outing in the place that held magical memories. The next year, Canadian football came to Memorial Stadium, with a CFL expansion team. That lasted two seasons, culminating in a Grey Cup championship in 1995 for the Stallions, modeled on the old Colts. In 1996 and 1997, the NFL's transplanted Ravens played there, giving fans yet more chances to relive their memories, albeit of the pigskin variety. It was not until 1998, when the Ravens moved into their own Camden Yards–style stadium, that Memorial was demolished. Before the destruction, there was a brisk trade in artifacts, including bleachers and bricks, for fans who wanted a piece of their past.

The next big change for the Orioles came in 1993, when Baltimore lawyer Peter Angelos purchased the team at auction following Eli Jacobs' managed bankruptcy. Among the competitors was the DeWitt family, of the old St. Louis Browns. Had they purchased the team, it would have been an unusual but fitting historical twist. But Angelos, who made his fortune as a tort attorney representing plaintiffs in asbestos and tobacco lawsuits, came away with the franchise for $173 million. He told the press his purchase was an act of civic pride, and his consortium of owners included Baltimore celebrities like tennis star Pam Shriver and author Tom Clancy. Angelos was Baltimore-born, with political experience, and would develop his own ownership style. He also announced plans to chase an NFL team. Fans appreciated his Baltimore-first rhetoric and attitude.

Angelos' Orioles enjoyed early success, with consecutive playoff appearances in 1996 and '97. Fans cherished Cal Ripken's pursuit of Lou Gehrig's consecutive-games record. The nights he tied and broke that hallowed mark were clearly the most magical moments to date in the new ballpark. More than one observer opined that Ripken's demeanor and the palpable love fans showed for him on September 6, 1995, helped to restore the emotional connection the major leagues sundered through their disastrous 1994 labor Armageddon. Angelos had earlier opposed a replacement player scheme that might have cheated Ripken out of the record. Later, as the 2,130 mark approached and was passed, the team unveiled numerical banners on the warehouse.

Another display of tact and respect for the team's past came when the Orioles resigned Eddie Murray in 1996. His return to Baltimore went far in erasing the memories of the onetime Oriole leader's bitter departure in 1988. It was fitting that Murray broke the 500-homer mark as an Oriole. Here again, the team counted down the chase with banners, and the fans responded with the old cheer, "Ed-die! Ed-die! Ed-die!" In these respects, Angelos' status as a Baltimorean coupled with his long record of hometown spirit and philanthropy demonstrated a connection to the team's past which fans could appreciate. At least there was official recognition of Orioles Magic. Angelos also developed a reputation for argumentativeness as a result of run-ins with other owners, as well as with his own managers. This boiled over with 1997 Manager of the Year Dave Johnson, brought in as part of yet another effort to restore the Oriole Way. Johnson was let go following a season in which he managed the team to baseball's best record but lost to Cleveland in the playoffs. Ray Miller was his replacement.

One of Angelos' major issues was the ultimate disposition of the Washington baseball question. What Kuhn termed a "solution for the moment" had moved well past that moment, especially as the Orioles began to rack up losing seasons. Their futility after 1997 loosened their grip on the loyalties of fans to the south, and brought into question their status as a regional colossus. At the same time, the Montreal Expos, whose fans never recovered from losing the 1994 season to a strike—a season in which Montreal posted the majors' best record—were languishing. After examining options, the major leagues settled on the obvious choice, returning a big league team to the nation's capital. The Nationals adopted the Senators' old curly W caps, adding blue to the red and white color scheme. Ironically, Frank Robinson was their manager. Angelos, who had fought the reintroduction of baseball into D.C., issued a set of barbed comments designed to ensure that Washingtonians would think twice before supporting a team he owned. Eventually, Angelos and the Nationals owners arrived at a negotiated cable-television-sharing arrangement. Later, they wound up arguing over the deal in court. The days of the Orioles serving as Washington's surrogate were finished. While there remained a distinct Oriole presence in the Maryland suburbs, the Nationals were more than happy to construct a fan culture of their own.

The Orioles suffered 14 straight losing seasons after 1997, prompting much nostalgia about whatever it was that made them so successful for so long. At the same time, fans took football's Ravens to heart, thanks largely to two Super Bowl victories and frequent playoff berths. Baltimore began to resemble a retooled version of itself from the late 1950s and early 1960s: a city with a great football team that also happened to have a baseball team. The words "Oriole Way" had come to sound folkloric, legendary. Fans were certain that there once was such a thing, but they had a hard time describing it. One of the saddest indications of the fruitless quest for a restoration was Mike Flanagan's term in the Orioles' front office. He served as vice president for baseball operations—a confusing title, but the hands-on Angelos did not believe in hiring General Managers. Flanagan's duties did resemble those of a GM, though, and he worked assiduously to help the organization turn the corner. In 2009, the team hired the respected Andy MacPhail, son of Lee, grandson of Larry, as President for Baseball Operations. Flanagan's responsibilities dwindled and he left the front office. Plagued by depression accentuated by his inability to end the team's struggles, the witty fan favorite committed suicide in 2011.

As for Orioles Magic, during the 14 years of losing, the fans cheered up whenever old clips from 1979–1983 were played on the video screen. If a former Oriole reappeared as part of a roster or coaching staff, he could count on a friendly welcome. But not until manager Buck Showalter arrived in 2012, taking the Orioles to an unexpected Wild Card berth, did the video clips spark anything beyond wistfulness. But the arrival of Showalter, along with the hiring of Dan Duquette, who continued MacPhail's system-wide overhaul, brought a new degree of professionalism to the Orioles organization. The losing finally stopped. Fans of the visitors gave way to orange-and-black-clad rooters, reminding observers that Baltimore was once a passionate baseball town. These fans contemplated the chance that those mysterious phenomena revered by the older generation—the Oriole Way and Orioles Magic—might return. Nervously, they allowed hope to reintroduce itself as Baltimore began to believe in the Orioles, and baseball, once again.

CHAPTER NOTES

Introduction

1. Peter Morris, "Excelsior/Pastime Base Ball Club of Baltimore," in Morris et al., *Base Ball Pioneers: The Clubs and Players Who Spread the Sport Nationwide* (Jefferson, NC: McFarland, 2012), 253.

2. James H. Bready, *The Home Team: Our O's, Baseball and Baltimore*, 4th ed. (Baltimore: James H. Bready, 1984), 4.

3. Harold Seymour and Dorothy Seymour Mills, *Baseball: The Early Years* (New York: Oxford University Press, 1960), 15–16; Gerald Astor, *The Baseball Hall of Fame 50th Anniversary Book* (New York: Prentice-Hall, 1988), 1.

4. David Nemec, Stephen Hanks, *et al.*, *The Baseball Chronicle: Year-By-Year History of Major League Baseball* (Lincolnwood, IL: Publications International, 2003).

5. Gerald Astor, *The Baseball Hall of Fame 50th Anniversary Book* (New York: Prentice-Hall, 1988), 4.

6. *Ibid.*, 5.

7. Bready, *Baseball in Baltimore: The First 100 Years* (Baltimore, Johns Hopkins University Press, 1998), 6–10.

8. *Ibid.*, 34–35.

9. Bready, *Baseball in Baltimore*, 44.

10. *Ibid.*, 39–40.

11. Bready, *Baseball in Baltimore*, 73.

12. Donald Dewey and Nicholas Acocella, *Total Ballclubs: The Ultimate Book of Baseball Teams* (Toronto: Sport Media, 2005), 29.

13. Bready, *Home Team*, 86.

14. Seymour and Mills, *Baseball: The Early Years*, 289–290.

15. *Bready, Baseball in Baltimore*, 115.

16. James A. Riley, *The Biographical Encyclopedia of the Negro Baseball Leagues* (New York: Carroll & Graf, 1994), 49.

17. Tom Flynn, *Baseball in Baltimore* (Charleston, SC: Arcadia, 2008), 83–85.

18. Lawrence S. Ritter, *Lost Ballparks: A Celebration of Baseball's Legendary Fields* (New York: Viking Studio, 1992), 187–191.

19. *Ibid.*, 191.

20. Fred Lieb, *Baltimore Orioles: The History of a Colorful Team in Baltimore and St. Louis* (Carbondale: Southern Illinois University Press, 2004), 214. First published 1955 by G.P. Putnam's Sons.

21. Bill Veeck, with Ed Linn, *Veeck as in Wreck: The Autobiography of Bill Veeck* (Chicago: University of Chicago Press, 2001), 213. First published 1962, Signet Books.

22. *Ibid.*, 213.

23. *Ibid.*, 224.

24. It is one of the great what-ifs of baseball history that the Browns, owned then by Donald Barnes, contemplated moving to Los Angeles in 1941. A meeting with major league owners to discuss the feasibility of the plan was scheduled for December 8, 1941, but Japan's attack on Pearl Harbor intervened. See Charles Kupfer, *Indomitable Will: Turning Defeat into Victory from Pearl Harbor to Midway* (New York: Continuum/Bloomsbury, 2012), 30–31.

25. *Ibid.*, 229.

26. James Edward Miller, *The Baseball Business: Pursuing Pennants and Profits in Baltimore* (Chapel Hill: University of North Carolina Press, 1990), 28–31.

27. William B. Mead, *Even the Browns: Baseball During World War II* (Mineola, NY: Dover Publications, 2010 c1978), 241.

28. Miller, *Baseball Business*, 31–35.

29. Ogden Nash, "You Can't Kill an Oriole," <http://www.baseball-almanac.com/poetry/po_you.shtml>.

30. *Baltimore Sun*, September 30, 1953.

31. *Washington Post*, September 30, 1953.

32. Bready, *Home Team*, 47 and 49.

33. Jim Henneman, *Baltimore Orioles: 60 Years of Orioles Magic* (San Rafael, CA: Insight, 2015), 37.

34. Joseph Reichler, *The Baseball Encyclopedia* (New York: Macmillan, 1982), 410.

35. Henneman, *Baltimore Orioles*, 36.

36. Vince Bagli and Norman L. Macht, *Sundays at 2:00 with the Baltimore Colts* (Centerville, MD: Tidewater, 1995), ix–xi.

37. Arthur Donovan, Jr., and Bill Drury, *Fatso: Football When Men Were Really Men* (New York: William Morrow, 1987), 135–136.

38. Dave Anderson, *Great Quarterbacks of the NFL* (New York: Random House, 1965), 16.

39. Michael MacCambridge, *America's Game: The Epic Story of How Pro Football Captured a Nation* (New York: Anchor, 2005), 92.

40. Warren Corbett, *The Wizard of Waxahachie: Paul Richards and the End of Baseball as We Knew It* (Dallas: Southern Methodist University Press, 2009), 157.

41. *Ibid.*, 111.

42. Paul Richards, *Modern Baseball Strategy* (New York: Prentice-Hall, 1955), 160.

43. *Ibid.*, 143.

44. Ted Patterson, *The Baltimore Orioles: Forty Years of Magic from 33rd Street to Camden Yards* (Dallas: Taylor, 1994), 38.

45. Corbett, *Wizard of Waxahachie*, 212.

46. Michael Olesker, *The Colts' Baltimore: A City and Its Love Affair in the 1950s* (Baltimore: Johns Hopkins University Press, 2008), 79.

47. Corbett, *Wizard of Waxahachie*, 183.

48. *Ibid.*, 183.

49. *Ibid.*, 176.

50. *Ibid.*, 163.

51. *Ibid.*, 176.

52. Richards, *Modern Baseball Strategy*, 1–10.

53. *Ibid.*, ix.

54. Patterson, *Baltimore Orioles*, 39.

55. Corbett, *Wizard of Waxahachie*, ix.

56. Ron Smith, *The Ballpark Book: A Journey Through the Fields of Baseball Magic* (St. Louis: Sporting News, 2003), 213.

57. Baltimore Orioles 1983 Media Guide, 53.

58. *Ibid.*, 39.

59. Reichler, *Baseball Encyclopedia*, 434.

60. *Ibid.*, 434.

61. Corbett, *Wizard of Waxahachie*, 239.

62. *Ibid.*, 239.

63. Bready, *Home Team*, 60–64.

64. Alexander Peters, *Heroes of the Major Leagues* (New York: Random House, 1967), 18.

65. Patterson, *Baltimore Orioles*, 82–83.

66. Miller, *Baseball Business*, 96–102.

67. Mike Gesker, *The Orioles Encyclopedia: A Half Century of History and Highlights* (Baltimore: Johns Hopkins University, 2009), 531.

68. *Ibid.*, 109–110.

69. *Ibid.*, 83.

70. Peters, *Heroes of the Major Leagues*, 18.

71. Gesker, *Orioles Encyclopedia*, 430.

72. *Ibid.*, 523.

73. *Ibid.*, 435.

74. Albert Sehlstedt and Rafael Alvarez, "Jerold C. Hoffberger, 80, Former Orioles Owner, Dies," *Baltimore Sun*, April 10, 1999.

75. Gesker, *Orioles Encyclopedia*, 13.

76. *Ibid.*

77. *Ibid.*, 437.

78. *Ibid.*

79. Frank Robinson with Al Silverman, *My Life in Baseball* (Garden City, NY: Doubleday, 1968), 180.

80. *Ibid.*

81. Dave Klein, *Great Infielders of the Major Leagues* (New York: Random House, 1972), 21–30.

82. Louis Berney, *Tales from the Orioles Dugout* (Champaign, IL: Sports Publishing, 2004), 94.

83. Earl Weaver with Barry Stainback, *It's What You Learn After You Know It All That Counts* (New York: Fireside, 1983), 79.

84. Roger Angell, *Once More Around the Park: A Baseball Reader* (New York: Ballantine, 1992), 103.

85. Gesker, *Orioles Encyclopedia*, 501.
86. *Ibid.*
87. Patterson, *Baltimore Orioles*, 91.
88. *Ibid.*, 114.
89. John Eisenberg, *From 33rd Street to Camden Yards: An Oral History of the Baltimore Orioles* (Chicago: Contemporary, 2001), 256.
90. Dan Nathan, *Baltimore Sports: Stories from Charm City* (Fayetteville: University of Arkansas Press, 2016), 218.
91. Smith, *Ballpark Book*, 99.
92 Ken Nigro, "Weaver, Ump Luciano Resume Trading Insults," *Sporting News*, March 10, 1979, 39.
93. Ron Luciano and David Fisher, *The Fall of the Roman Umpire* (NY: Bantam, 1986), 239–240.
94. Thomas Boswell, *Why Time Begins on Opening Day* (New York: Penguin, 1984), 25.
95. *Ibid.*, 24.
96. Thomas Boswell, *How Life Imitates the World Series* (New York: Penguin, 1983), 150.
97. *Ibid.*, 69.
98. *Ibid.*, 50.
99. *Ibid.*, 60.
100. George Will, *Bunts: Curt Flood, Camden Yards, Pete Rose and Other Reflections on Baseball* (New York: Scribner's, 1998), 50.
101. Will, *Bunts*, 45.
102. Dewey and Acocella, *Total Ballclubs*, 640–641.
103. Ted Leavengood, *Ted Williams and the 1969 Washington Senators: The Last Winning Season* (Jefferson, NC: McFarland, 2009), 7–15.
104. Shelby Whitfield, *Kiss It Goodbye* (New York: Abelard & Whitfield, 1973), X.
105. Leavengood, *Ted Williams*, 189–200.
106. *Ibid.*, 201–202.

Chapter 1

1. William Legget, "Birds Bug Off Toward a Title," *Sports Illustrated*, September 3, 1973, 20–21.
2. Eisenberg, *From 33rd Street*, 268.
3. *Ibid.*, 266–267.
4. Marvin Miller, *A Whole Different Ballgame: The Inside Story of the Baseball Revolution* (Chicago: Ivan R. Dee, 2004), 238–253.
5. Douglas S. Looney, "Smile for the Birdies," *Sports Illustrated*, June 18, 1979.
6. Thom Loverro, *Orioles Essential: Everything You Need to Know to Be a Real Fan* (Chicago: Triumph, 2007), 82–83.
7. Jim Henneman, *Baltimore Orioles*, 167.
8. Shirley Povich,"Orioles Sale Seen Imminent," *Washington Post*, January 17, 1979, D1.
9. *Ibid.*
10. *Ibid.*
11. Nancy Scannell, "Simon Withdraws Offer For Orioles," *Washington Post*, February 6, 1979, D1.
12. Shirley Povich, "Hoffberger Treats All Bidders Alike," *Washington Post*, February 7, 1979, D1.
13. *Ibid.*
14. Albert Theodore Powers, *The Business of Baseball* (Jefferson, NC: McFarland, 2003), 248–249.
15. Bob Maisel, "The Morning After: Renegotiation Is Name of Game," *Baltimore Sun*, February 22, 1979, B1.
16. Bob Maisel, "Baltimore Boosters Come to the Fore," *Baltimore Sun*, February 17, 1979, B7.
17. *Ibid.*
18. G. Jefferson Price III, "Hughes to Back $2.5 Million State Loan to Help Keep Orioles in Baltimore," *Baltimore Sun*, March 14, 1979, A1.
19. "Orioles Advocates, Inc.," *Orioles 1983 Media Guide*, 53.
20. Charles V. Flowers, "Schaefer Donates Aide to Orioles Ticket Drive," *Baltimore Sun*, March 14, 1979, A9.
21. "Ticket Pledges Grow; Snow Delays Bird Talks," *Baltimore Sun*, February 22, 1979.
22. Jim Henneman, "Drive Takes Wing to Keep Birds in Baltimore," *Sporting News*, February 24, 1979.
23. Jim Henneman, "Sale Rumors Upset Orioles' Players," *Sporting News*, February 3, 1979, 39.
24. Ken Nigro, "Orioles Need to Teach Flyhawks How to Talk," *Sporting News*, March 3, 1979, 31.
25. Thomas Boswell, "Feisty Operation Survives Crisis," Thomas Boswell, *Washington Post*, March 3, 1979, D1.

26. Richard Dozer, "Baltimore Orioles," *Street & Smith's Official 1979 Yearbook*," 24.

27. Ken Nigro, "Orioles are Billed as Mystery Contestant," *Sporting News*, April 7, 1979, 35.

28. *Ibid.*, 40.

29. Ken Nigro, "Orioles Need to Teach Flyhawks How to Talk," *Sporting News*, March 3, 1979, 31.

30. Boswell, *How Life Imitates the World Series*, 64.

31. *Ibid.*, 232.

32. "Insiders Say," *Sporting News*, 4.

33. Boswell, *How Life Imitates the World Series*, 233.

34. *Ibid.*, 103.

35. Jim Palmer and Jim Dale, *Palmer and Weaver: Together We Were Eleven Foot Nine* (Kansas City: Andrews & McMeel, 1996), 116.

36. *Ibid.*, 124–127.

37. Nola Breglio, "Earl Weaver: Hall of Fame Skipper," *Sports Illustrated*, September 25, 2000.

38. William Gildea, *When the Colts Belonged to Baltimore: A Father and a Son, a Team and a Time* (Baltimore: Johns Hopkins University Press, 1994), 253–261.

39. Bob Maisel, "Wild Bill and the Birds Are Two of a Kind," *Baltimore Sun*, September 30, 1979, C1.

40. "A.L. Flashes," *Sporting News*, August 18, 1979, 37.

41. Maisel, "Wild Bill and the Birds Are Two of a Kind," C1.

42. Kevin Cowherd, "Seventh Inning Stretch Belonged to Denver Orioles: Time After Time, 'Thank God I'm a Country Boy' Got the Stadium Rocking," *Baltimore Sun*, October 14, 1997.

43. *Ibid.*

44. Nigro, "'Grow Up!' Weaver Fumes as Palmer Lists His Pains," *Sporting News*, July 7, 1979, 7.

45. Palmer & Dale, *Palmer and Weaver*, 125.

46. Nigro, "'Grow Up!'" 7.

47. *Ibid.*

48. *Ibid.*

49. *Ibid.*

50. "O's Pennant Caps Record Smashing Attendance Year," *World Series 1979 Official Program*, Cardinal Publishing Company, 1979, 13.

51. *Ibid.*, 7.

52. Bready, *The Home Team*, 94.

53. Looney, "Smile for the Birdies," *Sports Illustrated*, June 18, 1979.

54. Kent Baker, "Birds Set Fast Pace at Gate, Too," *Baltimore Sun*, June 22, 1979, C7.

55. "Bill O'Donnell—Doug Decinces Homerun [*sic.*] June 22, 1979"; YouTube, uploaded October 3, 2012, accessed February 17, 2016.

56. Charley Eckman and Fred Neil, *It's a Very Simple Game* (Baltimore: Borderlands, 1995, 162–163.

57. Kent Baker, "Orioles Rally to Shade Tigers, 6–5," *Baltimore Sun*, June 23, 1979, B5.

58. *Ibid.*

59. Rob Kasper, "T.G.I.F.: Thanks for the Memories, Abner Doubleday," *Baltimore Sun*, June 22, 1979, B1.

60. Bob Maisel, "The Morning After, Oriole Baseball, Call It Unique," *Baltimore Sun*, June 24, 1979, C1.

61. Dave Kindred, "Williams Wants National League Team in DC," *Washington Post*, June 19, 1979, D1.

62. Nancy Scannell, "Columbia Stadium Proposed," *Washington Post*, June 26, 1979, D6.

63. Susan Dooley, "Entertaining: Take Me Out to the Ballgame," *Washington Post*, June 25, 1979, B5.

64. Thomas Boswell, "Old Ways Paying Off for Birds," *Washington Post*. June 29, 1979, D1.

65. *Ibid.*

66. *Ibid.*

67. *Ibid.*

68. *Ibid.*

69. Ken Nigro, "Singleton Super, But Voters Ignore Him," *Sporting News*, July 14, 1979.

70. Ken Nigro, "Big Test Ahead—Can Orioles Keep Lead?" *Sporting News*, August 11, 1979, 21.

71. Ken Nigro, "Winning? A Way of Life for Soaring Orioles," *Sporting News*, August 18, 1979, 3.

72. *Ibid.*

73. *Ibid.*

74. *Ibid.*

75. *Ibid.*

76. Evan Thomas, *The Man to See: Edward Bennett Williams, Ultimate Insider;*

Legendary Trial Lawyer (New York: Simon & Schuster, 1991), 378–391.

77. Ken Nigro, "Birds Sold for $12 Million," *Sporting News*, August 18, 1979, 6.
78. *Ibid.*
79. Ken Nigro, "Bird-Watching Newest Craze in Baltimore," *Sporting News*, August 25, 1979, 5.
80. Jane Leavy, "The Fans of Baltimore: Defiant Oriole Fans Await Decision," *Washington Post*, August 12, 1979, D1.
81. "81 at Memorial Stadium in '80," *Baltimore Sun*, September 1, 1979, A14.
82. Thomas, *The Man to* See, 397–398.
83. Theo Lippman, Jr., "Back in the Saddle Again," *Baltimore Sun*, October 1, 1979, A12.
84. Thomas Boswell, "Orioles Have Aces, but Playoff Deck is Stacked," *Washington Post*, October 2, 1979, D1.
85. Thomas Boswell, "Orioles, Angels, Open 'Scary' Playoff Tonight," *Washington Post*, October 2, 1979, D1.
86. Ken Denglinger, "Birds at a Pinnacle, Colts in the Pits: Rapture Over Birds, Despair Over Colts," *Washington Post*, October 2, 1979, D1.
87. Ken Nigro, "Birds Sweat it Out to Win," *Baltimore Sun*, October 5, 1979, A1.
88. Shirley Povich, "Orioles Win in 42 Minutes, then get Dose of Humility," *Washington Post*, October 5, 1979, D4.
89. *Ibid.*
90. Ron Fimrite, "A Series of Ups and Downs," *Sports Illustrated*, October 22, 1979, accessed at http://www.sivault.com.
91. *Ibid.*
92. *Ibid.*
93. *Ibid.*
94. *Ibid.*
95. Ron Fimrite, "Rising from the Ashes," *Sports Illustrated*, October 29, 1979, accessed at https://www.si.com/vault.
96. "Carter was 'Neutral,'" *Baltimore Sun*, October 18, 1979, C6.
97. "Carter was 'Neutral,'" *Baltimore Sun*, C6.
98. Bryan Burwell, "Cosell Faces Verbal Assault Everwhere he Goes," *Baltimore Sun*, October 18, 1979, C6.
99. C. Fraser Smith, "Gloom? You Could Almost Touch it as O's Fell," *Baltimore Sun*, October 18, 1979, A1.
100. "O's Pennant Caps Record Smashing Attendance Year," *1979 Official World Series Program*, 13–15.
101. *Ibid.*, 15.
102. Bob Maisel, "Bird Front Office Showed Lots of Class, Too," *Baltimore Sun*, October 20, 1979, B5.
103. Michael Olesker, "Now Orioles Begin Season of TV Spots, Pitfalls, Putting Down Roots," *Baltimore Sun*, October 18, 1979, D1.

Chapter 2

1. Dave Brady, "Williams vs. Rozelle: No Progress," *Washington Post*, January 17, 1980, E4.
2. Ken Nigro, "Oriole Fever Running Wild in Baltimore," *Sporting News*, January 12, 1980, 42.
3. *Ibid.*
4. Jackson Diehl, "Md. Leaders to Back Bills on Oriole Stadium Loans," *Washington Post*, February 12, 1980, C2.
5. "Hughes Eyes O's as Lever for Project," *Washington Post*, February 16, 1980, D8.
6. Stan Isle, "Wheel of Fortune," *Sporting News*, February 2, 1980, 22.
7. Gildea, *op. cit.* 131–161.
8. Angus Phillips, "Orioles, Having Gotten Even, Are Minus Only Stanhouse," *Washington Post*, February 24, 1980, F7.
9. "Orioles Magic—Feel it Happen," (record), Perfect Pitch, Incorporated of Maryland, 1980.
10. Ken Nigro, "O's Flanagan High and Wry: Southpaw Values Tradition," *Sporting News*, April 12, 1980, 8.
11. *Ibid.*, 8.
12. Ken Nigro, "Oriole 'Slap in the Face' Irks Smith," *Sporting News*, March 22, 1980, 44.
13. Ken Nigro, "Oriole Farm Show Takes Upward Turn," *Sporting News*, January 26, 1980, 54.
14. *Ibid.*
15. Ken Nigro, "Williams Won't Play Free Agent Game," *Sporting News*, February 25, 1980, 44.
16. Dick Young, "Young Ideas," *Sporting News*, February 16, 1980, 12.
17. "Insiders Say," *Sporting News*, April 5, 1980, 6.
18. Ken Nigro, "Sobering Sight in Nica-

ragua: Gun-Toting Kids," *Sporting News*, April 5, 1980, 50.

19. Christopher Dickey, "Orioles Win by Losing in Nicaragua; Birds Lose to Nicaragua But Win Over the Revolutionaries; Baltimore's Birds Pitch In to Polish Slumping US Image," *Washington Post*, March 16, 1980, A1.

20. Angus Phillips, "Orioles, Having Gotten Even, Are Minus Only Stanhouse," *Washington Post*, February 24, 1980, F7.

21. Miller, *op. cit.*, 285.

22. *Ibid.*, 290.

23. Ken Nigro, "Birds Go Through Motions," *Baltimore Sun*, April 6, 1980, C1.

24. Murray Chass, "Free Agency a Plus for All, Weaver Says," *Sporting News*, April 5, 1980, 30.

25. *Ibid.*, 30.

26. *Ibid.*, 30

27. Seymour Smith, "Singleton Says 'Experts' Underestimate Birds Again," *Baltimore Sun*, April 13, 1980, C1.

28. Ken Nigro, "Oriole No-Names Scoff at Skeptics," *Sporting News*, April 12, 1980, 20.

29. Thomas Boswell, "A Fundamental Oriole Spring: With the Blooms Comes Basics," *Washington Post*, March 20, 1980, G1.

30. *Ibid.*

31. *Ibid.*

32. *Ibid.*

33. Alan Goldstein, "Birds Have Much to Remember About 1981," *Baltimore Sun*, April 15, 1980, C1.

34. Furman Bisher, "Weaver Finally Feels Secure as a Manager," *Sporting News*, April 5, 1980, 16.

35. Ken Nigro, "Stone New Big Bird With Martinez Hurt," *Sporting News*, April 19, 1980, 27.

36. Bob Maisel, "Take a Tip from Weaver Fans, Don't Panic," *Baltimore Sun*, April 25, 1980, B1.

37. Ken Nigro, "Orioles Find New Weapon: Dynamite in Dempsey's Bat," *Sporting News*, May 10, 1980, 17.

38. Ken Nigro, "Orioles Leave Wakeup Call for Their Bats," *Sporting News*, May 17, 1980, 10.

39. *Ibid.*, 10

40. Jane Leavey and Peter Mehlman, "Witching Hour for Baseball is Just Days Away; Clock's Winding Down for Players,

Owners, Fans; Sides Still Deadlocked on Compensation Issue," *Washington Post*, May 18, 1980, F1.

41. *Ibid.*

42. Thomas Boswell, "Resignation, Guilt in Baltimore as Strike Sinks In," *Washington Post*, May 23, 1980, D1.

43. Thomas Boswell, "Williams Group Stirred Kuhn, Spurred Settlement; Flexibility Forged Formula of Truce," *Washington Post*, May 24, 1980, C1.

44. Ken Denglinger, "First Loud Chirp: Easy Schedule Beckons as Orioles Finally Show Signs of Life; Modest Surge Shows Ingredients of Old," *Washington Post*, May 25, 1980, F1.

45. Peter Gammons, "A.L. Beat," *Sporting News*, March 21, 1981, 40.

46. *Ibid.*

47. John Feinstein, "Orioles Flop, 10–6; Indians Tattoo Orioles; Indians Rout Disgusted Palmer," *Washington Post*, May 29, 1980.

48. Ken Nigro, "Graham Answers Oriole Prayer," *Sporting News*, June 7, 1980, 27.

49. Ken Nigro, "Good Dates, Bad Trips in Orioles' Schedule," *Sporting News*, March 1, 1980, 45.

50. Craig Carter, "Major League Attendance," *Sporting News*, June 21, 1980, 26.

51. Bob McCoy, "Keeping Score," *Sporting News*, September 27, 1980, 6.

52. Ken Nigro, "The State of the Orioles: Sad," *Sporting News*, July 5, 1980, 27.

53. Thomas Boswell, *How Life Imitates the World Series*, 244.

54. *Ibid.*, 240–241.

55. *Ibid.*, 253.

56. *Ibid.*, 239.

57. *Ibid.*, 261.

58. *Ibid.*, 277.

59. *Ibid.*, 277.

60. Bruce Markusen"Earl Weaver and the Cigarette Ejection," *Hardball Times*, January 28, 2013, available at http://www.hardballtimes.com

61. "Earl Weaver's legendary tirade at Bill Haller w/Optional Captions," Youtube, uploaded by Derek Wood

62. Bob Maisel, ""Give the Yankees Credit, but They Got the Breaks, Too," *Baltimore Sun*, October 5, 1980, October 5, 1980, C1.

63. Thomas Boswell, "There's a Tomato Patch in This Man's Future; Weaver Figures

it Out: 2 Years," *The Washington Post,* August 21, 1980, F1.

64. Michael Olesker, "Baseball's Just a Game, and Yet..." *Baltimore Sun,* October 5, 1980, B1.

Chapter 3

1. Byron Rosen, "Sports FanFare," *Washington Post,* February 12, 1981, D2.

2. Melvin A Barron, Letters to the Editor, "Big-Hearted Birds," *Baltimore Sun,* March 15, 1981, C5.

3. Ken Nigro, "Murray and Orioles Hum $1 Million Tune," *Sporting News,* January 17, 1981, 39.

4. John Steadman, "The Quarterback: Colts' Owner Irsay Must Keep Promise," *Sporting News,* January 24, 1981, 16.

5. Peter Gammons, "AL Beat," *Sporting News,* April 25, 1981, 7.

6. *Ibid.,* 39.

7. Ralph Ray, "Managing the Money: More Pro Athletes Are Getting Help With Their Finances," *Sporting News,* January 24, 1981, 21.

8. Thomas Boswell, "Orioles Carry Banner for Baseball Purity; Orioles Stay Patient, Keep Robust Health," *Washington Post,* February 22, 1981, E1.

9. *Ibid.*

10. *Ibid.*

11. Peter Gammons, "O's Prime Example of Good Management," *Sporting News,* January 31, 1981, 45.

12. *Ibid.,* 45.

13. Ken Nigro, "Orioles Next Pay Hurdle: Stoddard," *Sporting News,* January 31, 1981, 49.

14. Bob Maisel, "Baseball Must Learn It's Not Immune to Fiscal Suicide," *Baltimore Sun,* February 20, 1981, C9.

15. John Helyar, *Lords of the Realm: The Real History of Baseball* (New York: Ballantine Books, 1994), 274.

16. Associated Press, "Owners' Step Triggers Baseball Strike; Owners Implement Compensatio Scheme, Players Riled," *Baltimore Sun,* February 20, C9.

17. Helyar, *Lords of the Realm,* 276.

18. Ken Nigro, "Palmer Finds a New Ache," *Sporting News,* February 14, 1981, 38.

19. Ken Nigro, "Oriole Staff Best Ever— Palmer," *Sporting News,* March 14, 1981, 48.

20. Ken Nigro, "Orioles Puzzle Over Ripken's Role," *Sporting News,* February 21, 1981, 33.

21. Peter Gammons, "Top Rookies? Watch These in '81," *Sporting News,* March 7, 1981, 11.

22. Boswell, "Orioles Carry Banner for Baseball Purity," *Washington Post,* February 22, 1981, E1.

23. Dave Kindred, "Pop Now Rat-a-Tat-Tat for DeCinces," *Washington Post,* March 31, 1981, C2.

24. Helyar, *Lords of the Realm.,* 277.

25. *Ibid.,* 277–278.

26. *Ibid,* 278.

27. "Caught on the Fly," *Sporting News,* March 21, 1981, 51.

28. Thomas Boswell, "Batter Up: All's Right with World; Baseball Is Back," *Washington Post,* March 13, 1981, E1.

29. *Ibid.*

30. Thomas Boswell, "Each Step's Higher One for Murray: Orioles Murray Yet to Look Back, Fall Back," *Washington Post,* March 18, 1981, F1.

31. *Ibid.*

32. *Ibid.*

33. Dave Kindred, "Weaver Ahead of Schedule," *Washington Post,* March 23, 1981, D6.

34. *Ibid.*

35. "Let's Relish Hurdle's Hot Dogs," *Sporting News,* April 11, 1981, 8.

36. Mel Durslag, "Orioles' Weaver Gets No Respect," *Sporting News,* April 25, 1981.

37. Ken Nigro, "Deep O's Keep Weaver Smiling," *Sporting News,* April 11, 1981, 30.

38. *Ibid.*

39. Ken Nigro, "Earl Weaver Is Impressed with Dwyer," *Sporting News,* April 18, 1981, 28.

40. Bob Maisel, "AL East Talk Starting to Heat Up," *Baltimore Sun,* March 15, 1981, C1.

41. Ken Nigro, "Birds Brimming with Optimism," *Baltimore Sun,* April 9, 1981, C8.

42. Ken Nigro, "Dauer Blooms Early with April Hit Binge," *Sporting News,* May 9. 1981, 31.

43. Ken Nigro, "Singleton Drives in Four Runs," *Baltimore Sun,* May 16, 1981, B7.

44. Ken Nigro, "Singleton Eyes a Big Season," *Sporting News,* May 23, 1981, 33.

45. Nick Peters, "Mental Errors Put

Giants on Rocks, Robby on Fire," *Sporting News*, May 23, 1981, 40.

46. "Dennis Martinez Injured, " *Sporting News*, May 9, 40.

47. Ken Nigro, "Downdraft Traps Orioles Again," *Baltimore Sun*, May 16, 1981, 23.

48. "American League Flashes," *Sporting News*, May 16, 1981, 28.

49. "American League Flashes," *Sporting News*, May 9, 1981, 38.

50. Stan Isle, "Notebook: Palmer-Earl, Behind Closed Doors," *Sporting News*, May 16, 1981, 16.

51. Ken Nigro, "Feud Eased by Weaver," *Baltimore Sun*, June 5, 1981, C5.

52. Ken Nigro, "Ripper Roenicke—O's Hot Hitter," *Sporting News*, June 13, 1981, 23.

53. Dick Young, "Young Ideas," *Sporting News*, May 23, 1981, 14.

54. Thomas Boswell, "Umps Return Venom on Weaver; Umps Turn Purple at Mention of Weaver," *Washington Post*, May 19, 1981, D1.

55. *Ibid.*

56. Ken Nigro, "Steve Stone Between Rock and Hard Place; Bird Seed," *Sporting News*, June 6, 1981, 25.

57. Boswell, "Umps Return Venom," D1.

58. *Ibid.*

59. Ken Dengliner, "Message Clear: Strike Wanted," *Washington Post*, May 7, D1.

60. Murray Chass, "Secret Panel Seals Owners' Lips," *Sporting News*, May 23, 1981, 12.

61. Donald Huff, "Orioles Pleased by Strike Postponement," *Washington Post*, May 29, 1981, E4,

62. Associated Press, "Negotiators Wait On Judge's Ruling," *Baltimore Sun*, June 10, 1981, B5.

63. Ken Nigro, "Baseball People Aren't Talking: Owners May Scrub Their Meeting," *Baltimore Sun*, June 15, 1981, B7.

64. Murray Chass, "Owners Reject Player-Pool Ban," *Sporting News*, June 20, 1981, 13.

65. John Feinstein, "Reality Hits: Orioles Start a Long Trip Back Home;" *Washington Post*, June 13, 1981, D1.

66. *Ibid.*

67. Ken Nigro, "O's 'Family' Maintains a Healthy Relationship," *Sporting News*, July 4, 1981, 33.

68. *Ibid.*

69. Ken Nigro, "Orioles: 17 Scouts Cut," *Sporting News*, July 18, 1981, 28.

70. Stephen Krasner, "Curtain Falls on 33-Inning Drama," *Sporting News*, July 11, 1981, 45.

71. Murray Chass, "Bitter Stalemate—Is Season Over?" *Sporting News*, July 11, 1981, 26.

72. Ken Nigro, "O's Williams Take a Beating," *Sporting News*, July 11, 1091, 26.

73. Ken Nigro, "Williams Loses a Round—but Vows He'll Win the War," *Sporting News*, July 26, 1981, 16.

74. Ken Nigro, "Critic Palmer Takes His Shots," *Sporting News*, August 1, 1981, 28.

75. "Major League Flashes," *Sporting News*, August 1, 1981, 36.

76. Thomas Boswell, "Kuhn: Problem Solved, No DC Team in Sight," *Washington Post*, July 7, 1981, D1.

77. Jane Leavy, "Back from the Brink: How Season Was Saved; A Failure to Communiicate Haunted the Negotiations; The Baseball Strike of '81," *Washington Post*, August 2, 1981, F1.

78. Thomas Boswell, "Weaver Says Yanks Have No Incentive," *Washington Post*, August 3, 1981, D1.

79. Ken Nigro, "O's: Ripken Arrives; Bird Seed," *Sporting News*, August 29, 1981, 38.

80. "Caught on the Fly," *Sporting News*, November 21, 1981, 62.

81. Ken Nigro, "Murray looking for Batting Pals," *Sporting News*, October 3, 1981, 16.

82. *Ibid.*

83. Ken Nigro, "Bird Seed," *Sporting News*, 1981, 33.

84. Bob Maisel, "Crazy, Topsy-Turvy Season Ends Mercifully for the Orioles," *Baltimore Sun*, October 5, 1981, C1.

85. Ken Nigro, "Orioles Dave Ford on the Road Back; Bird Seed;" *Sporting News*, 51.

Chapter 4

1. E.M. Swift, "Now You See Him, Now You Don't," *Sports Illustrated*, December 1, 1986.

2. John Steadman, "The Quarterback: Colts," *Sporting News*, January 2, 1982, 23.

3. "Keep Jones, Trade Irsay," *Baltimore Sun*, February 14, 1982, C4.

4. Steadman, "The Quarterback," *Sporting News*, February 14, 1982, 23.

5. John Steadman, "The Quarterback: Kush Arrives—Colts' Party Over," *Sporting News*, January 16, 1982, 17.

6. Alan Goldstein, "Meet Dan Ford, A Bird with His Own Flight Pattern," February 9, 1982, B1.

7. *Ibid.*

8. Thomas Boswell, "Jackson, Templeton, Ford in Orioles' Plans," *Washington Post*, January 2, 1982, E2.

9. Ken Nigro, "Pieces Fall into Place for Earl's Last Stand," *Sporting News*, 10, 1982, 34.

10. Peter Gammons, "AL Beat: Pitching, Homers, and Earl Give O's an Edge," *Sporting News*, April 10, 1982, 45.

11. Ken Nigro, "Flanagan's Arm No Longer Tired," *Sporting News*, February 20, 1982, 34.

12. Murray Chass, "Flanagan's Salary Bid Is Under O's Figure," *Sporting News*, February 13, 1982, 45.

13. Peter Gammons, "Restructuring for Baseball, or Just a League of Nations?" *Sporting News*, January 9, 1982, 39.

14. Ken Nigro, "Swift Shelby Rated Top Orioles Prospect," *Sporting News*, January 16, 1982, 51.

15. Stan Isle, "Caught on the Fly: Singleton Wins Clemente Award," *Sporting News*, March 27, 1982, 30.

16. Ken Nigro, "Weaver May Alter Retirement Plans," *Sporting News*, February 27, 1982, 42.

17. *Ibid,* 42.

18. Thomas Boswell, "The Competition: Palmer, Stone vs. Age, Each Other," *Washington Post*, February 23, 1982, D1.

19. *Ibid.*

20. Shirley Povich, "Root, Root, Root for the What Team?" *Washington Post*, April 4, 1982, C8.

21. ESPN SportsCenter, January 13, 2013; available at "Earl Weaver Highlights," You Tube, uploaded January 19, 2013.

22. Ken Nigro, "A Rocky Getaway for Rookie Ripken," *Sporting News*, May 3, 1981, 27.

23. Ken Nigro, "Ripken Overcomes Slow Start at Bat," *Sporting News*, July 5, 1982, 21.

24. Jane Leavey, "Palmer, Orioles Make Return to Normalcy," *Washington Post*, April 30, 1982, D1.

25. *Ibid.*

26. Ken Nigro, "Sore Right Elbow Disheartens Stone," *Sporting News*, April 26, 1982, 16.

27. Thomas Boswell, "Sammy Stewart; Of Short Returns and Long Relief: Cleaning Up Despite the Dirty Work," *Washington Post*, May 16, 1982, D5.

28. *Ibid.*

29. *Ibid.*

30. Ken Nigro, "New Job Challenging to DH Singleton," *Sporting News*, May 31, 1982, 26.

31. Ken Nigro, "O's Murray a 'Regular' Superstar," *Sporting News*, May 10, 1982, 2–3.

32. Stan Isle, "Caught on the Fly," *Sporting News*, June 21, 1982, 38.

33. Ken Nigro, "McNamara Favorite to Succeed Weaver," *Sporting News*, June 7, 1981, 17.

34. Bob Nightengale, "Kuhn a Big Winner in 'Unified' Majors," *Sporting News*, June 28, 1982, 13.

35. Jonathan Yardley, "Champ's Chatter; Baltimore's Earl Weaver & His Love of Baseball," *Washington Post*, June 9, 1982, B1.

36. Dick Kaegel, "Weaver's Grand Finale: Earl Heading for Retirement, but Skeptics Doubt It's Final," *Sporting News*, July 26, 1982, 2–3.

37. Thomas Boswell, "Weaver May Join NBC for Color," *Washington Post*, September 6, D4.

38. Kent Baker, "Oriole Notes: Bumbry Goes Light," *Baltimore Sun*, August 10, D2, D1.

39. Thomas Boswell, "McGregor in Form as Orioles Win Again," *Washington Post*, September 6, 1982, D1.

40. Thomas Boswell, "It Was Weaver's Way on Weaver's Day," September 20, 1982, D1.

41. Bob Maisel, "Orioles Show Character as Brew(er) Masters," *Baltimore Sun*, September 27, 1982, C1.

42. Thomas Boswell, "Orioles Lose Again, Fall Four Games Behind; Homer in 9th Tiger Winner," *Washington Post*, September 19, 1982, E1.

43. Robert Markus, "American League: Milwaukee Brewers," *Street & Smith's Official Baseball Yearbook 1982* (New York: Conde Nast, 1982), 57–58.

44. Daniel Okrent, *Nine Innings: The Anatomy of Baseball as Seen Through the*

Playing of a Single Game (New York: Mc-Graw-Hill, 1986), *passim.*

45. Thomas Boswell, "Orioles Sweep Brewers, Reduce Lead to One," *Washington Post*, October 2, 1982, F1.

46. Angus Phillips, "Orioles Soar; Suddenly, It's One for the Money," *Washington Post*, October 2, 1982, G1.

47. Dave Kindred, "The Orioles Finish Second, but Weaver Comes First," *Washington Post*, October 3, 1982, A1.

48. Angus Phillips, "Orioles Soar,"G1.

49. Lee Kluck, "October 3, 1982: Brewers Hold Off Orioles' Charge in Season Finale," Society for American Baseball Research, accessed at http://www.SABR.org

50. "End of an Impossible Dream," *Baltimore Sun*, October 4, A12.

51. Jim Henneman, "Orioles Finally Run Out of Gas," *Sporting News*, 1982, 33.

52. Jim Henneman, "Peters Screening Pilot Candidates," *Sporting News*, 1982, 35.

53. Jim Henneman, "'I'm Qualified,' Says O's Pilot Altobelli," *Sporting News*, November 22, 1982, 39.

54. *Ibid.*, 39.

Chapter 5

1. Thomas Boswell, *Why Time Begins on Opening Day* (New York: Penguin, 1984), 67.

2. Baltimore Orioles, *In Appreciation of Baseball's Greatest Fans*, 1983, 68.

3. Baltimore Orioles, *1983 Orioles Media Guide*, 76.

4. Thomas Boswell, "After the Fall, Altobelli Takes the Plunge," *Washington Post*, February 5, 1983, D1.

5. Michael Olesker, " Every Forty Years or So, Washington Deserves a Break," *Baltimore Sun*, February 1, 1983, B1.

6. "Robinson, Marchial Elected to Baseball Hall of Fame," *Washington Post*, January 12, 1983.

7. Jim Henneman, "Brooks Praises His Early Pilots," *Sporting News*, January 24, 1983, 47.

8. Jack Clary, "Dr. Carter Saves Football at Holy Cross," *Sporting News*, November 22, 1982, 22.

9. Jim Henneman, "AL East," *Sporting News*, January 3, 1983, 39.

10. Jim Henneman, "O's Seek Clues in Winter Drills," *Sporting News*, January 17, 1983, 41.

11. Thomas Boswell, "The Moles of Memorial Take to Their Mounds," February 6, 1983, H1.

12. Bill James, *The Bill James Baseball Abstract* (New York: Ballantine Books, 1983), 1.

13. *Ibid.*, 83.

14. "Pinch-Homer Record," *Street & Smith's Official Baseball Yearbook 1983* (New York: Conde-Nast, 1983) 106.

15. *Ibid.* 56.

16. Kent Baker, "The Orioles' Winning Style," *Street & Smith's Official Yearbook 1984*, 15.

17. Jim Henneman, "Belanger, Lee May to Aid Altobelli," *Sporting News*, February 21, 1983, 39.

18. Loverro, 19.

19. Thomas Boswell, "The Sad-Happy Passing of Weaver's Reign," *Washington Post*, February 22, 1983, D1.

20. *Ibid.*

21. *Ibid.*

22. Jim Henneman, "Orioles Sign Nolan, Sakata, Stoddard," *Sporting News*, January 31, 1983), 41.

23. Jim Henneman, "Rodriguez Gives O's Infield Insurance," *Sporting News*, February 14, 1983, 40.

24. Jerry Coleman, Ernie Harwell, Ralph Kiner, Tim McCarver, Ned Martin, & Brooks Robinson, *The Scouting Report: 1983* (New York: Harper & Row, 1983), 25.

25. *Ibid.*, 28.

26. Stan Isle, "Caught on the Fly," *Sporting News*, April 11, 1983, 12.

27. Kent Baker, "Hatched in NY, 'Magic' Flops," *Baltimore Sun*, April 6, 1983, E2.

28. Thomas Boswell, "Fast-Breaking Orioles Keep Heat on, 4–1," *Washington Post*, April 18, 1983, E1.

29. *Ibid.*

30. Jim Henneman, "Dempsey Shooting for Four Decades," *Sporting News*, April 25, 1983, 26.

31. Thomas Boswell, "Dempsey: Orioles Catcher in the Wry," *Washington Post*, August 2, 1983, D1.

32. Thomas Boswell, "A Long Season Demands Some Enduring Qualities," *Washington Post*, June 28, 1983, D1.

33. *Ibid.*

34. Jim Henneman, "Dennis Struggles, Stoddard Squawks," *Sporting News*, May 9, 1983, 23.

35. Jim Henneman, "Bird Seed," *Sporting News*, May 23, 1983, 26.

36. Dave Kindred, "Cooke: Baseball Team for Washington 'as Inevitable as Tomorrow,'" *Washington Post*, June 17, 1983, E1.

37. "Robert Irsay: President and Treasurer," *Prolog—The NFL's Official 1982 Annual*, Baltimore edition, December 19, 1982, 4.

38. Thomas Boswell, "A Long Season," D1.

39. Alan Goldstein, "Jays Are Turning the Skeptics into Believers," *Baltimore Sun*, August 24, 1983, E1.

40. Thomas Boswell, "Umpires Louder, Maybe Better," *Washington Post*, August 24, 1983, D1.

41. Ray Parillo, "Sakata's HR Lifts Birds over Jays in 10th," *Baltimore Sun*, August 25, 1983, C1.

42. *Ibid.*

43. *Ibid.*

44. Ken Denglinger, "Tigers Have Williams Fretting to the End," *Washington Post*, September 21, 1983, D1.

45. *Ibid.*

46. America, "You Can Do Magic," *View from the Ground*, 1982, Capitol Records.

47. Thomas Boswell, "Orioles-White Sox: Equal and Dazzling," *Washington Post*, October 4, 1983, D1.

48. *Ibid.*

49. *Ibid.*

50. *Ibid.*

51. Michael Kernan, "Orioles: The Fever Builds, Playing It Cool on Home Ground," *Washington Post*, October 4, 1983, C1.

52. Bill Free, "Feud with White Sox Came to a Boil," *Baltimore Sun*, October 9, 1983, C6.

53. *Ibid.*

54. Frank Deford, "Knocking Their Sox Off," *Sports Illustrated*, October 17, 1983, accessed at http://www.si.com/vault/1983/10/17/620362/knocking-their-sox-off

55. "Championship Series Notes," *Sporting News*, October 17, 1983, 20.

56. Ken Denglinger, "Landrum Puts Orioles into Series," *Washington Post*, October 8, 1983, A1.

57. Bill Free, "Landrum Symbolizes Ori-oles' Style, Spirit," *Baltimore Sun*, October 9, 1983, C4.

58. Steve Wulf, "Philly Is Streaking for Home," *Sports Illustrated*, October 3, 1983, accessed at http://www.si.com/vault/1983/10/03/626906/philly-is-streaking-for-home.

59. Ron Fimrite, "The Old and the Relentless Beat the Young and the Restless," *Sports Illustrated*, October 17, 1983, accessed at http://www.si.com/vault/1983/10/17/620363/the-old-and-the-relentless.

60. Ron Fimrite, "He Was Moe Than Philly Could Handle," *Sports Illustrated*, October 24, 1983, accessed at http://www.si.com/vault/1983/10/24/627266/he/was/moe/than/philly/could/handle.

61. Thomas Boswell, "Phillies Go 1 Up On Home Run by Maddox," *Washington Post*, October 11, 1983, D1.

62. Thomas Boswell, "Boddicker's 3-Hitter, 1 RBI Tie Series for Orioles," *Washington Post*, October 12, 1983, C1.

63. *Ibid.*

64. *Ibid.*

65. George Will, "The Orioles and Civic Virtue," *Baltimore Sun*, October 13, 1983, A15.

66. Steve Parks, "On Artificial Turf, Birds Play Deep, Bunched", October 14, C1.

67. Dan Castellano, "Perez Surprised by Series Start," *Newark Star-Ledger*, October 15, 1983, 17.

68. Rich Chere, "Palmer Happy to Help," *Newark Star Ledger*, October 15, 1983, 17–18.

69. Moss Klein, "Tippy's Save in 9th Nets 3d in a row, 5–4" *Newark Sunday Star-Ledger*, October 16, 1983, Sports 1.

70. Steve Wulf, "The Orioles All Pitched In," *Sports Illustrated*, October 24, 1983, accessed at http://www.si.com/vault/1983/10/24/627265/the-orioles-all-pitched-in

71. Ron Fimrite, "He was Moe Than Philly Could Handle," *Sports Illustrated*, October 24, 1983, accessed at http://www.si.com/vault/1983/10/24/627266/he-was-moe-than-philly-could-handle.

72. *Ibid.*

73. *Ibid.*

74. David Nightengale, "McGregor, Murray End Phil Misery," *Sporting News*, October 24, 1983, 18.

75. Patrick A. McGuire, "In City's Streets, Bars, Fans Cheer their Champions," *Baltimore Sun*, October 17, 1983, A1.

76. Bill Free, "Amid The Bubbly, Dauer is Proud to be an Oriole," *Baltimore Sun*, October 17, C10.

77. *Ibid.*

78. Doug Struck, "Iowa Farm Town Can Claim a Hero," *Baltimore Sun*, October 17, A8.

79. "Orioles Prove It Take All to Win it All," *Baltimore Sun*, October 17, 1983, C8.

80. Patrick A. McGuire & Rafael Alvarez, "Mob Greets Conqueror at Stadium," *Baltimore Sun*, October 17, 1983, A1.

81. Thomas Boswell, "Orioles Take Series, Begin Celebration," *Washington Post*, October 16, 1983, A1.

82. Jim Henneman, "Birds Won't Stand Pat Despite Title," *Sporting News*, November 8, 1983, 51.

83. Moss Klein, "MVP Ripken: Murray Should Share Award," *Newark Star Leger*, November 17, 1983, 97.

84. Seymour Smith, "Consistency, Patience, Fairness Are Secrets of Oriole Success," *Baltimore Sun*, October 18, 1983, C3.

Chapter 6

1. 595. James Edward Miller, *The Baseball Business*, 286–287.

2. *Ibid.*, 289.

3. Evan Thomas, *The Man to See*, 472.

4. Steve Keplinger, *The Comeback Kids: A Fan Relives the Amazing 1989 Baltimore Orioles Season* (St. George, UT: Publisher's Place, 1989), 45.

5. Peter Richmond, *Ballpark: Camden Yards and the Building of an American Dream* (New York: Simon & Schuster, 1993), 54.

6. *Ibid.*, 117–118.

BIBLIOGRAPHY

Note on Statistics and Digital Sources: Statistics in this book come from Baseball-Reference.com (http://www.baseball-reference.com), Baseball Almanac.com (http://www.baseball-almanac.com), and resources available through the Society for American Baseball Research (http://www sabr.org). The 1982 edition of Macmillan's *Baseball Encyclopedia* (Joseph Reichler, ed.) was also a data source. YouTube videos are cited by title and upload date.

Periodicals

Newspapers: *Baltimore Evening Sun, Baltimore News-American, Baltimore Sun, Newark Star-Ledger, New York Times, Washington Post, Washington Star, Washington Times.*

Journals and Magazines: *The Baseball Research Journal; National Baseball Hall of Fame and Museum Yearbook, 1996; Prolog: NFL 1982; The Sporting News; Sports Illustrated; Street & Smith's Baseball Yearbook, 1970–1984; World Series 1979 Official Program; Baltimore Orioles Media Guides 1979–1984; Baltimore Orioles Game Programs, 1970–1983.*

Books

Aylesworth, Thomas, Benton Minks, and John Bowman, eds. *The Encyclopedia of Baseball Managers.* New York: Crescent, 1990.

Anderson, Dave. *Great Quarterbacks of the NFL.* New York: Random House, 1965.

Angell, Roger. *Once More Around the Park: A Baseball Reader.* New York: Ballantine, 1992.

Armour, Mark, and Malcolm Allen. *Pitching, Defense, and Three-Run Homers: The 1970 Baltimore Orioles.* Lincoln: University of Nebraska Press, 2012.

Astor, Gerald. *The Baseball Hall of Fame 50th Anniversary Book.* New York: Prentice-Hall, 1988.

Bagli, Vince, and Norman Macht. *Sundays at 2:00 with the Baltimore Colts.* Centreville, MD: Tidewater, 1995.

Baltimore Orioles. *Baltimore Orioles 1983 Media Guide.* Baltimore: Baltimore Orioles, 1983.

_____. *To the Best Fans in Baseball: A Celebration.* Baltimore: Baltimore Orioles, 1984.

Berney, Louis. *Tales from the Orioles Dugout.* Chicago: Sports Publishing, 2004.

Block, David. *Baseball Before We Knew It: A Search for the Roots of the Game*. Lincoln: University of Nebraska Press, 2005.
Boswell, Thomas. *Gameday: Sports Writings 1970–1990*. New York: Doubleday, 1990.
_____. *The Heart of the Order*. New York: Penguin, 1989.
_____. *How Life Imitates the World Series*. New York: Penguin, 1983.
_____. *Why Time Begins on Opening Day*. New York: Penguin, 1984.
Bready, James H. *The Home Team: Our O's, Baseball and Baltimore*. Baltimore: James H. Bready, 1984.
_____. *Baseball in Baltimore: The First 100 Years*. Baltimore: Johns Hopkins University Press, 1998.
Clary, Jack. ed. *1970 Baseball Guide*. Key Largo, FL: Snibbe, 1970.
Coleman, Jerry *Et Al*. *The Scouting Report: 1983*. New York: Harper & Row, 1983.
Corbett, Warren. *The Wizard of Waxahatchie: Paul Richards and the End of Baseball as We Knew It*. Dallas: Southern Methodist University Press, 2009.
Cord Communications. *Major League Baseball 1973*. New York: Pocket Books, 1973.
Cortina, Lou, ed. *Goal: A History of the Baltimore Blast Indoor Soccer Team*. Baltimore: Baltimore Sun, 2000.
Creamer, Robert W. *Babe: The Legend Comes to Life*. New York: Penguin, 1986.
Crunden, Robert M. *American Salons: Encounters with European Modernism, 1885–1917*. New York: Oxford University Press, 1993.
Davis, Mac. *Baseball's Unforgettables*. New York: Bantam Pathfinder, 1972.
Decaneas, Antony. ed.. *Negro League Baseball*. New York: Harry Abrams, 2004.
Dewey, Donald, and Nicholas Acocella. *Total Ballclubs: The Ultimate Book of Baseball Franchises*. Toronto: Sportclassicbooks, 2005.
Donavan, Arthur J. Jr. *Fatso: Football When Men Were Really Men*. New York: Avon, 1987.
Drucker, Peter. *The Essential Drucker*. New York: Collins Business, 2001.
Eckman, Charley, with Fred Neil. *It's a Very Simple Game: The Life and Times of Charley Eckman*. Baltimore: Borderlands, 1995.
Eisenberg, John. *From 33rd Street to Camden Yards*. New York: Contemporary, 2001.
Flynn, Tom. *Baseball in Baltimore*. Charleston, SC: Arcadia, 2008.
Fox, Bucky. *The Orioles Fan's Little Book of Wisdom*. New York: Taylor Trade, 2008.
Frommer, Harvey. *Baseball's Greatest Managers*. New York: Franklin Watts, 1985.
Gershman, Michael. *Diamonds: The Evolution of the Ballpark*. Boston: Houghton Mifflin, 1993.
Gesker, Mike. *The Orioles Encyclopedia: A Half Century of History and Highlights*. Baltimore: Johns Hopkins University Press, 2009.
Gildea, William. *When the Colts Belonged to Baltimore: A Father, a Son, a Town, and a Team*. Baltimore: Johns Hopkins University Press, 1994.
Hawkins, John C. *This Date in Baltimore Orioles & St. Louis Browns History*. New York: Scarborough. 1983.
Helyar, John. *Lords of the Realm: The Real History of Baseball*. New York: Ballantine, 1994.
Henneman, Jim. *Baltimore Orioles: 60 Years of Orioles Magic*. San Rafael, CA: Insight Editions, 2015.
Hogan, Kenneth. *The 1969 Seattle Pilots: Major League Baseball's One-Year Team*. Jefferson, NC: McFarland, 2007.
Irwin, Constance. *Strange Footprints in a Strange Land: Vikings in America*. New York: Harper & Row, 1980.
James, Bill. *The Bill James Baseball Abstract 1983*. New York: Ballantine, 1983.
_____. *The New Bill James Baseball Abstract*. New York: Free Press, 2001.
Johnson, Lloyd, and Miles. eds.) Wolff. *The Encyclopedia of Minor League Baseball*. Durham, NC: Baseball America, 1997.

Jordan, David M. *The Athletics of Philadelphia: Connie Mack's White Elephants, 1901–1954.* Jefferson, NC: McFarland, 1999.

Kasson, John. *Amusing the Million: Coney Island at the Turn of the Century.* New York: Hill & Wang, 1978.

Keplinger, Steve. *The Comeback Kids: A Fan Relives the Amazing Baltimore Orioles 1989 Season.* St. George, UT: Publishers Place, 1990.

Klein, Dave. *Great Infielders of the Major Leagues.* New York: Random House, 1972.

Kuhn, Bowie. *Hardball: The Education of a Baseball Commissioner.* Lincoln: University of Nebraska Press, 1997.

Kuklick, Bruce. *To Everything a Season: Shibe Park and Urban Philadelphia, 1909–1976.* Princeton, NJ: Princeton University Press, 1991.

Leavengood, Ted. *Ted Williams and the 1969 Washington Senators.* Jefferson, NC: McFarland, 2009.

Lieb, Frederick. *The Baltimore Orioles: The History of a Colorful Team in Baltimore and St. Louis.* Carbondale: Southern Illinois University Press, 2004. First published 1955 by G.P. Putnam's Sons.

Loverro, Thom. *Oriole Magic: The O's of 1983.* Chicago: Triumph, 2004.

_____. *Orioles Essential: Everything You Need to Know to Be a Real Fan.* Chicago: Triumph Books, 2007.

Luke, Bob. *The Baltimore Elite Giants: Sport and Society in the Age of Negro League Baseball.* Baltimore: Johns Hopkins University Press, 2009.

Luciano, Ron, and David Fisher. *The Fall of the Roman Umpire.* New York: Bantam, 1986.

_____ and _____. *The Umpire Strikes Back.* New York: Bantam, 1982.

MacCambridge, Michael. *America's Game: The Epic Story of How Pro Football Captured a Nation.* New York: Anchor Books, 2005.

Mead, William B. *Even the Browns: Baseball During World War II.* Mineola, NY: Dover, 1978.

Miller, James Edward. *The Baseball Business: Pursuing Pennants and Profits in Baltimore.* Chapel Hill: University of North Carolina Press. 1990.

Miller, Marvin. *A Whole Different Ballgame.* Chicago: Ivan R. Dee, 2004.

Milliken, Mark R. *The Glory of the 1966 Orioles and Baltimore.* Haworth, NJ: St. Johann Press, 2006.

Morris, Peter. "Excelsior/Pastime Base Ball Club of Baltimore." In *Base Ball Pioneers, 1850–1870: The Clubs and Players Who Spread the Sport Nationwide,* edited by Peter Morris, William J. Ryczek, et al., 253–262. Jefferson, NC: McFarland, 2012.

Mote, James. *Everything Baseball.* New York: Prentice-Hall, 1989.

Nemec, David, et al. *The Baseball Chronicle: Year-By-Year History of Major League Baseball.* Lincolnwood, IL: Publication International, 2003.

Nathan, Dan. *Baltimore Sports: Stories from Charm City.* Little Rock: University of Arkansas Press, 2016.

Okrent, Daniel. *Nine Innings: The Anatomy of Baseball as Seen Through the Playing of a Single Game.* New York: McGraw-Hill, 1985.

Olesker, Michael. *The Colts' Baltimore: A City and Its Love Affair in the 1950s.* Baltimore: Johns Hopkins University Press, 2008.

Palmer, Jim, and Jim Dale. *Palmer and Weaver: Together We Were Eleven Foot Nine.* Kansas City: Andrews & McMeel, 1996.

Parillo, Stephanie, ed. *Cal Ripken Jr. Official Commemorative.* Baltimore: Baltimore Orioles, 1996.

Patterson, Ted. *The Baltimore Orioles: Forty Years of Magic from 33rd Street to Camden Yards.* Dallas: Taylor, 1994.

_____. *The Golden Voices of Baseball.* Chicago: Sports Publishing, 2002.

Peters, Alexander. *Heroes of the Major Leagues.* New York: Random House, 1967.

Powers, Albert Theodore. *The Business of Baseball.* Jefferson, NC: McFarland, 2003.

Preston, Joseph G. *Major League Baseball in the 1970s: A Modern Game Emerges.* Jefferson, NC: McFarland, 2004.

Reichler, Joseph. *The Baseball Encyclopedia.* New York: Macmillan, 1982.

Richards, Paul. *Modern Baseball Strategy.* New York: Prentice-Hall, 1955.

Richmond, Peter. *Ballpark: Camden Yards and the Building of an American Dream.* New York: Simon & Schuster, 1993.

Riley, James A. *The Biographical Encyclopedia of the Negro Baseball Leagues.* New York: Carroll & Graf, 1994.

Ripken, Cal Jr., with Rick Wolff. *Parenting Young Athletes the The Ripken Way.* New York: Gotham Books, 2006.

Ripken, Cal. Jr., and Mike Bryan. *The Only Way I Know.* New York: Viking, 1997.

Ritter, Lawrence S. *Lost Ballparks: A Celebration of Baseball's Legendary Fields.* New York: Viking Studio, 1992.

Robinson, Frank, with Al Silverman. *My Life in Baseball.* Garden City, NY: Doubleday, 1968.

Robinson, George, and Charles Salzburg. *On a Clear Day They Could See Seventh Place: Baseball's Worst Teams.* New York: Dell Trade, 1991.

Robinson, Ray, ed. *Baseball Stars of 1975.* New York: Pyramid, 1975.

Rogosin, Donn. *Invisible Men: Life in Baseball's Negro Leagues.* New York: Macmillan, 1985.

Rossi, John P. *The 1964 Phillies: The Story of Baseball's Most Memorable Collapse.* Jefferson, NC: McFarland, 2005.

Seidel, Jeff. *Baltimore Orioles: Where Have You Gone?.* New York: Sports Publishing, 2014.

Seymour, Harold, and Dorothy Seymour Mills. *Baseball: The Early Years.* New York: Oxford University Press, 1960.

_____ and _____. *Baseball: The Golden Age.* New York: Oxford University Press, 1971.

Silvia, Tony. *Baseball Over the Air: The National Pastime on the Radio and in the Imagination.* Jefferson, NC: McFarland, 2007.

Siwoff, Seymour, Steve Hirdt, and Peter Herdt. *The 1987 Elias Baseball Abstract.* New York: Collier Books, 1987.

Smiley, Jane. Preface to *The Sagas of the Icelanders.* New York: Penguin, 2000.

Smith, Ron. *The Ballpark Book: A Journey Through the Fields of Baseball Magic.* St. Louis: The Sporting News/Vulcan Media, 2003.

Stallings, Jack, and Bob Bennett. *Baseball Strategies: Your Guide to the Game Within the Game.* Champaign, IL: Human Kinetics, 2003.

Steadman, John F. *From Colts to Ravens: A Behind-The-Scenes Look at Baltimore Professional Football.* Baltimore: Schiffler, 1997.

Sullivan, Neil J. *The Minors: The Struggles and the Triumph of Baseball's Poor Relation from 1876 to the Present.* New York: St. Martin's Press, 1990.

Thomas, Evan. *The Man to See: Edward Bennett Williams, Ultimate Insider; Legendary Trial Lawyer.* New York: Simon & Schuster, 1991.

Thorn, John, ed. *The National Pastime.* New York: Warner Books, 1987.

Thorn, John, and Bob Carroll, eds. *The Whole Baseball Catalogue: The Ultimate Guide to the Baseball Marketplace.* New York: Simon & Schuster, 1990.

Usereau, Alain. *The Expos in Their Prime: The Short-Lived Glory of Montreal's Team, 1977–1984.* Jefferson, NC: McFarland, 2003.

Veeck, Bill, with Ed Linn. *Veeck as in Wreck.* Chicago: University of Chicago Press, 2001. First published 1962 by Signet Books.

Voigt, David Quentin. *From the Commissioners to Continental Expansion.* Volume 2 of *American Baseball.* University Park: Penn State University Press, 1992.

Ward, John Montgomery. *Base-Ball: How to Become a Player*. Cleveland: SABR, 1993. First published 1888 by the Athletic Publishing Company.

Weaver, Earl, with Barry Stainback. *It's What You Learn After You Know It All That Counts: The Autobiography of Earl Weaver*. New York: Simon & Schuster, 1982.

Whitfield, Shelby. *Kiss It Goodbye*. New York: Abelard Schuman, 1973.

Wiggins, Robert Peyton. *The Federal League of Base Ball Clubs: The History of an Outlaw Major League, 1914–1915*. Jefferson, NC: McFarland, 2009.

Will, George F. *Bunts: Curt Flood, Camden Yards, Pete Rose, and Other Reflections on Baseball*. New York: Scribner, 1998.

_____. *Men at Work: The Craft of Baseball*. New York: Macmillan, 1990.

INDEX

197